IΘ123576

THE RED RECORD OF THE SIOUX.

LIFE OF

SITTING BULL

AND

HISTORY OF THE INDIAN WAR

OF 1890-'91

A GRAPHIC ACCOUNT OF THE LIFE OF THE GREAT MEDICINE MAN AND CHIEF
SITTING BULL; HIS TRAGIC DEATH: STORY OF THE SIOUX NATION;
THEIR MANNERS AND CUSTOMS, GHOST DANCES AND MESSIAH
CRAZE; ALSO, A VERY COMPLETE HISTORY OF THE
SANGUINARY INDIAN WAR OF 1890-'91.

BY W. FLETCHER JOHNSON,

Author of "The Johnstown Flood," "Stanley in Africa," etc., etc.

PROFUSELY ILLUSTRATED.

EDGEWOOD PUBLISHING COMPANY

PUBLISHERS.

COPYRIGHTED, 1891, BY H. W. STRINGER.

PREFACE.

There is in all the checkered history of America no chapter of more general interest than that which tells of the Aborigines and our dealings with them. It narrates a story often shameful, often noble, sometimes pusillanimous, sometimes heroic, now causing us to blush with shame for fallen human nature, now kindling us with enthusiastic admiration for humanity that seems almost divine; but always full of power to thrill the heart, of romance to captivate the fancy, and of rich food to nourish earnest thought. To the man of war and to the man of peace, to the statesman and to the Christian teacher, to the scientist, and to the romanticist, it makes with equal directness its irresistible appeal.

It is the object of the present volume to relate the story of the Sioux, more properly the Dakota Indians, and our relations with them. Of all the aboriginal people, they were the greatest,—the bravest in war, the wisest in peace, the most powerful in body, the most advanced in mind. As possessors of the famed Red Pipe Stone Quarry, the Indian Mecca, where Gitche Manito the Mighty, revealed himself to man, they have cherished and developed more than any others the myths and legends of the Indian race. The foremost leaders of aboriginal civilization, they have longest resisted the inflowing tide of alien civilization brought hither by the Puritan and the Cavalier. And to-day, he who would study the red race in its noblest remnant and in its best estate, must do so among the scattered lodges of the Sioux.

The name of Sitting Bull must be as famous as that of Tecumseh, of Red Cloud, as that of Black Hawk or Massasoit. The Sioux massacres of 1862, make Wyoming seem commonplace, and the last rally of Custer at the Little Big Horn fight has no parallel in all the annals of our Indian wars. Nor is the long drama drawn to an unworthy close by the weird Ghost Dances, the death of Sitting Bull and the mad slaughtering at Wounded Knee.

It is the present purpose to record this history before the blood of the last grim chapter shall have grown dry. The tale is told chiefly in the words of those who could truly say, *magna pars quorum fuimus.* The views of both friends and foes of the Indian are given a fair hearing, nothing extenuated, nothing set down in malice. In years to come, when some metempsychosis shall have translated passion into philosophy, a more discerning judgment may record in other terms these same events. For this day and this generation we can only tell the story as it comes to us in the echoes of war, in the prayer for relief, in the cry of despair.

CONTENTS.

CHAPTER I.

AUTOBIOGRAPHY.

CHAPTER II.

MEDICINE MAN AND WARRIOR.

CHAPTER III.

THE SAVAGE IN SOCIETY.

CHAPTER IV.

THE FOE OF THE WHITE MAN.

CHAPTER V.

THE LITTLE BIG HORN.

CONTENTS.

CHAPTER VI.

CUSTER'S LAST RALLY.

CHAPTER VII.

THE DEATH OF CUSTER.

CHAPTER VIII.

CUSTER.

CHAPTER IX.

IN EXILE.

CHAPTER X.

THE MIGHTY FALLEN.

CHAPTER XI.

THE LAST CAMPAIGN.

CONTENTS.

CHAPTER XII.

DEATH OF THE GREAT CHIEF.

CHAPTER XIII.

TRIBUTES TO HIS MEMORY.

CHAPTER XIV.

THE SIOUX NATION.

CHAPTER XV.

LEGENDS AND CREEDS.

CHAPTER XVI.

IN PEACE AND WAR.

CHAPTER XVII.

FEASTING AND DANCING.

CONTENTS.

CONTENTS.

CHAPTER XXIV.

THE SEAT OF WAR.

CHAPTER XXV.

LIFE AT PINE RIDGE.

CHAPTER XXVI.

INDIANS AND SETTLERS.

CHAPTER XXVII.

RED CLOUD.

CHAPTER XXVIII.

THE LEADERS OF THE SIOUX.

CHAPTER XXIX.

THE BEGINNING OF WAR.

CONTENTS.

CONTENTS.

CHAPTER XXXVI.

DOUBT AND FEAR.

CHAPTER XXXVII.

IN AT LAST.

CHAPTER XXXVIII.

WHO SHALL BE THE VICTIM?

CHAPTER XXXIX.

THE INDIAN IN CONGRESS.

CHAPTER XL.

THE INDIAN BUREAU.

CHAPTER XLI.

DOCUMENTS IN THE CASE.

CONTENTS.

CHAPTER XLII.

INDIAN EDUCATION.

CHAPTER XLIII.

WHAT OF THE FUTURE.

LIST OF ILLUSTRATIONS.

LIST OF ILLUSTRATIONS.

CHAPTER I.

AUTOBIOGRAPHY.

A Unique History in Pictures—The Chief's Own Story of His Bloody and Lawless Career—Killing Enemies and Stealing Mules—Many Different Stories of his Life—Was he a West Point Graduate?—Startling Theory of an Army Officer.

Among the countless relics and records in the Army Medical Museum at Washington, most of them ghastly and tragic in their nature, is conspicuous the Autobiography of Ta-tan-kah-yo-tan-kah, the Sioux chieftain best known to fame as Sitting Bull. The work is unique, and it has itself a curious history. In the fall of 1870, a Yankton Sioux brought to the army officers at Fort Buford an old roll-book of the Thirty-first Regiment of Infantry, U. S. A., which bore, on the backs of the leaves, originally blank, a remarkable series of portraitures, representing the doings of a mighty Indian warrior. The pictures were outlined in ink, and shaded with colored chalks and pencils, brown, blue, and red. In the corner of each picture was a "totem," or Indian signature, just like the "remarque" on an etching. This totem was a buffalo

17

bull on its haunches, and it revealed at once the authorship of the work. The Yankton Indian wanted to sell it, and finally did so, for one dollar and a half, confessing, frankly, that he had stolen it from Sitting Bull himself, whose autobiography it was, down to date.

This literary and artistic work, which is now likely to be famous, fell into the hands of Assistant Surgeon James C. Kimball, of the army, who was then stationed at Fort Buford, Dakota. He had the pictures translated and sent them, with the translation and an index, to the curator of the Army Medical Museum, Washington, Surgeon George A. Otis, United States Army, who filed them, in book shape, among the archives of the museum. The introduction, written by Dr. Kimball, says that the autobiography contains a description of the principal adventures in the life of Sitting Bull, an Unk-pa-pa chief. It was sketched by himself in the picture language in common use with the Indians.

The index, explanatory of the drawings, was prepared through the assistance of Indians and interpreters. The word "coup," which occurs frequently in the index, has been appropriated by the Sioux from the French. "Counting coup" signifies the striking of an enemy, either dead or alive, with a stick, bow, lance, or other weapon. The number of "coups" counted are enumerated along with the number of horses stolen and scalps taken in summing up the brave deeds of a warrior. Sitting

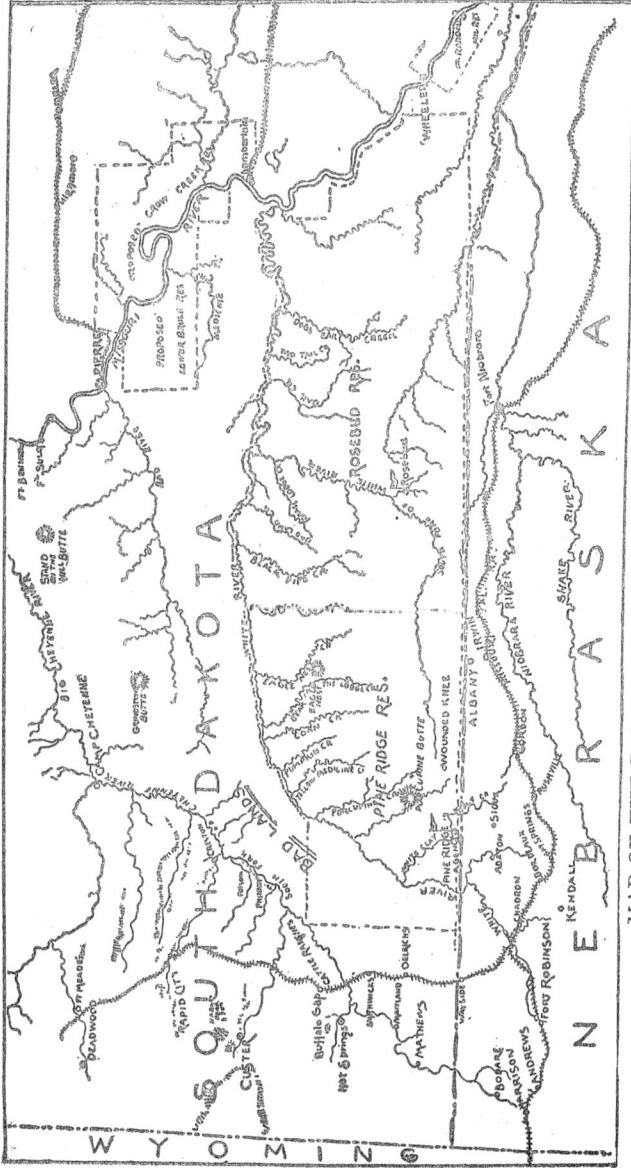

MAP OF THE BAD LANDS AND SCENE OF THE INDIAN WAR.

HORSE RACING.

Bull was not at all modest in recounting his deeds for the edification of posterity. The scalping of a soldier and the theft of a mule are pictured with equal pride and with an equally artistic display of pigments. The plates are enumerated and described in the index as follows :

No. 1. Sitting Bull, a young man without reputation and therefore wearing no feather, engages in his first battle and charges his enemy, a Crow Indian, who is in the act of drawing his bow, rides him down and strikes him with a "coup" stick.

Sitting Bull's autograph, a buffalo bull sitting on his haunches, is inscribed over him. His shield suspended in front has on it the figure of an eagle, which he considers his medicine, in the Indian sense of the term.

No. 2. Sitting Bull, wearing a war bonnet, is leader of a war party who take a party of Crows, consisting of three women and a man, so completely by surprise that the man has not time to draw his arrows from the quiver. Sitting Bull kills one woman with his lance and captures another, the man meanwhile endeavoring to drag him from the horse, from which it is supposed he is forced to destroy others of the war party.

The fate of Sitting Bull and his victims is given in this history.

No. 3. Sitting Bull pursuing his enemy, a Crow Indian, whom he strikes with his lance.

No. 4. Lances a Crow woman.

No. 5. Lances a Crow Indian.

No. 6. Sitting Bull twice wounded and unhorsed ; his enemy, a Crow, at length killed by a shot in the abdomen and his scalp taken and hung to Sitting Bull's saddle.

No. 7. In an engagement with the Crows, Sitting Bull mortally wounds one of the enemy, and, dropping his lance, rides up and strikes him with his whip. The lines and dashes in the picture represent the arrows and bullets that were flying in the air during the combat.

No. 8. Counts "coup" on a Gros Ventre de Prairie by striking him with his lance. Gros Ventre distinguished from Crow by manner of wearing his hair.

No. 9. Lances a Crow Indian.

No. 10. A Crow Indian attempts to seize Sitting Bull's horse by the bridle ; Sitting Bull knocks him down with a "coup" stick, takes his scalp and hangs it to his bridle.

No. 11. Sitting Bull, with his brother mounted behind him, kills a white man, a soldier.

No. 12. Counts "coup" on a white man by hitting him with a "coup" stick.

No. 13. In a warm engagement with the whites, as shown by the bullets flying about, Sitting Bull shoots an arrow through the body of a soldier, who turns and fires, wounding Sitting Bull in the hip.

No. 14. Sitting Bull counts "coup" on a white man by striking him with his bow. Sitting Bull wears a red jacket and bandanna handkerchief taken from some of his victims.

Nos. 15 to 22 are repetitions of No. 14, Sitting Bull in each counting "coup" on a white man.

No. 23. Sitting Bull shoots a frontiersman wearing a buckskin shirt, takes his scalp, which he hangs to his own bridle, and captures his horse. Sitting Bull wears a blanket.

No. 24. Sitting Bull strikes a white soldier with his "coup" stick, takes his scalp and mule.

No. 25 counts "coup" on a soldier mounted, with overcoat on, gun slung across his back, by riding up and striking him with his riding-whip.

No. 26. Kills a white man and takes his scalp.

No. 27. Captures a mule and a scalp.

No. 28. In a warm engagement captures a horse and a scalp.

No. 29. Steals a mule.

No. 30. Captures two horses in action.

No. 31. Steals a horse.

No. 32. Steals and runs off a drove of horses from the Crows.

No. 33. In an engagement captures a government horse and mule and a scalp.

No. 34. Steals a horse.

No. 35. Captures three horses and a scalp.

No. 36. Steals a drove of horses from the Crows.

No. 37. Steals a government horse.

No. 38. Steals a drove of horses from the Crows.

No. 39. In an engagement captures a mule. Sitting Bull first appears here as chief of the band of Strong Hearts, to which dignity his prowess had raised him. The insignia of his rank, a bow having on end a lance head, he carries in his hand.

No. 40. Sitting Bull, chief of the band of Strong Hearts, captures two horses in an engagement, in which his horse is wounded in the shoulder.

No. 41. Captures a horse in a fight.

No. 42. Steals a mule.

No. 43. Captures two horses in a fight, in which his horse is wounded in the leg.

No. 44. Mounted on a government horse captures a white man.

No. 45. Steals two horses.

No. 46. Captures four mules in a fight, in which his horse is wounded in the hip.

Nos. 47 and 48. Counts "coup" on white men.

No. 49. Steals a government horse.

No. 50. Fastens his horse to his lance, driven into the earth, and in a hand-to-hand fight kills a white man with his own gun. The black marks show the ground fought and trampled over.

No. 51. A fort into which his enemies, the Crows, have retreated, and from which they maintain a hot fire, through which Sitting Bull charges the fort.

No. 52. In a fight with Crows, Sitting Bull kills and scalps one Indian and counts "coup" on another, and fires at him, barely missing him.

No. 53. Steals a drove of mules.

No. 54. Sitting Bull, at the head of his band, charges into a camp of Crows and kills thirty of them. This happened in the winter of 1869–70.

No. 55. Kills one Crow and counts "coup" on two others, who run from him disgracefully.

Such was the self-told story of this red desperado's career down to the summer of 1870, and in it he doubtless did himself no injustice. Rather was his life more venturesome and lawless than even that criminal calendar would indicate. Since the establishment of Fort Buford, in 1866, Sitting Bull, at the head of from sixty to seventy warriors, had been the terror of mail-carriers, wood-choppers and small parties in the vicinity of the post, and from 100 to 200 miles from it either way, up and down the Missouri River. During the time from 1866 to 1870, when the biography was written, this band had several times captured and destroyed the mail, and had stolen and run off over 200 head of cattle and killed near a score of white men in the immediate vicinity of the fort.

Despite this autobiography, however, the origin and early life of Sitting Bull are involved in much of mystery. Many different stories have been told concerning him, and he has himself told the story of his early years on various occasions in various versions. Once he said:

"I was born near old Fort George, on Willow Creek, below the mouth of the Cheyenne River. Cannot tell exactly how old I am. We count our years from the moons between great events. The event from which I date my birth is the year in which Thunder Hawk was born. I have always been running around. Indians that remain on the same hunting grounds all the time can remember years better. I have nine children and two living wives and one wife that has gone to the Great Spirit. I have two pairs of twins. I think as much of one as the other. If I did not I would not keep them. I believe if I had a white wife I would think more of her than the other two. My father's name was The Jumping Bull, and he was a chief. At the age of fourteen I killed an enemy and began to make myself great in battle and became a chief."

Again, in 1877, after the Custer massacre, and while he was in the British territory for safety, a correspondent wrote as follows concerning the famous chief:

"The mystery that has hitherto shrouded the person of the great Sioux warrior has been removed. In conversation after dinner with one of the police officers, the other day he said that he was a native of Fort Garry, and an alumnus of St. John's College there—statements which he himself afterward confirmed. Several old traders who have had a look at him declare that they remember him well as Charlie Jacobs, a half-breed, who attended the college in its infancy thirty years ago. This young Jacobs was of Ojibway birth, and was a remarkably intelligent lad, with ambition to become a 'big

Injun.' He disappeared from Fort Garry about 1853.

"When asked by the police officer if he recollected anything about Fort Garry, Sitting Bull laughed heartily and said he knew the principal people there, among others Donald A. Smith, the Hudson Bay factor; James Sutherland, and Father Vary, now a missionary at the Sault. He was also well acquainted with the late James Ross, Chief Justice of the Riel-Lepine Government in 1869–70; indeed, he says, they were boys together. Ross was a half-breed, who, after graduating at St. John's College, went to Toronto University, where he was a gold medalist. Sitting Bull says his father, Henry Jacobs, was at one time employed as interpreter by Father Proulx on Manitoulin Island, but whether the old gentleman is dead or not he does not know. Sitting Bull is thoroughly familiar with French and English and several Indian languages. He is about forty-two or forty-three years of age, a medium-sized, athletic-built man, of no distinguishing traits beyond those always found in the half-breed. He is an excellent conversationalist, and will talk on every subject but his plans for the future."

Captain McGarry, of an Upper Missouri steamboat, knew Sitting Bull well for many years, and in August, 1876, gave this account of him:

"Sitting Bull is a Teton-Sioux, and is thirty-

A ROMAN CATHOLIC.

five years old. He is a Roman Catholic convert, and said to be a firm believer in all the tenets of that church. He was convertd by Father de Smet. By this priest he was taught French, and he is able to read and speak that tongue with fluency. He has always doggedly refused to learn English. He is well versed in the Delaware language also, and is pronounced by the native tribes a greater orator than Little Pheasant, chief of the Yanktonnais. Sitting Bull has read French history carefully, and

APEING NAPOLEON.

he is especially enamored of the career of Napoleon, and endeavors to model his campaigns after those of the "Man of Destiny." In 1868 Sitting Bull became a chief. Previously he had been repudiated by the other chiefs, and had been for several years a malcontent and at variance with the other chiefs of the Sioux nation, often coming into open conflict with them. After he contemplated his present war with the whites his ranks were filled by hundreds of young braves, who were seduced into revolt by his persuasive eloquence. At length the other chiefs deemed it policy to recognize him, and from that moment his supremacy was insured. Every summer, for years, he has been North into the country of the Assiniboins and Crees, and the acquaintance and friendship which he cultivated there are ripening into a harvest."

About the same time a well-known resident of Manitoba, made another contribution to the history of Sitting Bull. He described him as a Sac or Fox, and not a Sioux at all. He attended, says this historian, the school at Fort Garry, when a young man, having moved thither from Prairie du Chien. He acquired a good education, especially in French, and was noted as a superb marksman with pistol or rifle. While in Manitoba, his great object in life seemed to be the establishment of a great Indian commonwealth, governed exclusively by aborigines or half-breeds. In the summer of 1869, he made a proposition to Louis Riel, looking to the establishment of an independent province either on British or Canadian soil, stating at the same time that he could obtain money from London and through the Hudson Bay company, in support of such a governmental enterprise. He

INTRIGUING WITH REIL.

told Reil that he would stand at his back with 5,000 Sioux warriors, if he would only enter into an agreement providing that none but Indian and half breed officers should be chosen to govern his proposed independent province. This proposition was declined by Reil on the ground that the church authorities of Manitoba would refuse any sanction to the programme, being opposed to an independent principality in Northern America. Nor does this conclude the catalogue of conflicting records. An army officer, in the summer of 1876, propounded the startling inquiry, "Is Sitting Bull a West Point graduate?" "This question," he continued, "is asked in sober earnest, with the view of eliciting information, there being reasons

for believing that this formidable warrior and so-
called savage, now occupying so much of public
attention, from the unquestioned skill and extraordinary courage with which he has met our sol-

GRADUATE OF WEST POINT.

diers, is really a graduate of the Military Academy.
There may be some foundation for the reports as
to his reading French and being familiar with the
campaigns of the great Napoleon. Graduates of
West Point, between 1846 and 1850, will remember
the new cadet of both singular and remarkable appearance, hailing from the western borders of Missouri, who reported for duty in 1845, 1846 or 1847.
Above medium height, apparently between eighteen and twenty years old, heavy set frame, long,
bushy hair, growing close to his brow and over-
hanging his neck and shoulders, his face covered
with thin patches of fuzzy beard, the general get-up
of this plebe was such as to cause the old cadets to
hesitate in the heretical jokes usually played off on
new cadets. Nicknames are often applied to
cadets that they carry with them among their friends
into the army, and even to their graves. The thick
neck, broad shoulders, and long, bushy hair, caused

NICKNAMED " BISON."

the name of " Bison " to be applied to this new
comer, and it adhered to him ever afterward. The
West Point course he learned with ease, graduating
in the upper third of his class. He had no disposition to be social, kept to himself, talked but little

and was never known to either smile or laugh.
During hours of recreation he did not mingle with
his classmates, but was often seen in solitary walks
around the plain or scaling the neighboring mountains, even to their very summits. He was often
out of his quarters after night, eluding successfully
the vigilance of sentinels and officers, visiting the
neighboring villages in quest of strong drink, but
never seen under its influence until he had graduated.

"This remarkable character passed his graduating examination creditably, received his diploma,
but before doffing the cadet gray, visited the village
of Buttermilk Falls, below West Point a short distance, got intoxicated and became involved in a
broil, in which stones and sticks were used freely.

IN A DRUNKEN BROIL.

Several of the participants were badly hurt, and the
Bison himself much bruised. This conduct was regarded as so unbecoming and discreditable that on
the recommendation of the academic board he was
refused a commission in the army. He was heard
of three times after leaving the academy, once at
Galveston, Texas. There he had a terrible fight
with some desperadoes, and was forced to leave.
He was next seen on one of the California steamers,
and going upon the western coast he got into an
altercation with the officers of the steamer, and was
placed under guard down in the hold, and made to
work. The third and last time, as far as we know,
he was seen and recognized under the following

circumstances; In 1858, about ten years after the Bison had graduated, Lieutenant Ives, of the Topographical Engineer Corps, was engaged in making an exploration and survey of the Colorado River, emptying into the Gulf of California. While engaged in this work he would quite often leave his boat in the afternoon and go on shore and bivouac till morning. On one of these occasions a party of Mohave Indians came into his camp, and after talking some time in Spanish, the chief says, in English, "Ives, do you know me?" The Lieutenant was startled at hearing his name called so distinctly in English by this naked and painted-face chief; he replied that he did not, and asked the chief where he had learned to speak English so well. The chief replied: "Never mind that, but do you know me, Ives?" The Lieutenant scanned closely the huge painted chief, with feathers in head, rings through his nose and ears, and again answered he did not, and again asked the chief where he had learned English, and how did it happen that he knew him. The chief replied that he did not wonder at his not knowing him, as his change of nationality had brought with it a great change in habits, dress and appearance, and then added: "I am the Bison; we were together at West Point. I have with this little party been watching you for several days. My band wanted to

WANTED TO KILL HIM.

kill you and your little party, but I told them we had better wait and see, and try and talk; that we might do better than kill you. I have made them understand that after you have left and gone back trade will spring up, and we can then do better by trading or robbing the boats loaded with goods and supplies of all kinds." The Indians retired and were seen no more, nor did I bivouac on land any more. A year or two before this, Captain Lyon (killed in the late war) of the army, had a desperate fight with the Indians on an island in the Colorado River, the Indians supposed to have been commanded by the Bison. He was successful for years in raiding on the settlements and extending as far off as Arizona. It may be, and we think it probable, with the settlements extending from the West to the East, and from East to West, and the Indian area diminishing constantly, that this Indian chief may have gone as far North as the Black Hills, and may be even the veritable Sitting Bull, for to the close observer, Sitting Bull has shown as much skill and judgment as any educated civilized soldier could have done. It would not be strange if Sitting Bull proves to have been educated at West Point, and it seems to us probable that such is the case."

To this remarkable story the following was added by another West Pointer:

"Bison" McLean was a cadet at West Point from Missouri from 1844 to 1848, and stood *well intellectually* in a large and bright class. His diploma was refused him when his class graduated in 1848, he, having been convicted before a court-martial of dishonorable conduct.   During the Summer of 1852 I

JOINING THE INDIANS.

met him in New Mexico.   He had joined the Gila
Apache Indians, had been adopted into the tribe,
and had with him a wife or two from among the
squaws.   At this meeting he declared to me that he
would never forget nor forgive the injustice and injuries he conceived he had received from his classmates and the academic authorities at West Point.   If
"Bison" McLean is living he is forty-nine or fifty
years old.   In character he is strong and rugged.
His nature is untamed and licentious, his courage
superb, and his physical qualities almost herculean,
except in size.   He is fair-complexioned, light colored hair, very full-bearded and hairy-bodied man,
with a large head, and bold, irregular, full face.   His
height is five feet ten or eleven inches, and twenty-
four years ago he would have weighed about 175 or
180 pounds.

   "When a cadet there was no disguise he would

HAZARDOUS NATURE.

not assume and no hazard he would not venture for
the gratification of his appetites.   He never used
strong drink when I knew him, and notwithstanding
the great circumspection and vigilance of West
Point authority, he thwarted it until the very end of
his career at that institution, and was then brought
to grief by the testimony of his own classmates,
against whose watchfulness he had perhaps taken
no precaution.   Such a man, after near thirty years

or experience among the savages, might well fill the position of Sitting Bull. While he was a cadet, under the cloak of a false marriage, he ruined a pretty girl, Effie Conklin, who lived at Buttermilk Falls, a mile or two below West Point."

This startling theory, however, was generally discredited. A correspondent writing from Huntsville, Mo., to *The St. Louis Republican,* thus inveighed against it:

"Bison, as he was known at West Point, was born and raised in this (Randolph) county. He was of highly respectable parentage. A nephew of John McLean, once a U. S. senator from Illinois, and brother of Finis M. McLean, a prominent citizen of this county. He entered West Point about the year 1846, and, I think, graduated in the class of which Stonewall Jackson was a member. He (Bison) was killed by Indians near Tubac, Arizona, about the year 1870. A gentleman then living in Tucson, Arizona, who had formerly lived here, and who knew Bison here and there, informed his relatives of his death, and sent them what money he left. Lieut. Hall of the Fifth cavalry, who was with Crook in Arizona, and now with him, and who is well acquainted with Bison's relatives here, confirms the statements received by his relatives of his death and the manner of his death. Of Bison I suppose it may be said that his greatest fault was that of hav-

VIOLENT TEMPER.

ing an ungovernable temper, which he knew, and

which no doubt led him to pass his life beyond the
confines of civilization. It was through the influence of Senator Benton that he received the appointment as a cadet to West Point, though his father,
Charles McLean, was a zealous Whig. As to who
Sitting Bull is, the writer of this does not know.
But certain it is that he is not Bison."

CROW FOOT.—Son of Sitting Bull.

CHAPTER II.

MEDICINE MAN AND WARRIOR.

The True Story of Sitting Bull's Life—Son of a Rich Chief—
A Buffalo Hunter at Ten Years Old—His Three Wives and
Nine Children, Including Twins— How He Gained Supreme
Sway Among the Sioux—What it is to be a Medicine Man.

The fragmentary and often contradictory narratives rehearsed in the foregoing chapter contain much fiction and some fact. The general concensus of opinion now is that Sitting Bull was born at a camp on Willow Creek, near the mouth of the Cheyenne River, and near old Fort George, about 1830. He was the son of Jumping Bull, a Sioux chief, and a nephew of Four Horns and Hunting His Lodge, who were also chiefs. His father was, for an Indian, a wealthy man, and was "the owner of a great many ponies in four colors." Although not destined to be a warrior, Sitting Bull, who was at first called Sacred Standshot, soon became a famous hunter. At ten years old he was famous all through the tribe as a killer of buffalo calves. As his father was rich and did not need the meat, the boy gave away all the game he killed to the

39

poorer members of the tribe, and thus gained great

popularity. When he was thirteen years old his father died, and he thereupon "killed buffaloes and fed his people." The next year he fought with and killed a young Indian a few years older than himself, and his name was then changed to Lame Bull or Sitting Bull, on account of a wound which he then received, which made him permanently lame.

Before he reached his fifteenth year Sitting Bull began to develop those traits which afterward made him a terror to the white settlers of the frontier. He is described by an old Western scout as a boy of rather stocky appearance, not "straight as an arrow" like the traditional Indian, and not given to any of those boyish sports which Fennimore Cooper has set up as a standard. He was lazy and vicious, and never told the truth when a lie would serve better. But with all these traits he was fearless under all circumstances, a magnificent rider, an accurate shot, and capable of enduring an extraordinary amount of fatigue. As he approached 21

the cruelty of his nature became more marked, but he did nothing to indicate that he had in him the making of one of the representative men of his race.

He was three times married, one of his wives dying soon after the wedding. The other two wives were named She That Was Seen by the Nation, and

She That Had Four Robes. They bore in all nine children, including a pair of twins—a most unusual thing among Indians. When, after the Custer massacre, Sitting Bull at last surrendered at Fort Buford, one of his sons, a young man of 18, was at school in Chicago. Another, a boy of six years, was with the chief, and at the formal pow-wow the chief put his heavy rifle in the little fellow's hands and ordered him to give it to Major Brotherton, saying:

SURRENDERING HIS RIFLE.

"I surrender this rifle to you through my young son, whom I now desire to teach in this way that he has become a friend of the whites. I wish him to live as the whites do and be taught in their schools. I wish to be remembered as the last man of my tribe who gave up his rifle. This boy has now given it to you, and he wants to know how he is going to make a living."

Sitting Bull is commonly thought of as a warrior. In point of fact he was not. He was a "medicine man;" which means that he included within himself the three professions of the priesthood, medicine and law. He inherited from his father the chieftanship of a part of the Sioux tribe. But his remarkable ascendancy over the whole tribe or nation was due

A MIRACLE WORKER.

to his miracle-working and to his talents as a politician. He played upon the credulity of the Sioux with his "medicine" or pretended miracles, until they believed him to possess supernatural powers,

and were ready to follow his lead in everything.
Some other chiefs inherited wider authority, such as
Red Cloud and Crazy Horse, and some minor chiefs
were inclined now and then to dispute his sway,
such as Gall, Rain-in-the-face, and Broad Trail. But
when Sitting Bull made an appeal to the religious
fanaticism of the people, there was no withstanding
him. To the day of his death he was the principal
chief of all the Sioux and leader of 6,000 braves,
who at all times were ready at his command to commit any crime from murder up or down. As a med-

CONTROL OF THE SQUAWS.

icine man he had the squaws of his tribe abjectly
subservient, and through them was assisted in maintaining control of the bucks.

"Just what sort of a man a "medicine man" is,
not many people are prepared to say. Even those
who have traveled in the Indian country have not
the most definite ideas. As explained by a well-
versed writer in *The New York Sun*, every tribe has
many of these personages, some of them chiefs, and
all important men. They may be either young or
old ; and they are the leaders in all religious and
social functions. No one can visit any Indians at
any festival time, or time of general excitement from
any cause, without seeing the medicine men figuring
very conspicuously in whatever is going on. Sometimes they are merely beating drums, or perhaps
they are only crooning, while a dance or feast *is* in
progress. At other times they appear in the most

grotesque costumes, painted all over, hung with feathers and tails and claws, and carrying some wand or staff, gorgeous with color, and smothered with Indian finery.

The term medicine is a white man's expression which the Indians have adopted. It was applied to the priests of the tribes—for that is what they really are—because the first white men often found them making their incantations at the side of the sick, the wounded, or the dying. In reality they were exor-

EXORCISING EVIL SPIRITS.

cising the evil spirits of disease or death, but the white travelers, seeing them in the presence of the sick, put two and two together and called them medicine men. The term is two centuries old, and the Indians have so fully adopted it that when one of these officials is at his offices they say he is " making medicine."

The medicine-man is a conjurer, a magician, a dealer in magic, and an intermediary between the men of this world and the spirits of the other. He may know something of the rude pharmacopœia of his fellows, and may prescribe certain leaves or roots to allay fever, to arrest a cold, or to heal a wound. That is not his business, however, and such prescriptions are more apt to be offered by the squaws or by any member of the patient's family.

FEELING FOR THE DYING.

The medicine-man's work comes in when medicine fails, and it is pursued until death is seen to be cer-

tain, when—among most of the tribes—the sick or
wounded man is abandoned to meet his fate. Far
from thinking the only good Indian is a dead one,
the Indians themselves have little regard for one who
is half dead or seems certain to die.

In the Spring of 1890 as many medicine men as
could crowd into a tepee of the largest size, beat
their tomtoms and rattled their gourds all day and
night for nearly a week to save the life of a dying
plain chieftain, and then, as he seemed to get worse,
deliberately withdrew from the tepee and turned the
chief over to the ministrations of a Roman Catholic
priest, whom they had excluded while they thought
the man might live. They secured the best horse
the old man had, and, leading it to the side of the
tent, shot it through the head, that its carcass might
be buried with him. Then they engaged in the politics of the situation and made themselves warmly
friendly in the eyes of the heir apparent to the leadership. The old chief lived two or three days and
was dosed with the physics of both the whites and
red men. He begged for more " medicine," but
the conjurors had diagnosed his case and decided it
to be a waste of time to bother the spirits any longer in his behalf.

A WEIRD SIGHT.

No more weird sight is to be seen on the face of
this continent than a view of such a group of medicine men at work to save a life. Seen at night the
effect is awesome. They sit in a circle, broken only

by the body of the invalid stretched on a blanket, at the head of the tent opposite the door or tent opening. The wavering light is from a candle stuck ingeniously in a loop of birch bark, fastened tight in a slit in the end of a stick that has been thrust in the earth. The medicine men are painted in their own colors, green and yellow predominating. They are in full regalia, but their hair falls over their hideous faces as they bend forward to swing to and fro or to

HIDEOUS ORGIES.

beat their drums. All are singing. Often they sing only the tunes of ancient songs, the words being forgotten or having grown tiresome. Now and then one leaps to his feet, waving his befeathered rattle and yelling louder than the others. He sings the words that occur to him as suiting the case. He has on no clothing but moccasins and a breech-clout, or "gee-string," as they call that garment on the plains.

His thin, bony, bare red legs have the effect of their nakedness increased by the jumping, dangling tail of feathers that flutters down from his head and mixed its colors with the paint stripes on his flesh. His dancing is rather more like pounding something beneath him than like what we call dancing. He lifts his feet by bending his knees; lifts them and thumps them down monotonously, though he turns his body first to one side and then to the other. When the dancer tired and fell back in his place in the circle the spirit moved another to take his place.

The queer resemblances between the Indians and those Hebrew bands of whose history the Old Testament is a record have often been pointed out, but the writer has never seen attention called to the similiarity of certain of the Hebrew incidents to the common practices of Indian medicine men. In their

HEBREWS LIKE INDIANS.

early history the Hebrew leaders were continually holding converse with the Almighty. They went apart from their followers, up in mountains or in secret places and talked with Jehovah. That is precisely what the medicine men do to-day, or pretend to do. Every man who knows the Indians knows that during all this Messiah craze the medicine men of the various tribes have with great formality prepared to talk with Gitchie-Manitou or whatever they happen to call the Good Spirit. In some tribes they have built little wickiups of saplings and leaves and have gone into them and held conversations that were audible, though not intelligible, to the red men listening outside. The savages have heard the medicine man's voice and then have heard the voice of some other person replying to him in a jargon they could not unravel. In other tribes the medicine men have merely reported having held such conversations precisely as the Israelitish leaders did. It is

CONVERSE WITH JEHOVAH.

not for us to say that the grounds for such reports of the words of the Almighty were as slight in one case as the other, but it is true that the Indians have believed that their priests have really believed such conversations took place.

Those that have followed Sitting Bull's history know that his tribe has long been divided as to his power. One contingent has held that his "medicine" is no good, by which they mean that if he ever had genuine power to converse with spirits that power has left him. This often happens. Medicine men have their day and their decline, and he is a very sagacious Indian who can keep up faith in his ministrations for many years at a time or until he dies.

IN TERROR OF HIM.

The following authentic story illustrates how much Sitting Bull was feared in his tribe. In January, 1876, when Major Alderson was Indian agent at Fort Peck, he received from the government a letter which he was ordered to convey to Sitting Bull, commanding that worthy to come into the reservation or consider himself an outlaw. Alderson was in a quandary. His instructions were clear and peremptory. He sent for Sitting Bull, but Sitting Bull was just then too busy to visit Fort Peck; so the letter had, if possible, to be sent to him. A gentleman of unquestioned bravery, who could speak the Indian language fluently, was sent for and offered $500. and an escort if he would take the letter to the Indian camp. After consideration, however, the offer was declined. "For," said he, "if I could see Sitting Bull myself, I believe my life would be safe, but he would cut my ears off, sure." Finally, a party of Indians were dispatched with the missive after it had been very carefully explained and interpreted. After an absence of five days they returned and confessed that their hearts "were not big enough" to carry such a message to Sitting Bull. Consequently the benevolent intentions of the government were never conveyed to the contumacious chief.

And yet he was often magnanimous, from an Indian's point of view. For example, it is told that in 1873 he was coming with a small band to Fort Peck, and he found a short distance from the fort,

SAVED THEIR LIVES.

three white men lying asleep under a tree. His followers wanted to kill and scalp them on the spot, and secure their arms and horses. This the chief would not allow, and stood over them till all his band had passed. Next day in the fort, Sitting Bull walked up to the leader, Mr. Campbell, and shook hands. Campbell said he did not know him. "I am Sitting Bull," was the reply, "and I gave you your life yesterday." "How was that?" said Campbell. The chief proceeded to explain in a manner that satisfied Campbell that what he said was true, and, in gratitude, offered rewards, but Sitting Bull declined all such proffers, and after another hand-shaking, strode away.

CHAPTER III.

THE SAVAGE IN SOCIETY.

His Visit to a Camp at Fargo—Ashamed of His Primitive Garb—His First Suit of White Man's Clothes—A Discomfited Young Clergyman—The Indian at Dinner—His First Look in a Mirror—Autograph Selling.

Away back in the '70's, what is now the city of Fargo, North Dakota, was a mere camp of civil engineers. Among its occupants was one who had his wife and daughter with him. And that wife has related in the Denver *Republican* some interesting reminiscences of frontier life at that time, and especially of Sitting Bull's visit to their camp. "Our camp," she says, "had many visitors that year. It chanced that two well-known French gentlemen, heavy bondholders in the Northern Pacific, were making the tour to judge of the wisdom of their investments. Two or three New York stockholders were spending a few days in camp, also, and a couple of St. Paul wholesale merchants, on the lookout for possible contracts for supplies.

"I heard an unusual commotion outside the tent before rising in the morning, and, peeping out, saw a party of eight or ten Indians, full-blooded Sioux,

49

from the Missouri Valley, on their way to pay a visit
to the 'Great Father' in Washington. Among
them was the wily, keen-witted, merciless savage
who afterward became so famous—Sitting Bull.
They had left their native haunts clad only in their
native garb, but at Bismarck two or three of them
had succeeded the evening before they left in in-
ducting themselves into some of the cast-off clothes

GORGEOUS APPAREL.

of Fort Lincoln soldiers. Over these they had
thrown their own blankets, so Sitting Bull had not
discovered the change until the next morning.
While openly scoffing at such degeneracy, the interpreter accompanying them told us the chief was
secretly chagrined at not having procured such
gorgeous raiment for himself, and upon his arrival
at Fargo he declined to be presented to the poten-
tates of the Northern Pacific Railroad until properly
attired.

"As he was resolute in his desire to have white
man's clothes, a contribution was levied on different
members of the encampment, the result of which,
although satisfactory to him, struck the rest of us
as inexpressibly ludicrous. The only pair of trousers whose waist-band was suited to his girth belonged to a very short man, and gave to their present wearer that laughable appearance inseparable

A QUEER OUTFIT.

from abbreviated nether garments. As no ordinary
masculine sock was long enough to fill the gap be-

tween shoes and trousers, Aunt Venny, the huge old negro cook, was called to the rescue, and a pair of snow white stockings were given to him. There was, of course, some difficulty in giving these the smooth, unwrinkled appearance desirable, but the ebony aunty (whom I have always suspected of presiding over that extraordinary toilet) got round the difficulty by fastening hose and trousers together with those useful little articles known as safety pins.

"One of our brawny teamsters contributed a shirt. Flannel shirts were in general wear among our engineers, and a white one (commonly known as a boiled shirt) was an almost unknown luxury. However, one of the men resurrected one long buried in a hidden trunk, and, to Sitting Bull's great satisfaction, he was instructed as to the approved manner of entrance and exit. A waistcoat was not to be found, and it seemed for a time that civilization, as represented by a coat, was for him still in the dim future. But here again his good genius in the shape of the fat old negress intervened. A coat having been found whose only objection was its extreme narrowness across the back, this ingenious woman energetically ripped the centre seam

A LUCKY EXPEDIENT.

and inserted a broad stripe of vivid red, cut from a heavy blanket. A stove-pipe hat polished to the last degree was found, and thus equipped the famous chieftain made his début before the presiding officials of the encampment.

" The wives of several of the officers had been at various times resident in the camp, but just then I chanced to be left alone with my little girl to represent our sex. I had been warned of the impending call, but had been told nothing of the change of raiment, and when this astounding toilet appeared before me, the keeping of the muscles of my face under control, and maintaining a gravity befitting the occasion was the great triumph of my life. My little daughter was not so fortunate, and at once gave utterance to an uproarious burst of mirth, causing her father to instantly seize and bear her ignominiously from the tent.

SITTING BULL'S LANGUAGE.

" Sitting Bull's language was a compound of pure Sioux, mongrel English, bespattered here and there with a word or two of French, picked up in his intercourse with post traders. As these traders generally use language adapted to the strength of their emotions when their stores are pillaged by the half-breeds, the ejaculations picked up and embalmed by Sitting Bull were occasionally startling to ladies. But women on the frontier learn to exhibit great fortitude in matters of this sort. So I proudly felt that I was acquitting myself very creditably during the interview, and as I had been instructed to invite the chieftain to dine with us in due form and state, I did so. He evidently viewed the idea of sitting down to a meal at the same time with a woman with

HIS IDEA OF WOMEN.

much disfavor. His creed taught him that I should stand meekly behind his chair, bringing to him his nectar and ambrosia as represented by bean soup and venison, myself thankfully swallowing at intervals such morsels as he might see fit to toss me.

"Among our guests that day was a young Eastern clergyman, making his first trip over the prairies. He was a very zealous youth, strongly imbued with the missionary spirit, albeit sadly lacking in experience. I soon saw he looked upon the meeting with these Indians as a special providence, and burned with a desire to turn it to account in their behalf spiritually. Still no opportunity seemed to offer, and we took our places at the table. Now, clergymen were rare visitors in those regions at that date, and we had become lamentably thoughtless as regarded many of the religious observances of civ-

A SERIOUS DILEMMA.

ilization. No sooner had we seated ourselves than the dreadful consciousness came over me that my husband was entirely oblivious of the fact that when a minister of the gospel was present grace was a customary preliminary to a meal. He prepared to carve the substantial roast of venison, and there was no lull in the conversation of the gentlemen. In vain I fixed my gaze upon his face and strove to send him a mental telegram. In desperation I thrust my foot across, seeking his beneath the table, hoping in this way to give him an intimation of what should be done. But, alas! when I did succeed in touching him, he, with that depraved obtuseness seen only in man, looked up with a cheerful 'pardon me,' as though he had trespassed beyond his boundaries beneath the table.

"The poor young clergyman had given one or two loud 'ahems' in vain, and now in despair rose from his seat, and, with arms extended over the

SAYING GRACE.

table, loudly invoked a blessing upon our feast. Despairing of any other chance, I suppose, he dexterously interwove a petition for the conversion of the grim old savage before him, making in all a rather lengthy preamble. Sitting Bull's eyes had been fixed eagerly on the venison, wandering only to the motions of the carving knife in the hands of my husband, who, finding his hospitable efforts suddenly suspended by the unexpected prayer, sat with the carving implements in his hands, gazing helplessly at me with an air of mild reproach as if to say, 'Why didn't you warn me?'

"The old warrior evidently regarded this devout exercise as some sort of incantation by a medicine man of the pale-faces, designed to affect food, for as

SUSPICIOUS OF EVIL.

our minister, in his eagerness to offer a suitable petition, wildly waved his hands over the various dishes, Sitting Bull glanced suspiciously from one

article of food to another, then to the faces of the white men, and finally sank sullenly back in the unaccustomed chair.

"When at length his plate was filled and sent round to him, he glowered over it, muttered and grunted, but made no attempt to eat. In distress I beckoned to the half-breed, who served as interpreter, and who hung about the tent awaiting his turn to eat. After a series of grunts exchanged with the savage, the half-breed informed us: 'Great chief say white medicine man put bad spirit in meat and potatoes. If chief eat, maybe he be weak and never travel to see the Great Father.'

"A long explanation ensued, and at last our grim guest fell upon his long-delayed dinner with fierce appetite. I regret to say, however, that in the training of his childhood table manners must have been sadly neglected. The only possible use he could see for a fork was to reach forth with his grimy hands and spear various articles of food which appeared to him desirable.

"At the close of the meal the persevering little minister was on the watch for his opportunity, and, as we were now better prepared, a decent silence ensued, and we bowed our heads with due reverence for the return of thanks. The poor man opened his mouth and had uttered but a word or

SITTING BULL OBJECTS.

two of adjuration when Sitting Bull arose and with one stride reached him, placed his hand over the parson's mouth, and with an emphatic, 'No, no; once enough; no more call down the Great Spirit to crush the chief,' he marched out.

"For the remainder of the day he strutted about the camp with the most absolute self-satisfaction, his confidence and pleasure in the loveliness of his new attire being unbounded. Furthermore, upon strolling into my tent and peering about at the various unknown articles, he espied a small hand-mirror. Now, Sitting Bull, equipped as he was that day, squatted on the floor surveying himself in the little mirror, is about as different an object from the Sitting Bull of the Record of the War Department as it is possible to conceive, but the one is as much of a reality as the other.

"Nothing could induce him to return the glass. He deposited it somewhere beneath his vestments and went out, but justice compels me to state that

A FEATHER FOR A MIRROR.

he returned to the tent with the tall war plume worn when arrayed for battle, and, plucking one heavy quill from it, bestowed it as a great treasure upon my little girl. It was white, apparently from the wing of some huge white bird, but its tip was stained with crimson, and he haughtily explained it was the blood of 'Wah-ton-set, chief of the Arickarees.'

"I saw him at Bismarck long after this episode, the centre of a group of Eastern curiosity hunters, where he was driving a thriving business disposing of his autographs at twenty-five cents apiece. Re-

gard for my sex should, I suppose, induce me to refrain from recording the fact, but it is true that I saw
a New York belle in the crowd around him, who,
not content with the autograph, aspired to bear away
some more novel memento, and mincing up to him
whispered something in his ear. The old chief
grinned and shook his head, then something heavy
passed from her hand to his, and with another grin
to the crowd the grimy, dirty, smoke-scented old
heathen bent his head down and kissed her."

Such, then, was the formidable personage around
whom the disaffected Sioux rallied, in hope of win-
ning by force redress for their many grievances.

CHAPTER IV.

THE FOE OF THE WHITE MAN.

FORT BUFORD'S GHASTLY TRAGEDY—AN ACCOMPLISHED CATTLE THIEF
—CONTEMPT FOR PALE FACES—OPPOSING INVASION OF HIS TERRI-
TORY—THE FORT ELLIS EPISODE—A PEN-AND-INK SKETCH OF THE
SAVAGE CHIEF.

Sitting Bull first became widely known to the
white people of America in 1866. In that year he
led a terrible raid against the settlers and military
post at Fort Buford. His path was marked with
blood and made memorable by ruthless savagery.
As the marauders approached the fort, the com-
mandant of the post shot and killed his own wife,
at her earnest request, to save her from the more
cruel fate of falling into the hands of the Sioux.
After that awful introduction to public notice, the
chief kept himself conspicuous by his daring, his
cunning, and his implacable hostility to the whites.
He seldom went further than to steal horses and
cattle, but in that he was very successful, and no
man was ever more agile in eluding pursuit.

His influence throughout the whole tribe was bad,
and he was gathering about him constantly increasing numbers of young men, whose morals were

corrupted and who were "spoiling for a fight." His attitude toward white men was impudent and defiant; even toward the military authorities. To emphasize his contempt for the "pale-faces," he would never speak a word of English, or admit for a moment that he understood it. He even objected to having it spoken in his presence. General Morrow was in command of Fort Buford in 1869, and when numerous depredations were committed and stock stolen, Sitting Bull was accused because of his general character, although he was then a chief. He denied the charge with great vigor, and not long afterward one of his men was killed. He charged

DEMANDING SATISFACTION.

that the killing was unprovoked and had been done by a soldier. He made a demand for some sort of a settlement, and displayed such powers of argument that General Morrow piled up blankets on the dead Indian until the chief declared himself satisfied.

His success in obtaining such a concession drew around him some of the bolder members of the tribe who had before held aloof, although they did not dare to dispute his authority. From that day forward Sitting Bull became a great chief among his people. It was conjectured by some of the white scouts at the time that the wily young buck had been playing a part, and that his laziness was only assumed. At all events, the chief began at once to display a deliberative turn of mind altogether at variance with his previous character.   In a very few

RECOGNIZED LEADER.

months his perspicacious view of events became so well known that he had every buck in the tribe under his thumb, and those who had been bold enough to consider themselves possible rivals were heard of no more.   He was of more than an ordinarily restless nature, even from an Indian standpoint, and as soon as he felt that his power was absolute he gave orders to strike camp and go to the Yellowstone River.   There the tepees were put up, the stock tethered, and orders issued that no white man

SITTING BULL'S CLAIM.

should be permitted to enter the camp.   Sitting Bull set up a claim to all the land for forty rods on both sides of the Yellowstone and all its tributaries.

Notwithstanding this embargo, several white men did get into the camp and get out again with whole skins and proper quota of scalps.   The big chief was crafty enough to impress upon these men the

ADMIRATION FOR THE CHIEF.

strength of his mental make-up.   He gave them exhibitions of his judicial wisdom in determining disputes, of the fairness of his decisions, of the regard in which he was held by his people, of his skill as a hunter and a rider.   When these men returned to civilization their praise for Sitting Bull was extravagant. One of them went back and spent several days more in the Indian camp, and when the butchery of Custer and his command took place some years later wrote an extensive and impassioned defense of Sitting Bull's work on that bloody field. Another white man who formed an intense admiration for the chief was John Nelson, a scout, who afterward became connected with Buffalo Bill's Wild West show as an interpreter.

In the latter part of ·1875 a party of fifty white men from Montana invaded Sitting Bull's territory and built a fort. The chief ordered them to leave, and some accounts are to the effect that he enforced the demand by killing one of the party. The historians favorable to the Indian side, however, assert that an Indian was killed first, and that two white men were killed in retaliation. It is certain, however, that there were two deaths in the fort from

BESIEGING THE PALE-FACES.

bullets fired by the Indians. Sitting Bull immediately put the fort under fire, and there were desultory attacks daily, lasting through the months of December and January. Six white men were killed and eight wounded. Five hundred warriors surrounded the fort, and their persistent patience soon convinced the besieged that the intention was to starve them to death. Two of the imprisoned men volunteered to attempt to reach the nearest point where help could be obtained. They got out safely at midnight, and after great hardship and suffering reached Fort Ellis in the latter part of February, after having traveled afoot for seventeen days, half starved and badly frozen. Four companies of United States cavalry, three companies of Montana militia, and about seventy-five friendly Indians were put under marching orders at once. The chief heard of their coming through his outposts, and sent word that he was glad that the white men were to be taken away. Knowing he could not hope to compete with the reinforcement, he withdrew his force to a safe distance and was not attacked. The wretched survivors were rescued, and after the evacuation Sitting Bull fired the fort, and had the bodies of the six dead men dug from their shallow graves and scalped.

HIS INVETERATE HATRED.

This hatred for the whites distinguished Sitting Bull above all other Sioux. When he was engaged in hostilities he was as ferocious and bloodthirsty as a beast of prey, and his atrocities, or those directed by him, have earned him death a thousand times. In peace he was a smooth liar, and, professing the utmost friendship, never failed to be insolent and insulting when the opportunity offered. His personal appearance is described by John Finerty, who paid the chief a visit at his camp on Mushroom Creek, Woody Mountains, Northwest Territory. The noted chief had taken a trip into the British possessions to remain until he could arrange for amnesty for his connection with the uprising of which the Little Big Horn or Custer massacre was

A VIVID PICTURE.

one of the sanguinary incidents. Mr. Finerty thus paints the picture:

"Soon afterward an Indian mounted on a cream-colored pony and holding in his hand an eagle's wing which did duty as a fan, spurred in back of the chiefs, and stared stolidly for a minute or two at me. His hair, parted in the ordinary Sioux fashion, was without a plume. His broad face with a prominent hooked nose and wide jaws was destitute of paint. His fierce, half-bloodshot eyes gleamed from under brows which displayed large perceptive organs, and as he sat there on his horse regarding me with a look which seemed blended of curiosity and insolence, I did not need to be told that he was Sitting Bull. . . . After a little the noted savage dismounted and led his horse partly into the shade. I noticed that he was an inch or two over the medium height, broadly built, rather bow-legged, and limped slightly, as though from an old wound. He sat upon the ground, and was soon engirdled by a crowd of young warriors with whom he was an especial favorite as representing the unquenchable hostility of the aboriginal savage to the hated pale-faces."

CHAPTER V.

THE LITTLE BIG HORN.

SITTING BULL AT THE HEIGHT OF HIS POWER—THE RUSH FOR THE BLACK
HILLS—INEFFECTUAL NEGOTIATIONS—SITTING BULL'S DEFIANT ANS-
WER TO A SUMMONS—PREPARATIONS FOR A GREAT STRUGGLE—HOW
THE THREE DIVISIONS OF THE ARMY MARCHED INTO THE INDIANS'
COUNTRY.

Sitting Bull reached the zenith of his fame and
power in the Sioux war of 1876. That conflict began more like a civil war than any other of our In-
fightings. There were diplomatic hagglings, breaches
of faith on both sides, deliberate preparations for a
long campaign, an finally an ultimatum. The inspiring cause of the trouble was the discovery of
gold and silver in the Black Hills. This was then
an almost unknown region, girt by the famous Bad
Lands. Even the Indians went there seldom, re-

CUSTER EXPEDITION.

garding it as a "medicine country," or haunted
region. But when it became known that precious
metals were to be found there, pressure was brought
to bear upon the Government, and an expedition
was sent. Ostensibly it was a military reconnais-

66

sance. In reality, it was a prospecting party. It was led by General George A. Custer, and consisted of more than 1200 men, with sixty Indian guides. The expedition found the hills rich with precious metals, and forthwith there was a great rush of miners and other settlers.

This greatly annoyed the Indians, to whom all that region belonged. Red Cloud, Spotted Tail, and other chiefs visited Washington to protest against the invasion, which was a clear violation of existing treaties. The Government agreed to keep the prospectors out, but failed to do so, and by the fall of 1875 there were a thousand miners at work in the Black Hills. Then the Indians demanded payment for the land of which they were being robbed, and a Government Commission visited them to agree on terms. But the Commission returned with its work undone, and reported that it would be impossible to settle the matter without force. The Indians, too, came to the conclusion that they would have to fight for their rights. Accordingly they began to desert

FLOCKING TO SITTING BULL.

Red Cloud and the other more conservative chiefs, and to flock about Sitting Bull, who had all along been truculent and had opposed parting with the land at any price.

For many years a number of hostile Sioux had been roaming through the northern portion of Dakota under the leadership of Sitting Bull, Crazy Horse, and a few other chiefs. In 1874 their num-

ber was estimated at 7,000, but subsequently about
4,000 of these Indians went into the agencies at
Standing Rock, Spotted Tail, and Cheyenne River
reducing the number who might be properly called
hostile to about 3,000. The War Department estimated Sitting Bull's band at about 3,500 Indians.
The number of warriors in these bands could not
originally have exceeded between 400 and 500. All
attempts to induce these Indians to go upon reservations had thus far failed. In 1875, Gen. Crook
visited Washington for the purpose of consulting
the Administration in regard to its future treatment
of them. With the Secretary of War and Gen.
Cowen, acting Secretary of the Interior, Gen. Crook

PLANNING AN EXPEDITION.

visited the President and proposed that an expedition be sent against these Indians during the Winter, when they would be less prepared than at any
other time to resist. His recommendation was fav-
orably considered. A message was sent to Sitting
Bull and the chiefs who were operating with him,
ordering them to report at their reservations before
the 1st of January, 1876, the alternative being that
if they did not the United States would make war
against them.

The hostile Sioux paid no attention whatever to
the orders directing them to report at reservations,
and preparations were made to send an expedition
against them. The first engagement occurred in
January, 1876, but resulted in no advantage to

either side. A vigorous compaign was accordingly organized in the Spring of 1876, against the hostile

WAR AGAINST THE SIOUX.

tribes of the Sioux, who under the leadership of Sitting Bull refused to leave their camps on the Big Horn and Tongue Rivers, in the Valley of the Yellowstone, and enter upon the reservations which the Government had set apart for them. The Government dispatched scouts into the Big Horn country with a peremptory notice of ejection, and the threat that if they should not heed the summons, troops would be sent into the valley to drive them out. Sitting Bull received the message with contempt,

AN OMINOUS REPLY.

saying : "When you come for me you need bring no guides. You will easily find me. I shall be right here. I shall not run away." This answer was ominous, and the military authorities at once prepared for serious action. All available troops were ordered into active service. Three columns under the command of Gen. Gibbon, Gen. Terry, and Gen Crook, were equipped and placed under marching orders. The objective point was Sitting Bull's camp, in the Big Horn country. The three columns were to meet on the Powder or Tongue River, and combine their forces in the heart of the enemy's country. Gen. Crook at Fort Reno, was to strike north ; Gen. Terry, with Gen. Custer's cavalry, at Fort Lincoln, was to march west; and Gen. Gibbon, at Fort Buford, was to descend the Yellowstone Valley and join Gen. Terry.

General Terry's command followed the proposed line of the Northern Pacific Railroad, from Fort Lincoln on the Missouri River to the Yellowstone, at the mouth of the Powder River. The total fighting strength was 1,007 men, including the 7th Cavalry, two companies (C and G) of the 17th Infantry, Company B of the 6th Infantry, a battery of Gatling guns, commanded by Lieutenant W. H. Low, Jr., and a detachment of Indian scouts. The strength of the cavalry was 28 commissioned officers and 747 men; of the infantry, 8 officers and 135 men, and of the battery, 2 officers and 32 men. The train was a large and expensive one, giving employment to 179 men in various capacities, and including 114 six-team mules, 35 pack mules, and 37 two-horse

STARTING OUT.

teams. The expedition set out on May 17th, General Custer commanding the cavalry and General Terry being in advance with the infantry and train. The line of march from Fort Lincoln led almost directly west to the Little Missouri. The Mauvaises Terres were reached in ten days, and twelve bridges were built over Davis Creek, which the column was compelled to cross fourteen times. On May 29th, camp was pitched on the Little Missouri, and General Custer after an extended reconnaissance reported that there were no signs of Indians, and that it would be safe to resume the march on the morrow.

On June 1st, there was a hard snow storm and the expedition halted. Two days afterward three scouts entered the camp on Big Beaver Creek and brought word that General Gibbon's column was on the north bank of the Yellowstone, opposite Rosebud River; and that steamers loaded with supplies had arrived at the stockade below Powder River. The original plan had been to march directly to the

CHANGE OF PLAN.

stockade, but inasmuch as this would involve a circuitous route, and as there was high water in the Yellowstone, General Terry ordered Colonel Moore to send the supplies to Powder River, and then led his own column to the valley of that stream by a shorter detour. Scouts were also sent to General Gibbon with instructions for him to remain where he was until General Terry's command should join him. General Custer, after a ride of fifty miles, marked out a road for the wagons, and conducted the column to the banks of Powder River, about 25 miles from its mouth. General Terry with a cavalry escort pushed down stream and found the steamers with the supplies moored to the bank. Learning that General Gibbon's force was encamped 35 miles up the river, and that the country was swarming with Indians, General Terry embarked on one of the steamboats and steamed up the river to hold a conference with him. General Gibbon's

INDIAN CAMP DISCOVERED.

scouts reported that there was a large Indian

5

camp strongly posted in the valley of Rosebud
River.   After a brief conference the two command-
ers agreed upon a plan of operations, and General
Terry returned to the Powder River.

The main column reached the Yellowstone on
June 11th, and went into camp.   General Terry
sent Colonel Reno with six companies of cavalry
and a Gatling gun to ascend Powder River Valley,
and striking across to Tongue River, descend to the
Yellowstone, where, according to the plan, the rest
of the command would be encamped.   The scouting party was detained by rain until June 10th, when
it started in a north-westerly direction along the
north bank of the Powder River.   At that time no
tidings had been received from General Crook's
force, but the columns of General Terry and General Gibbon were within 35 miles of each other on
opposite sides of the Yellowstone.   The Generals

PLAN OF CAPTURE.

had arranged that the northern column should return to its former camp opposite the mouth of the
Rosebud River and prevent the escape of Sitting
Bull's Indians across the river if they should be
routed or hard pressed by the cavalry.   General
Terry's force was to ascend the Yellowstone as far
as the Tongue River, and there await the return of
Colonel Reno's scouting party.   General Custer was
then to take nine companies of cavalry and a detachment of Indian scouts, and with a large train of
pack mules, loaded with supplies for fifteen days,

was to pass up the valley of the Tongue River, make a forced march across the country to Rosebud River, where the Indians were reported to be in strong force, and to rejoin the main column at the mouth of the river. Meanwhile, four companies of General Gibbon's cavalry were to be ferried across the Yellowstone, and with the three companies of the 7th, that were left with General Terry, were to march up the river to the mouth of the Rosebud River and up the valley in the direction of General Custer's force. This was the plan of operations on June 12th.

On July 3, advices were received at Bismarck, on the Missouri, from Gen. Terry's command. They

COLONEL RENO CENSURED.

were to the following effect: " Col. Reno with his cavalry command had returned from the work assigned him, and was censured for not fully obeying instructions. Gen. Custer with twelve companies of cavalry, took the trail of the 1,500 Indians where Col. Reno had abandoned it, and pushed into Rosebud Valley, where the Indians had been congregated

RUMORS OF BATTLE.

for some time. Rumors prevail that Gen. Custer had since had a battle with the Indians. Gen. Custer, on the 21st, was at the mouth of the Rosebud and a fight with the Indians was expected about the 24th. Gen. Custer carried ten days' rations. Gen. Terry was to supply Gen. Custer from the mouth of the Big Horn, should his pursuit of Indians lead

'him that way.   Otherwise, Gen. Custer **may go to**
Fort Fetterman for supplies.   Gen. Terry retains
two steamboats, carrying troops and supplies.   The
Yellowstone being high, boats have no difficulty in

ROUGH COUNTRY.

running to Big Horn.   The country is so rough that
even Gatling guns cannot be easily moved by land.
Col. Reno, on the 20th, was near the mouth of
Tongue River.   Moore, with six companies of in-
fantry, was at the mouth of the Powder River, Gen.
Gibbon's command was at the mouth of the Big
Horn.   Two hunters were killed by the Indians near
Powder River.   No other casualties had occurred.
The health of the command was good.   Gen. Terry
had mounted 200 infantry on the mules of the
wagon train.   He had not heard from Gen. Crook."

General Gibbon's force was concentrated at Fort
Buford, at the junction of the Yellowstone and the
Missouri, and was under marching orders about the
middle of May.   The line of March extended up
the right or north bank of the Yellowstone, and the
force comprised six companies of the 7th Infantry

INDIANS HOVERING AROUT.

and four companies of cavalry.   Indians were frequently seen hovering about the camp, and three
soldiers who had strayed from the main force were
shot.   The column advanced as far as the Rosebud
River and went into camp.   Learning from scouts
that General Terry's force was approaching, General

Gibbon resolved to descend the Yellowstone in order to form a junction with the main command. After consulting with General Terry 35 miles west of Powder River and receiving supplies, General Gibbon retraced his steps to his former camp, and subsequently pressed on to the Big Horn, where he was stationed when the Custer massacre occurred.

Brigadier-General Crook had led soldiers in an attack upon the hostile Sioux Indians twice during the Centennial year. Leaving Fort Fetterman in Wyoming Territory early in March, he succeeded, after a fortnight's march in very inclement weather, in surprising the village of Crazy Horse on the Pow-

SCATTERING THE SAVAGES.

der River. The soldiers entered the Indian camp early in the morning of March 17th, quickly scattered the savages, killed many, and destroyed a large amount of ammunition stored in the tents. Owing to a lack of sufficient supplies and the exhaustion of the troops, General Crook was then compelled to return to Fort Fetterman. This return march the Sioux Nation interpreted as a retreat caused by fear, and many Indians at the Red Cloud and Spotted Tail Agencies have since left the agencies and joined their kindred in the revolt.

General Crook was occupied during May in gathering a large force of soldiers at Fort Fetterman, and in organizing a pack train of sufficient size to carry supplies to feed the little army for two months, it being his intention to make another and more de-

termined attack upon the Indians. Toward the end
of May the preparations for the expedition were
completed. The force numbered in all about 1100
men.

The expedition marched from Fort Fetterman on
May 29th. For a week the march was continued in
a north-westerly direction. The ruins of two forts,
now known as Old Fort Reno and Old Fort Kearney, were reached and passed, but no Indians were
encountered. Occasionally columns of smoke were
seen rising in the distance, indicating the presence of
an Indian camp, but no enemy was seen. The
Tongue River, over 190 miles from Fort Fetterman
was crossed on the morning of June 7th, and a camp

COUNCIL OF WAR.

was established. At midnight an Indian speaking
the Sioux language was heard shouting from the
summit of a high bluff near the camp. Other Indians soon joined him, and apparently there was a
war council. They warned the members of the expedition to return to Fort Fetterman if they valued
their lives, as before two suns rolled round the camp
would be attacked by a multitude of the Sioux. A
day and a night passed, however, before the threatened attack was made. It was late on the afternoon
of June 9th when an infantry picket saw a band of
Indians creeping to good positions behind rocks on
a bluff near the camp. The infantry were immediately formed into order of battle, and the cavalrymen mounted their horses. The infantry soldiers

fired several volleys and the Indians returned the fire. Four companies of cavalry then ascending the bluff, routed the Indians.

On the following day, it being thought that the camp was in an unsafe position, the troops marched sixteen miles to the junction of Goose Creek with the Tongue River, where a favorable position was found. Here, on June 14th. the band of Crow and

RESOLVED TO FIGHT.

Snake scouts joined the expedition. General Crook now resolved to seek and attack the Sioux. The five companies of infantry were mounted on mules belonging to the pack train, and four days' rations and one blanket were allowed to every man. No means of transportation were taken except riding horses and mules. The Snakes and Crows, 250 in number, were provided with Government arms and ammunition. The march·was resumed on the morning of June 16th. A distance of 35 miles was made and the force encamped at the headwaters of the Rosebud River, between high bluffs. A hollow square was formed in anticipation of a night attack, the Crows reporting that there were signs of the presence of the Sioux. The camp was astir at five o'clock the following morning, and the march was

QUIETLY ADVANCING.

continued down the valley of the Rosebud. The advance was made as quietly as possible, and the column was divided so as to avoid raising dust, and thus give warning to the enemy. The Crows marched in front and on the flanks of the column of soldiers, but they had forgotten to send forward their scouts during the night before, and this omission was to cost the army many lives that day.

The expedition had marched ten miles, when at 7.30 A. M., the Crow scouts suddenly came running in from the front and declared that the Sioux were about to make an attack, A halt was made and an order was given to unsaddle the animals, it being supposed that the scouts had merely seen some of the scouts near their village on the hills engaged in herding their ponies. Yells were soon heard, however, beyond a low hill to the north, and a Crow

CROW SIGNAL HEARD.

chief soon appeared over the hill and gave a signal to the Crows that meant to them that the Sioux were near at hand. The Crows instantly dashed forward and disappeared over the hill. At this moment the two battalions of the 3d Cavalry were resting on the south side of Rosebud Creek, and the battalion of the 2d Cavalry on the north side, The cavalry made ready to mount, scouts came galloping back and said that the Sioux were about to charge, and shots began to be heard. The valley in which the troops were stationed is surrounded by hills, rising ridge above ridge on every side, and these ridges are frequently cut through with deep ravines. If the expedition had continued its march a mile further in the same track it would have entered one of the deepest of these ravines, and here probably the Sioux had intended to make their at-

DANGER SHUNNED.

tack. If it had happened as they wished, the troops would have had great difficulty in forming any line of defense, and doubtless hundreds of them would have perished. Gen. Crook on receiving the news of the advance of the Sioux, rode to a small hill at the front and saw that the hostile Indians were indeed coming forward with the evident intention of attacking the troops clustered in the valley below. Gen. Crook immediately formed his plan of battle. He ordered Col. Royall on the left with the 3d Cavalry to advance and occupy the hills in his front and Capt. Mills, with another portion of the 3d Cavalry with two infantry companies, to advance on the right.

DRIVING THE SAVAGES.

The columns drove the Indians from hill to hill, but in the advance the left, under Col. Royall became separated from the infantry. The Indians from the higher ridges discovered the unfortunate position of the left wing, and entering the gap between it and the center attacked the cavalrymen not only on that flank, but also in the rear. Col. Royall was compelled to retreat, and in the endeavor to consolidate his line with the center his troops were forced to descend into a deep ravine. The Indians immediately took possession of the abandoned hill, and poured a galling fire into the ranks of the soldiers as they retreated. while Indians at either end of the hollow

HAND TO HAND CONFLICT.

boldly attacked the soldiers. A hand to hand conflict followed between many of the soldiers and the Indians. Several of the soldiers in the hurried retreat down the hill and across the hollow were cut off from their comrades, were surrounded by the Sioux, and after a desperate resistance were killed and scalped. One of the soldiers who surrendered his musket to a Sioux Indian was instantly brained with the weapon by the Indian. The main body of Col. Royall's force regained the main body of the expedition, however, and the troops were reformed and again pushed forward to the line of battle. The troops now advanced three miles, clearing the hills on either side of the Rosebud. At 1 P. M., Gen. Crook decided to halt, the Crow scouts not knowing in which direction the great Sioux village could be found.

RESULTS OF THE BATTLE.

In the battle 10 soldiers had been killed and 19 wounded, and one Snake Indian killed and several Crow Indians wounded. Gen. Crook resolved to continue his pursuit the following day, but learned with dismay from his Indian allies that they intended to go home. The Crows said that they had captured a pony, which they had left in their native village, and feared that the Sioux had attacked the village.

The snakes complained that they had not been well supported by the soldiers in their attack upon the Sioux. It being impossible to pursue the Sioux without scouts, Gen. Crook reluctantly retreated to the Goose Creek camp.

CHAPTER VI.

CUSTER'S LAST RALLY.

DEPARTURE OF THE CAVALRY—MARCH OF THE INFANTRY—FIRST NEWS
OF THE DISASTER—THE RESCUE—STORY OF THE BATTLE—RENO'S
FORCE RESCUED TWICE—HOW CUSTER FOUGHT TO THE END.

It was the Year of a Hundred Years. The
American people had just celebrated the National
Anniversary with unparalleled pomp and enthusiasm.
The International Exposition at Philadelphia was
open and thronged with myriads of visitors from
all parts of the world. Suddenly, upon the scene
of universal festivity and rejoicing, fell a shadow of
a great tragedy. The first news of disaster was
received with incredulity. But fuller tidings "followed fast and followed faster," until there was no
doubting them. Here is the story, as written to
The New York Tribune from the camp at the mouth
of the Big Horn River, Montana, on July 3d, 1876:

"It is the eve of Independence Day—the Centennial Fourth—and all the land is ablaze with enthusiasm. Alas! if the tidings of General Custer's

A GREAT SHADOW.

terrible disaster could be borne on the wings of the
four winds, dirges and not anthems would be heard

84

in the streets of Philadelphia, New York, and San Francisco to-morrow! A great shadow has fallen upon the valley of the Big Horn. The youngest of our generals, the *beau sabreur* of the Army of the Potomac, the golden-haired chief whom the Sioux had learned to dread, has fought his last fight. Surrounded by over two hundred and fifty brothers-

FOUGHT HIS LAST BATTLE.

in-arms, Custer lies buried on the field where he fought and fought and fought until he could fight no longer.

"Let me make the story of his death as simple as I can. You already know that before Gen. Terry reached the mouth of Powder River he had sent Major Reno with six companies of the Seventh Cavalry to scout along the headwaters of the stream and to join the main column at the mouth of Tongue River. Major Reno went as far as the Rosebud, and on his arrival at the mouth of Tongue River brought word that he had discovered a heavy Indian trail. The command at once set out for the Rosebud. Gen. Gibbon's column was met on the left bank, and was soon on the march in the same direction. On June 22d, after a full consultation between Gens. Terry, Gibbon, and Custer, a plan of operations was arranged, and Gen. Custer started on his fatal errand. It was high noon when his regiment set out. Never were troops in better spirits than those bold riders!

VALLEY OF DEATH.

As they disappeared from our view, half of them forever, an old soldier remarked: 'There goes a command of which even a corps commander might have been proud during the Civil War!' Poor fellows! They little thought, as they spurred their horses out of camp, that the valley beyond was the Valley of Death!

"Gen. Terry had assured Gen. Custer that he would be at the forks of the Big Horn and the Little Big Horn by the evening of June 26th, and that Gen. Gibbon's column would be with him. Gen. Terry and his staff, with Gen. Gibbon, steamed up the Yellowstone, and on Saturday, June 24th, arrived at the mouth of the Big Horn. Freeman's, Sanno's, Clifford's, Logan's, and English's companies of the Seventh Infantry were ferried across the Yellowstone. Major Brisbin, with Ball's, Thompson's, Whelan's, and Roe's companies of the Second Cavalry, and Lowe's Gatling Battery, which had been added to Gen. Gibbon's column at the Rosebud,

OFF FOR THE FRAY.

were soon under marching orders. The whole command, with five day's rations, marched that evening to Tullock's Creek.

"On the next day we made an early start and marched with the infantry 23½ miles to the Big Horn. It was an exceedingly hot day, and there were no streams on the way, so that all the men suffered terribly from thirst. Many of the soldiers fell by the way. Our Indian scouts had reported that smoke was visible in the distance, and hence this forced march was necessary. We left the infantry at the river, with orders to follow in the morning, and pushed on with the cavalry and battery until we reached the Little Big Horn at midnight, thus being about 24 hours in advance of the time set by

DIFFICULTIES ENCOUNTERED.

Gen. Terry. It was a night of toil and suffering. Up and down bluffs, amid drenching showers and abyssmal darkness, we pressed on; yet all were in hopeful mood, for we expected to strike the hostile Sioux. We little knew what a day of wrath it had been for our brave companions!

"We finally bivouacked, after having marched over 12 miles. On Monday, June 26th, our scouts were sent in advance, and soon after we had resumed our march a report was brought in that a

A TRAIL STRUCK.

small trail had been struck. Subsequently Lieut. Bradley, Chief of Scouts, reported that he had followed the trail, and had met two Crows who had joined Custer's command at the Rosebud, and who now reported that he had been cut to pieces on the Little Big Horn. The story was incredible. We could not believe it—we would not believe it. We admitted that Custer might have struck an Indian village and have had a fight, but we would not listen to tidings of his defeat. We pressed on with eager enthusiasm. The infantry marched 29 miles that day—indeed, until they were ready to drop. As the twilight faded away we saw heavy columns of smoke in the distance and felt sure that Custer was ravag-

'ing the valley. During the night we encamped by our arms, and it was apparent to those who knew him that a shade of anxiety hovered over the face of our commander. Night had come, and the promised

ANXIOUS FOREBODINGS.

scout from Custer had not reported, although we were far in advance of our promised position. We had crossed the Little Big Horn almost a day's march from its mouth.

"On Tuesday, June 27th, clouds of smoke hung in front of us. The command hastened on and soon entered a beautiful plain over three miles long. On the east was a line of bluffs, on the west was the Little Big Horn with bluffs beyond it. Two tepees were still standing, and in them lay nine Indian chiefs with their dead horses close by. As we advanced hundreds and hundreds of tepee poles could be counted. Buffalo robes, cooking utensils, clothing, and tools of all kinds had been abandoned in hot haste. There was no time to peer about and take notes. There might be serious work for us to do. The shadow of a great calamity had already fallen upon us. As we drew rein for a moment we noticed some United States regulation saddles of the new pattern. Some one picked up a blood-stained glove—it had been worn by Yates. And close by were the riddled clothes of Porter and

A TERRIBLE REALITY.

Sturgis. A moment more and we were aghast with horror. Two hundred of our cavalrymen lay dead in the ravines and on the bluffs on the right bank of the river. Bradley had gone to the front and counted them, and now brought us the news. The Crow scouts had not lied to us. It was the awful truth. Faces paled, eyes moistened, teeth were set.

"An advance was now ordered. At every step we found tokens of the dreadful carnage. Here was brave McIntosh; here lay Isaiah, our negro scout; close by, Charley Reynolds, the chief scout, had bravely met his fate ; and here, close together, were the bodies of our cavalrymen and their horses. As we were supping on these horrors and asking ourselves whether any one had been left to describe the fate of the regiment, Lieutenants Wallace and Hall drew near and informed us that the survivors of seven companies under Reno and Benteen were intrenched on the east bluff of the ridge at the end of the plain, on the right bank of the river.

"'Where is Custer?' cried a dozen voices.

"'He left us Sunday morning with five companies, and we have heard nothing from him since.'

"Our commander with a small escort forded the stream, and scaling the almost perpendicular bluffs joined Reno's force. He was greeted with cheer upon cheer. Stout-hearted soldiers who had not flinched in the hour of peril now wept like children, and smiles returned to the wan faces of the wounded men. The Indians had retreated when they saw our line of infantry approaching. We had rescued these despairing soldiers.

6

"Now we had time to hear the story of the
THE AWFUL STORY.
battle. General Custer's regiment had marched seventy-eight miles without leaving the saddle. Suddenly the Indian village was discovered on a plain three miles long. It was on Sunday morning; Custer could not wait, although the odds were five to one. He ordered Benteen to make a detour to the left with three companies, and instructed him to go as far as he could into the Indian camp. He left one company, McDougall's, to protect the packs. With the other eight companies he pressed on. As he approached the high bluffs surrounding the plain where the village was situated, he divided his force. Reno, with three companies—French's, Moyland's, and McIntosh's—was directed to advance, ford the Little Big Horn, and enter the southern end of the village. Custer himself, with five companies— Yates's, Keogh's, Tom Custer's, Smith's, and Calhoun's—marched around the bluffs facing the village on the right bank of the stream. His plan of battle was very simple. While Reno was attacking the village from the south, his own force would assault the Indians on the flank and in the rear. It was a
THE PLAN OF BATTLE.
shrewd plan, but he overrated the endurance of his soldiers; they were faint and weary; they had been in the saddle twenty-four hours.

"Reno advanced along the plain, meeting with no opposition until he reached a little grove. Here his

HOSTILES ATTACKING FRIENDLIES.

line was attacked. He immediately deployed his skirmishers and dismounted. The horses were led into the wood, and the cavalrymen engaged the enemy. The Indians appeared in immense numbers. They attacked him fiercely in front, and at the same time turned his left flank and compelled his force to retreat into the woods. The Indians followed in hordes and drove the force before them to the river. The bluffs on the opposite side were steep and high, but the water in the river was low.

HAND-TO-HAND FIGHTING.

The Indians, flushed with success, rushed upon our men, and a hand-to-hand conflict ensued. Here McIntosh was shot. Hodgson was shot midway in the stream, and fell before he could reach the opposite bank. Dr. DeWolf crossed in safety, but was killed on the bluffs. The rest of the command fought their way up the heights, with the Indians in hot pursuit. Death seemed to stare every man in the face, when suddenly Benteen came to the rescue.

"Benteen, with his three companies, had gone to the left, according to Custer's instructions. He soon became convinced that further progress in that direction was impossible, and he turned back to join the main body. As he neared the plain he received Custer's last order—to hurry up the packs. Satisfying himself that they were approaching safely under McDougal, he resumed his march. Suddenly he caught sight of Reno's men rushing up the bluffs

with the Indians on all sides of them. He dashed
to the right, charged up the bluffs, drove back the

THE RESCUE.

Indians, and saved his despairing comrades from
death. The Indians were kept at bay until night
fell, and then the command began to intrench itself
on the top of the bluff.

"Meanwhile where was Custer? He had gone
around the bluffs and had attempted to ford the
river at the northern end of the village. The Indians were massed in his front and on his flanks.
The whole command dismounted and made a determined resistance, which checked momentarily the
onset of the Indians. Then Custer ordered a retreat, his force dividing in order to take advantage
of two ravines on the left flank. The enemy had
already appeared in large force on the right and
closed the door of escape in that direction. At the
head of the upper ravine Calhoun's company was
apparently thrown out as skirmishers to defend the
entrance. Here their bodies were found after the
battle; the skirmish lines were clearly marked by

DISCOVERY OF THE SLAIN.

the rows of the slain; with heaps of empty cartridge
shells; Calhoun and Crittenden were in their places
—in advance of the files. The Indians, baffled for
a moment, immediately flanked the force on the left,
rushed up another ravine which led into the main
one, and attacked Keogh's company. That gallant
Irish officer fell surrounded by his solders. Retreat

was cut off from this ravine, and the soldiers were then killed off one by one. Meanwhile, the soldiers in the other ravine had been subjected to a severe fire. The line of retreat led through a deep gully, at the mouth of which 28 men were killed. They fought desperately, but the Indians had surrounded

A DEATH TRAP.

them and there was no escape. Capt. Smith fought his way to a peak, where a last stand was made. They must have known that their hour had come. Here were Custer and his brother, Adjutant Cook, Capt. Yates, Lieut. Riley, Capt. Smith, and a few soldiers. Making ramparts of their fallen horses, they fought to the end. Here their bodies were found. Custer himself seemed to be sleeping; his attitude was natural, his expression sweet and serene.

"There was only one survivor—a Crow scout. He crossed the river, dashed into the village, seized a horse, covered himself with a Sioux blanket, and escaped. From his account, it is safe to estimate

3,000 WARRIORS.

the force of Indians at 3,000 warriors and their loss in battle at many hundreds.

"Benteen and Reno strengthened their position during the night and awaited the attack of the Indians. It was made at daybreak, and was resumed at intervals during the day. In the evening Gibbon's column appeared in the distance, and the Indians retreated in great haste, abandoning the vil-

lage and a large quantity of provisions and ammunition. Two days were spent by the troops on the
battle-field. The dead were buried, and horse litters
were constructed for the transportation of the
wounded to the supply steamer. The troops were
in no condition to follow the Indians, and a retreat
was ordered to the mouth of the Big Horn, after the
ammunition and stores in the village had been destroyed."

A few days later another correspondent wrote as

ANOTHER ACCOUNT.

follows, giving further details of the awful tragedy :

"At noon on the 22d day of June, Gen. Custer,
at the head of his fine regiment of twelve veteran
companies, left camp at the mouth of the Rosebud
to follow the trail of a very large band of hostile
Sioux, leading up the river and westward in the direction of the Big Horn. The signs indicated that
the Indians were making for the eastern branch of
the last-named river, marked on the map as the
Little Big Horn. At the same time Gen. Terry,
with Col. Gibbon's command of five companies
of infantry, four of cavalry, and the Gatlin battery,
started to ascend the Big Horn, aiming to assail the
enemy in the rear. The march of the two columns
was so planned as to bring Col. Gibbon's forces
within co-operating distance of the anticipated scene

PLAN OF ACTION.

of action by the evening of the 26th. In this way
only could the infantry be made available, as it would

not do to encumber Gen. Custer's march with foot soldiers. On the evening of the 24th, Col. Gibbon's command was landed on the south bank of the Yellowstone near the mouth of the Big Horn, and on the 25th was pushed twenty-three miles over a country so rugged that the endurance of the men was tasked to the uttermost. The infantry then halted for the night, but the department commander with the cavalry advanced twelve miles farther to the mouth of the Little Big Horn, marching until midnight in the hope of opening communication with Gen. Custer.

"The morning of the 26th brought the intelligence, communicated by three badly frightened Crow scouts, of the battle of the previous day and

STARTLING REPORT.

its results. The story was not credited, because it was not expected that an attack would be made earlier than the 27th, and chiefly because no one could believe that a force such as Gen. Custer commanded could have met with disaster. Still the report was in no way disregarded. All day long the toilsome march was plied, and every eye bent upon a cloud of smoke resting over the southern horizon, which was hailed as a sign that Gen. Custer was successful, and had fired the village. It was only when night was falling that the weary troops lay down upon their arms. The infantry had marched twenty-nine miles. The march of the next morning revealed at every step some evidence

of the conflict which had taken place two days before.

"At an early hour the head of the column entered
a plain half a mile wide, bordering the left bank of
the Little Big Horn, where had recently been an immense Indian village extending three miles along

EVIDENCE OF SLAUGHTER.

the stream, and where were still standing funeral
lodges with horses slaughtered around them, and
containing the bodies of nine chiefs. The ground
was strewn everywhere with bodies of horses, cavalry equipments, buffalo robes, packages of dried
meat, and weapons and utensils belonging to the
Indians. On this part of the field was found the
clothing of Lieuts. Sturges and Porter pierced
with bullets, and a blood-stained gauntlet belonging
to Col. Yates. Farther on were found bodies
of men, among whom were recognized Lieut.
McIntosh, the interpreter, from Fort Rice, and Reynolds, the guide. Just then a breathless scout arrived with the intelligence that Col. Reno, with
a remnant of the 7th Cavalry, was entrenched on a

RESCUING COMRADES.

bluff near by waiting for relief. The command
pushed rapidly on, and soon came in sight of a
group surrounding a cavalry guard upon a lofty
eminence on the right bank of the river. Gen.
Terry forded the stream, accompanied by a small
party, and rode to the spot. All the way the slopes
were dotted with the bodies of men and horses.

The General approached and the men swarmed out of the works and greeted him with hearty and repeated cheers. Within was found Major Reno with the remains of seven companies of the regiment, with the following named officers, all of whom are unhurt: Cols. Benteen and Wier, Capts. Felix, Moylan, and McDougal, Lieuts. Godfrey, Mathey, Gibson, Dernded, Edgerly, Wallace, Varnum, and Hare. In the centre of the inclosure was a depression in the surface in which the wounded were sheltered, covered with canvas. Major Reno's command had been fighting from Sunday noon, the 25th, until the night of the 26th, when Terry's arrival caused the Indians to retire. Up to this time Major Reno and those with him were in complete ignorance of the fate of the other five companies, which had been separated from them on the 25th to make an attack under Gen. Custer on the village at another point.

"While preparations were being made for the removal of the wounded, a party was sent on Gen. Custer's trail to look for traces of his command.

HEART-RENDING SIGHT.

They found awaiting them a sight fit to appal the stoutest heart. At a point about three miles down the right bank of the stream Custer had evidently attempted to ford and attack the villages from the ford. The trail was found to lead back up to the bluffs and to the northward, as if the troops had been repulsed and compelled to retreat, and at the same time had been cut off from regaining the forces under Major Reno. The bluffs along the right bank come sharply down to the water and are interspersed by numerous ravines. All along the slopes and ridges and in the ravines, lying as they had fought, line behind line, showing where defensive positions had been successively taken up and held till none were left to fight, lay the bodies of the fallen soldiers; then huddled in a narrow compass horses and men were piled promiscuously.

"At the highest point of the ridge lay Gen. Custer, surrounded by a chosen band. Here were his two brothers and his nephew, Mr. Reed, Col. Yates and Col. Cooke, and Capt. Smith, all lying in a circle of a few yards, their horses beside them. Here, behind Col. Yates's company, the last stand had been made, and here, one after another, these last survivors of Gen. Custer's five companies had met their death. The companies had successively thrown themselves across the path of the advancing enemy and had been annihilated.

FEARFUL SLAUGHTER.

Not a man has escaped to tell the tale, but the story was inscribed on the surface of the barren hills in a language more eloquent than words. Two hundred and sixty-one bodies have been buried from Gen. Custer's and Major Reno's commands. The last one found was that of Mr. Kellogg, correspondent of *The Bismarck Tribune* and also, I believe, of *The New York Herald.*

"The following are the names of the officers whose remains are recognized: Gen. Custer, Col. Keogh, Col. Yates, Col. Custer, Col. Cooke, Capt. Smith, Lieut. McIntosh, Lieut. Calhoun, Lieut. Hodgeson, and Lieut. Reilly. All of these belonged to the 7th Cavalry. Lieut. Crittenden, of the 20th Infantry, was serving temporarily with the regiment. Lieuts. Porter, Sturges, and Harrington, and Assistant Surgeon Lord are reporting missing, as their remains were not recognized; but there is small ground to hope that any of them survived, as it is obvious that the troops were completely surrounded by a force of ten times their number.

"The history of Major Reno's operations comprises all that is now known of this sanguinary affair. It seems that Custer with eight companies reached the river in the forenoon of the 25th, having marched continuously all the previous day and night. Seeing the upper or southern extremity of the village, and probably under-estimating its extent, he ordered Major Reno to ford the river and charge the village with three companies, while he, with five companies, moved down the right bank and behind the bluff to make a similar attack at the other end. Major

GREATLY OUTNUMBERED.

Reno made his charge, but finding that he was dealing with a force many times his own in number, he dismounted his men and sought shelter in the timber which fringed the river bank. The position appearing to him untenable, he remounted and cut his way to the river, forded under a murderous fire, and gained the bluff where he was subsequently found.

"Here he was afterward joined by Col. Benteen with three companies which had just reached the field, and by Capt. McDougal with his company and the pack mules. The position was immediately after completely invested by the Indians, who for more than 24 hours allowed the garrison no rest

TIMELY RELIEF.

and inflicted severe loss. Except for the timely arrival of relief, the command would have been cut off to a man. The number saved with Major Reno was 329, including 51 wounded. The loss among the Indians was probably considerable, as bodies have been found in every direction, and they left behind only a small portion of their dead.

"He remained nearly two days on the scene of the disaster to bury the dead and prepare for transporting the wounded to a place of safety. The neighboring country was still full of scattering bands of Indians watching our movements, and doubtless prepared to take advantage of any want of vigilance to add to the number of their victims. A species of rude horse-litter was constructed of poles and strips of hide, and on these the disabled were carried twenty miles to the forks of the Big Horn, where they were placed on board the steamer."

CHAPTER VII.

THE DEATH OF CUSTER.

Two Stories of the Grim Tragedy—General Terry's Official Report—The Desperate March to the Relief of Reno—Narrative of Old Nick Genneiss—A Picture Record by Little Big Man.

Two accounts of the Little Big Horn Massacre are worthy of rehearsal here, for sake of contrast. One is the official report, made by Brigadier-Gen. Alfred H. Terry, on June 27th, 1876, which was as follows:

"It is my painful duty to report that day before yesterday, the 25th inst., a great disaster overtook Gen. Custer and the troops under his command. At 12 o'clock on the 22d he started with his whole regiment and a strong detachment of scouts and guards from the mouth of the Rosebud. Proceeding up that river about twenty miles he struck a very heavy Indian trail which had previously been discovered, and pursuing found that it led as was supposed to the Little Big Horn River. Here he found a village of almost unexampled extent, and at once attacked it with that portion of his force which

was immediately at hand. Major Reno, with three
companies, A, G, and M, of the regiment, was sent
into the valley of the stream at the point where the
trail struck it. Gen. Custer, with five companies,
C, E, F, and L, attempted to enter it about three
miles lower down. Reno forded the river, charged
down its left bank, and dismounted and fought on
foot until finally, completely overwhelmed by numbers, he was compelled to mount, recross the river,
and seek a refuge on the high bluffs which over-
looked its right bank. Just as he recrossed, Capt.
Benteen—who, with three companies, D, H, and K,
was some two miles to the left of Reno when the
action commenced, but who had been ordered by
Gen. Custer to return—came to the river, and
rightly concluding that it would be useless for his
force to attempt to renew the fight in the valley, he
joined Reno on the Bluffs. Capt. McDougal, with
his company (B) was at first at some distance in the
rear with a train of pack-mules. He also came to

SURROUNDED BY INDIANS.

Reno soon. This united force was nearly surrounded by Indians, many of whom, armed with
rifles, occupied positions which commanded the
ground held by the cavalry—ground from which
there was no escape. Rifle-pits were dug and the
fight was maintained, though with heavy loss, from
about half-past 2 o'clock of the 25th till 6 o'clock of
the 26th, when the Indians withdrew from the valley,
taking with them their village.

" Of the movements of Gen. Custer and the five companies under his immediate command scarcely anything is known from those who witnessed them,

NONE FOUND ALIVE.

for no soldier or officer who accompanied him has yet been found alive. His trail from the point where Reno crossed the stream passes along and in the rear of the crest of the bluffs on the right bank for nearly or quite three miles ; then it comes down to the bank of the river, but at once diverges from it, as if he had unsuccessfully attempted to cross ; then turns upon itself, almost completes a circle, and closes. It is marked by the remains of his officers and men, the bodies of his horses, some of them dropped along the path, others· heaped where halts appear to have been made. There is abundant evidence that a gallant resistance was offered by the troops, but they were beset on all sides by overpowering numbers.

KNOWN TO HAVE FALLEN.

" The officers known to be killed are : Gen. Custer, Capts. Keogh, Yates, and Custer ; Lieuts. Cooke, Smith, McIntosh, Calhoun, Porter, Hodgson, Sturgis, and Reilley, of the cavalry ; Lieut. Crittenden, of the 20th Infantry, and Acting Assistant Surgeon DeWolf. Lieut. Harrington, of the cavalry, and Assistant Surgeon Lord are missing. Capt. Benteen and Lieut. Varnum, of the cavalry, are slightly wounded. Mr. Boston Custer, a brother, and Mr. Reed, a nephew of Gen. Custer were with him and were killed. No other officers than those whom I have named are among the killed, wounded, and missing. It is impossible yet to obtain a reliable list of the enlisted men who were killed and wounded, but the number of killed, including officers must reach 250. The number of wounded is 51.

"At the mouth of the Rosebud I informed Gen. Custer that I should take supply steamer "Far West" up the Yellowstone to ferry Gen. Gibbon's column over the river; that I should personally accompany that column, and that I would in all probability reach the mouth of the Little Big Horn on the 26th inst. The steamer reached Gen. Gibbon's troops near the mouth of the Big Horn early in the morning of the 24th, and at 4 o'clock in the afternoon all his men and animals were across the Yellowstone.

PUSHING FORWARD.

At 5 o'clock the column, consisting of five companies of the 7th Infantry, four companies of the 2d Cavalry, and a battery of Gatling guns, marched out to and across Tullock's Creek, starting soon after 5 o'clock on the morning of the 25th. The infantry made a march of 22 miles over the most difficult country which I have ever seen, in order that scouts might be sent into the valley of he Little Big Horn. The cavalry with the battery was then pushed on 13 or 14 miles further, reaching camp at midnight. The scouts were sent out at 4.30 on the morning of

INDIANS DISCOVERED.

the 26th. The scouts discovered the Indians. who

were at first supposed to be Sioux, but whenever taken they proved to be Crows, who had been with Gen. Custer. They brought the first intelligence of the battle. Their story was not credited. It was supposed that some fighting, perhaps severe fighting, had taken place, but it was not believed that disaster could have overtaken so large a force as 12 companies of cavalry. The infantry, which had broken camp very early, soon came up, and the whole column entered and moved up the valley of the Little Big Horn. During the afternoon efforts were made to send scouts through to what was supposed to be Gen. Custer's position, and to obtain information of the condition of affairs, but those who were sent out were driven back by parties of Indians who, in increasing numbers, were seen hovering in Gen. Gibbon's front.

"At twenty minutes before nine o'clock in the evening the infantry had marched between twenty-nine and thirty miles. The men were very weary, and daylight was fading. The column was, therefore, halted for the night at a point about eleven miles in a straight line above the stream. This morning the movement was resumed, and, after a march of nine miles, Major Reno's intrenched position was reached. The withdrawal of the Indians from around Reno's command and from the valley was undoubtedly caused by the appearance of Gen. Gibbon's troops. Major Reno and Capt. Benteen, both of whom are officers of great expe-

7

rience, accustomed to see large masses of mounted

men, estimate the number of Indians engaged at
not less than two thousand five hundred. Other
officers think that the number was greater than this.
The village in the valley was about three miles in
length and about a mile in width. Beside the
lodges proper, a great number of temporary brush-
wood shelters were found in it, indicating that many
men beside its proper inhabitants had gathered together there. Major Reno is very confident that
there were a number of white men fighting with the
Indians. It is believed that the loss of the Indians
was large."

A second version of the story, brief, epigrammatic,
and thoroughly Indian-like, was given many years
afterward by Old Nick Genneiss, of the Pine Ridge

Reservation. He related it to Miss Sickels, an accomplished teacher, who spent much time among
the Sioux, as they rode through the Black Hills
country along the edge of the Bad Lands, among
the wash-outs and buttes, " like the lay of the land
where the Custer fight was," he said.

"Folks blame me for putting Red Cloud up to
things. I've been with him so much. He talks to
me, and many times has told me what he aims to
do, and many times I've helped him, but he is a very
set kind of man. He don't stand out for nobody,
'cept, perhaps, his squaw. She makes it lively for

MAJOR-GENERAL SCHOFIELD, U. S. A.

him sometimes. She won't 'low no other squaw to his house. One come once, but she didn't stay. I've been with him off-and-on most of the time for twenty years, when the tribe has been movin' from place to place, first on the Platte River, then over to the Missouri, then back again to the White, near the Bad Lands, where we be now. I was with them up in Montana, where Custer got killed. It was in a place something like that." He pointed to a kind of ravine that had been the bed of a creek. The country is full of abrupt gulches or "wash-outs," some overgrown with grass, others immense masses of alkali clay, deeply seamed by the inroads of wind and water. Frequently the road follows the bed of the "dry creek," winding for miles between banks so high that they shut out the prospect of the country on both sides, and vividly suggest the stories of ambush and the possibilities of invisible foes lurking on either hand or concealed among the many ragged recesses that lie along the way.

POSITION OF THE SIOUX.

"The Sioux was camped in one of the loops of the creek where there was grass and trees and water. It was in so deep you couldn't see 'em 'til you got there. The creek turned so sudden and the banks was so high you had to go along the creek if you started that way. Custer's scouts hadn't seen nor known of our bein' there. He come along down the path of the creek, slap onto 'em, before he knew anythin' 'bout it. They seen him comin' and closed together 'cross the openin' of the loop, so he couldn't get back. He couldn't get out, 'cause the wash-outs was too high. It was all done so quick the soldiers didn't have time to shoot. Nobody got away. No white man, 'cept us as belongs to the tribe, went into that country for over a year. There was lots o' arrows lyin' 'round and only few bullets. When everything was all over I went to Washington with the chief, actin' as interpreter."

Nick Genneiss now lives with his Indian wife and children on his ranch, a prosperous cattle dealer, sharing the rations. He has invested them quite successfully. There are also good indications of thrift among the full-blooded Indians, who raise stock and till the land—so far as it is possible to raise anything in that arid country. A number have devoted the same energy to a life of peace and industry which made them famous on the war-path.

One of these was Little Big Man, one of the most active participants in the terrible massacre. He was a frequent visitor at Miss Sickels's school, having been one of the first to bring children. His daughter Oohoola was a very attractive child of sweet disposition, pretty and plump, notwithstanding the significance of her name, "Bones." She said plaintively, "Me not Oohoola; me Maud." The teachers had at first spoken of changing her name to Maud, but thinking Oohoola musical, retained it until her sensitiveness at the boys' teasing

MAUD LITTLE BIG MAN.

prompted her request. Maud Little Big Man became one of the brightest pupils. Her father was
very proud of her progress. " Our mutual interest
in her," says Miss Sickels, " was the foundation of
quite a friendship. He always took great satisfaction in showing his silver-headed cane given him by
the Great Father, and in displaying his silver medal,
on which was inscribed, ' Given to Little Big Man
for valiant services at the death of Crazy Horse.'
He very readily conversed about his trip to Washington and of school or agency matters, but he was
reticent about any allusions to former escapades on
the war-path. Any question or reference to that
was met by that impenetrable, uncomprehending
look by which the Indian can so perfectly conceal
his thoughts. I do not know whether it was a wish
to bury the past or reluctance to commit himself to
any confidences. He had promised to be a good
citizen and fulfilled his promise so long as he lived,
although it may be a matter of doubt what side he
would have taken in an outbreak. Personal spites
slumber until a general insurrection with its attending lawlessness gives an opportunity to wreak the
delayed vengeance.

" Tanka Cical Wacasa (Little Big Man) was

LITTLE BIG MAN.

called Little on account of his size—he measured
five feet four. The appellation Big was given on
account of his valor. Whenever he made his ap-

pearance among a group of young bucks they immediately recognized his authority by rising and
standing until he was seated.   One day he showed
me a document that was given him by the President,
setting forth his good qualities and allowing him
especial privileges.   I asked him to tell me about

INDIAN PICTURE OF THE CUSTER FIGHT—THE CAVALRYMEN.

Crazy Horse and the 'time the great white chief
was killed.'   He did not seem to understand me, so
I said, 'If you cannot tell me anything about it, will
you make a picture showing your idea of it?'   He
promised to do so.   I provided him with pencils and
paper.   A few weeks after he brought me two

sketches, one representing the Custer fight, the other a personal encounter he had had with the hereditary enemies of his tribe—the Crows. I asked him where he was ; he pointed to the solitary brave wearing two horns.

" ' Where are the other Indians ?'

SAME—THE INDIANS.

" ' Back there. Then arrows come.'

" Making due allowance for their inordinate love of praise that prompts them to draw on their imagination to supply what deficiency opportunity has failed to provide it is probable that the idea of the sketch is not exaggerated and that he rushed into the fight wherever the fray was thickest."

CHAPTER VIII.

CUSTER.

George A. Custer, the hero and the victim of the Little Big Horn, was a native of Ohio, and seemed born to be a soldier. He was barely of age when he began active service in the conflict which was destined to bring him so much honor, and was but 36 years of age when he fell at the head of his column, after a short life crowded with brilliant deeds. His birth-place was New-Rumley, Harrison County, Ohio; the date, December 5th, 1839. Before entering West Point he had received an ordinary English education and had taught in schools. The history of his life at the Military Academy he has told himself in one of the most recent of his many contributions to periodical literature. His appointment was obtained through the Hon. John S. Bingham, the Representative of his district, and the official notification of his appointment was signed by Jefferson Davis, President Buchanan's Secretary of War. He entered the Academy in 1857, when Colonel Richard Delafield was Superintendent, and Lieutenant-Colonel Wm. J. Hardee, who afterward became Lieutenant-General of the Confederate Army, commanded the corps of cadets. A large number of those who were in the institution during the period

DESTINY.

of his continuance there was destined, like himself, to take a prominent part in the approaching struggle. Thirteen of his instructors during that time afterward reached the rank of Major-General in the Union Army, and five others attained high rank in the Confederate forces. Among the former were " Lieutenant William B. Hazen, instructor of infantry tactics ; " "Lieutenant John M. Schofield, instructor of natural philosophy ;" Lieutenants George L. Hartsuff, O. O. Howard, Alexander Webb, and Godfrey Weitzel. Fitzhugh Lee was best known of the Confederates. Of Custer's fellow cadets, a number arrived at early distinction on both sides. Among those who choose to serve the Union cause were Hardin, Kilpatrick and Upton. Rosser and Young were among the Confederates. Seven, including Custer, won the rank of brigadier on the Union side within three years after graduation, and five became general officers in the Confederate army. Of these twelve, nine attained rapid promotion in the cav-

alry service. Cadet Custer did not make a brilliant
record either for scholarship or discipline. He grad-

NOT BRILLIANT.

uated at the foot of a class of 34, and spent 66 Sat-
urdays during the four years of his academic term
in doing extra guard duty in penance for various
offenses. His stay terminated with an incident characteristic of the man. It was when most of the
Southern cadets had withdrawn from the Academy,
and Custer' own class were waiting for the order
from Washington announcing their admission to the
roll of officers of the army. Custer was officer of
the guard, and came upon a group of disputants
who were just resorting to blows. Instead of putting
the brawlers under arrest, he even restrained those
who were attempting to restrain them, and called

FAIR PLAY.

out, "Stand back, boys; let's have a fair fight."
His appeal was heard by Lieutenants Hazen and
Merrell; he was placed under arrest and kept behind to be court-martialed, while the rest of his class
went on to Washington to enter active service. The
court-martial was as slow and formal as a trial of
impeachment, and it was only through the exertions
of his fellow cadets in Washington that the proceeding was cut short by a telegraphic order summoning
him there. Presenting himself at the War Department, he had the good fortune to obtain a personal
interview with General Scott, whom he asked to
send him to the front at once for active duty, and

by whom he was intrusted with dispatches for Gen-

FIRST EXPERIENCE.

eral McDowell. The all-night ride which bore these dispatches was his first work as an officer. This was the 20th of July, 1861, the day before the battle of Bull Run. Custer was just of age, and was now second lieutenant, Company G, of the 2d United States Cavalry, once commanded by Robert E. Lee.

His first day's service was a memorable one. It was 3 o'clock in the morning on the day of the battle of Bull Run when he reached General McDowell's headquarters, and after delivering his dispatches and eating a hasty breakfast—the last thing he was to eat for thirty hours—he joined his company while it was still dark. It was not long before he was stationed in the line of battle. It is not necessary to rehearse the incidents of this well-remembered engagement, though General Custer himself has given a graphic description of it. The sudden change in the fortunes of the day brought about by the unlooked for arrival of rebel re-enforcements, came just when Custer and a companion— so says General Custer in his account—were congratulating themselves "upon the glorious victory which already seemed to have been won." They were at that moment on a high ridge near the advancing line. Suddenly " our attention was attracted by a long line of troops appeariug behind us on the edge of the timber already mentioned. Before doubts could arise we saw the Confederate flag

floating over a portion of the line just emerging
from the timber; the next moment the entire line
leveled their muskets and poured a volley into the
backs of our advancing regiments." In the frantic
retreat that followed, Custer's company came among
the last, in good order, and bringing with it General
Heintzelman, who had been wounded.

After the appointment of McClellan to the command of the army—who Custer always insisted,
would have suppressed the Rebellion, if he had proper help from Washington—Lieutenant Custer was

PROMOTED.

chosen as a staff officer by Phil. Kearney, who had
just been commissioned a Brigadier-General, and
placed at the head of the Jersey Brigade. He was the
first staff officer detailed by Kearney, and was first
made aid-de-camp, and afterward assistant adjutant-
general. This position he continued to hold until
deprived of it by a general order prohibiting service on the staffs of volunteer officers by officers
of the regular army, but Kearney did not allow him
to leave his staff without a handsome acknowledg-
ment of his services. When Manassas was evac-
uated by the Rebels his company formed part of
that detachment of the Army of the Potomac which
marched to Manassas. The cavalry was under the
command of General Stoneman, in whose hands
the work of organizing and drilling the cavalry of
the Army of the Potomac had been placed, but who
" proved himself deficient," in Custer's opinion, "in

almost every necessary quality requisite to the success of a calvary leader."

It was of the branch of the service with which he

CRITICISM OF STONEMAN.

was immediately connected that General Custer said, in one of his articles : " The record of the cavalry while operating under Stoneman, contains nothing to its credit as a separate organization, and worse than nothing if successes are looked for upon which to base its leader's claim to the title of chief of cavalry." On the march just referred to, the cavalry met the enemy's cavalry near Catlett's Station, and when volunteers were called for to lead the charge, Lieutenant Custer came to the front. Here he made the first of that series of brilliant charges, the last of which carried him to a bloody grave. He drove the Rebels across Muddy Creek, and they had the honor of " drawing the first blood" in McClellan's campaign. He seems to have been first pretty much everywhere, Before Yorktown he planned and threw up the earthwork which was nearest to the enemy's lines; he was in the advance of the pursuit of the Confederate forces from Yorktown. and at the battle of Williamsburg, where he was aid-de-camp to General Hancock, he effected the first

THE FIRST BATTLE-FLAG CAPTURE.

capture of a battle-flag made by the Army of the Potomac; and he was the first man to cross the Chickahominy, " wading up to his armpits," under the fire of the enemy, and being rewarded for this act of bravery by General McClellan with a promotion to the rank of captain, and an appointment as personal aid to that general. He was an active participant in the whole of the Peninsular campaign, and was in every battle, and was also in the campaign which closed with the battles of South Mountain and Antietam. He followed General McClellan into retirement, and did not re-enter active service until the battle of Chancellorsville.

His gallantry in this battle procured him an appointment from General Pleasanton as a personal aid, under whom he fought on many fields, notably at Beverly Fords, Upperville, and Barbour's Cross

A GREAT PROMOTION.

Roads. Custer now received his great promotion, going at one bound to a brigadier-generalship. His appointment was made through General Pleasanton, who had been made a Major-General and placed in command of a cavalry corps, and wished to have Custer as one of his four brigadiers. It was Custer's brigade that routed Hampton's cavalry at Gettysburg and protected the Union train. It was Custer's brigade, too, that pursued the Confederate train when in retreat after Gettysburg, destroyed more than 400 wagons and captured more than 1,800 prisoners. It was Custer's brigade, too, that attacked the rear guard while it was crossing the Potomac, routing it with a loss of 1,300 prisoners, to say nothing of battle-flags and cannon. He was engaged in the opening battle of the Wilderness in the Spring of 1864, and accompanied General Sheridan in the raid toward Richmond, on which they set out on May 9th. Naturally his brigade led the column, and capturing Beaver Dam set free 400 Union prisoners. Coming back to Grant's army he fought

DESPERATE BATTLES.

in several battles. One was a most desperate conflict, in which this brave General showed all his indomitable bravery and pluck. It was at the battle of Trevillian Station, where he surprised the enemy's rear, but the attack that was to have been made at the same time in front was delayed, and the enemy closed in on Custer. There were five brigades against one, but the fierce fight lasted three hours. Guns were captured only to be recaptured, and Custer, when his standard-bearer had been killed, only saved his flag from capture by tearing it from the staff and wrapping it around his own body. Help finally came, and he was able to withdraw in good order.

He marked the closing months of the war by a succession of brilliant achievements. At Winchester his brigade fought from dawn until after dark, and was first through the lines of the enemy. Nine battle-flags and more than one prisoner to every man in the brigade were the trophies of the day.

LARGER COMMAND.

He was then put in command of the second and then the third division of cavalry of the Army of the Shenandoah. When Sheridan reached the field of

Cedar Creek, after the ride which has become famous, Custer's division was alone ready for action,
and Sheridan's order was "Go in, Custer!" Custer
hardly needed the order.   He drove the enemy off
the field, captured 45 out of their 48 cannon and
several hundred prisoners.   For this achievement
he was brevetted major-general.   On the 9th of
October he encountered one of his former fellow
cadets, General Rosser, and routed him, taking
many prisoners and trophies, and for this the War
Department thanked him in a special order.   At
Waynesboro, in February, 1865, Custer, with about
1,000 men, routed Jubal Early with 2,000, and captured 1,800 prisoners and 200 wagons, besides flags
and cannon.   All this at an expense of one
man killed and four wounded.   In the final campaign before Richmond, Custer converted the battle
of Dinwiddie C. H. from an impending rout into
actual victory.   At Five Forks his division was first
in crossing the works of the enemy,   At Sailor's
Creek, when two unsuccessful attempts had been
made to delay the enemy's retreat, Sheridan cried

SHERIDAN'S COMPLIMENT.

out, "I wish to God old Custer was here; he would
have been into the enemy's train before this time."
(Custer was 25; Sheridan ten years his senior.)
What followed is thus described in "Ohio in the
War:"

Accordingly, "Old Custer's" was ordered into the fight.   The men charged gallantly, and actu

ally leaped their horses over the breastworks.
Lieutenant T. W. Custer, the General's brother and
aid (also killed at the Little Horn), was among the
first to enter the works, which he did in the manner
described: He snatched a rebel standard from its

SHOT IN THE NECK.

bearer, and received a Minnie ball through his
cheek and neck. He, however, retained his trophy,
and shot down his opponent with a pistol. The division destroyed a large number of wagons, captured 16 pieces of artillery. 31 battle-flags, and
5,000 prisoners, including seven general officers,
among them Custis Lee, a son of Robert E. Lee ;
Semmes, brother of pirate Semmes, and Ewell.
After the battle Custer was riding up to General
Sheridan, who was surrounded by his staff and other officers of rank, when the latter and all the staff
with caps waving, proposed three cheers for Custer,
which were given with a will."

At Appomattox Court House, Custer was in the
advance and was the first to receive General Lee's
white flag, which he retained. The table upon
which the terms of surrender were signed was presented to Mrs. Custer by General Sheridan, with a
letter in which he said to her, that he knew "of no
person more instrumental in bringing about this
most desirable event than her own most gallant husband." For these last exploits he was made Major-
General of Volunteers, and was given an important
command in Texas, from which he was relieved Feb-

8

ruary 15th, 1866. In the reorganization of the army he was made Lieutenant-Colonel of the 7th Cavalry, with the brevet rank of Major-General in the regular service.

After the war, General Custer was engaged in a number of expeditions against the Indians. The

FIRST EXPEDITION.

first of those was organized and led by General Hancock in the opening of 1867. Its object was, in General Hancock's own words, "to convince the Indians that we were able to punish any of them who may molest travelers across the plains, or who may commit other hostilities against the whites." There was considerable fighting, but the losses of the Indians were comparatively slight. Another was sent out in October, 1868, south of the Arkansas, toward the Wichita Mountains. On this expedition the battle of the Washita was fought in which General Custer destroyed a Cheyenne village and took a number of prisoners, the Indians having 103 warriors killed. Others followed without special incident. In 1873 he commanded the Yellowstone Expedition, sent out as an escort to a surveying party, which was to mark out the uncompleted portions of the road. This expedition did some fighting

TONGUE RIVER BATTLE.

with the Sioux. One battle was on the Tongue River, a branch of the Yellowstone, flowing into it from the south in a direction parallel with the Big Horn, of which the Little Horn is a branch, having

its source in the country between the parallel
streams and flowing northerly. The engagement
on the Tongue River took place on August 4th,
1873. General Custer had proceeded up the
Yellowstone as far as the mouth of the Tongue
River, with a squadron of 90 men, to explore a
route over which the main column of his forces
could pass. When waiting at that point for the
arrival of the forces of the expedition, and his men
being dismounted, six Sioux Indians on horseback
dashed before them and attempted to stampede
their horses. Failing in this, they retired as though
tempting pursuit, and on seeing that the squadron
did not fall into the net they had prepared, with

ATTACK OF 300.

characteristic yells over 300 mounted warriors
dashed in line from the woods and attacked the
Government soldiers. With the river on one side,
they were able to entirely encompass the squadron
by forming a semi-circle on the other. But after a
fight of three and one-half hours, the Indians were
compelled to take flight, carrying their dead with
them, but leaving five ponies on the field, besides
throwing away in their flight breech-loading arms,
saddle equipments, clothing and other articles belonging to an Indian's outfit.

Another battle was fought one week later near
the mouth of the Big Horn River. The Indians had
been followed in their fight down the Yellowstone
and, on receiving additions to their number until

their force amounted to between 800 and 1,000
men, halted on the banks of the river as though
ready for an attack, Sitting Bull was in command
and upon the mounds and high bluffs, along the
river were gathered large numbers of squaws, old
men, and children, who had assembled to witness
what they evidently believed would result in the destruction of General Custer's force of 450 men.
After some skirmishing, General Custer gave the
order for an attack, and the assurance soon gained
by the savages that the charge was made in earnest

FLIGHT OF THE SAVAGES.

led them to a speedy and complete flight. The loss
of the Indians in these engagements was upward of
40 warriors, together with a large number of ponies,
while the loss of General Custer was only four men
killed, one wounded, and one officer seriously
wounded. Four horses were killed and four
wounded, one of the killed being General Custer's,
which was shot from under him.

General Custer was brave, even to recklessness,
as the manner of his death showed. He was a bold,
dashing officer, who did not know what fear, and
not always what discretion, was. His success was a
rule without exceptions, and his progress an advance
almost without pauses. He was the youngest Brigadier and the youngest Major-General in the army,
" He never lost a gun or a color," and " captured
more guns, flags, and prisoners than any other general not an army commander," and these guns and

flags " were all taken in action and field service."
His personal appearance was singular. Col. New-
hall, who wrote " With Sheridan in Lee's Last Cam-

NEVER LOST A GUN OR A COLOR.

paign," describes him thus : " Custer of the golden
locks, his broad sombrero turned up from his hard-
bronzed face, the ends of his crimson cravat floating
over his shoulders, gold galore spangling his jacket
sleeves, a pistol in his boot, jangling spurs on his
heels, and a ponderous claymore swinging at his
side, a wild dare-devil of a general, and a prince of
advance guards, quick to see and act." While he
fought brilliantly and bravely, he does not seem to
have been a soldier capable of real generalship. As
a subordinate working under sympathetic direction
he did his best. He died as he lived—fighting his
hardest and at the head of his men.

One of his comrades, at the time of his death, paid
this tribute to his memory : I accompanied General
Custer on the Yellowstone and Black Hills expedition. He was a born cavalryman. He was never
more in his element than when mounted on Dandy,
his favorite horse, and riding at the head of his regiment. He once said to me. " I would rather be a
private in the cavalry than a line officer in the infantry." He was the personification of bravery and
dash. His most bitter enemies never accused him
of cowardice. If he had only added discretion to his
valor he would have been a perfect soldier. His
impetuosity very often ran away with his judgment.

He was impatient of control. He liked to act independently of others and take all the risk and all the glory to himself. He freque itly got himself into trouble by assuming more aut.ority than really belonged to his rank. It was so on the Yellowstone expedition, where he came into collision with General Stanley, his superior officer, and was placed under arrest and compelled to ride at the rear of his column for two or three days, until General Rosser, who fought against Custer in the Shenandoah Valley during the war, but was then acting as engineer of the Northern Pacific Railroad, succeeded in effecting a reconciliation. Custer and Stanley afterward got on very well, and perhaps the quarrel would never have occurred if the two generals had been left alone to themselves without the intervention of camp gossips, who sought to foster the traditional jealousy between infantry and cavalry. For Stanley was the soul of generosity, and Custer did not really mean to be arrogant; but from the time when he entered West Point to the day when he fell on the Big Horn, he was accustomed to take just as much liberty as he was entitled to.

For this reason, Custer worked most easily and effectively when under general orders, when not hampered by special restrictions, or his success made dependent on anybody else. General Terry under-

UNBOUNDED CONFIDENCE.

stood his man when, in the order directing him to march up the Rosebud, he very liberally said: "The

Department Commander places too much confidence in your zeal, energy, and ability to wish to impose upon you precise orders which might hamper your action when nearly in contact with the enemy." But General Terry did not understand Custer if he thought he would wait for Gibbon's support before attacking an Indian camp. Undoubtedly he ought to have done this; but with his native impetuosity, his reckless daring, his confidence in his own regiment, which had never failed him, and his love of public approval, Custer could no more help charging this Indian camp than he could help charging just so many buffaloes. He had never learned to spell the word "defeat;" he knew nothing but success, and if he had met the Indians on the open plain, success would undoubtedly have been his; for no body of Indians could stand the charge of the 7th Cavalry when it swept over the plains like a whirlwind. But in the Mauvaises Terres and the Narrow Valley of the Big Horn he did it at a fearful risk.

With all his bravery and self-reliance, his love of independent action, Custer was more dependent than most men on the kind approval of his fellows.

LOVED DISPLAY.

He was even vain; he loved display in dress and in action. He would pay $40 for a pair of troop boots to wear on parade, and have everything else in keeping. On the Yellowstone expedition he wore a bright red shirt, which made him the best mark for a rifle of any man in the regiment. I remonstrated with him for this reckless exposure, but found an appeal to his wife more effectual, and on the next campaign he wore a buckskin suit. He formerly wore his hair very long, letting it fall in a heavy mass upon his shoulders, but cut it off before going out on the Black Hills, producing quite a change in his appearance. But if vain and ambitious, Custer had none of those great vices which are so common and so distressing in the army. He never touched liquor in any form; he did not smoke or chew or gamble. In early life he had been addicted to some of these habits, but was entirely won from them by the loving, purifying influence of his devoted wife. He was a man of great energy and remarkable endurance. He could outride almost any man in his regiment, I believe, if it were put to a test. His men had many nicknames for him, which celebrated this hardihood. When he sat out to reach a certain point at a certain time, you could be sure that he would be there if he killed every horse in the command. He was sometimes too severe in forcing marches, but he never seemed to get tired himself, and he never expected his men to be so. In cutting our way through the forests of the Black Hills, I have often seen him take an axe and work as hard as any of the pioneers. He was

NEVER IDLE.

never idle when he had a pretext for doing anything. Whatever he did he did thoroughly. He

would overshoot the mark, but never fall short. He
fretted in garrison sometimes, because it was too inactive; but he found an outlet here for his energies
in writing articles for the press. He made some
enemies in the army by the freedom with which he
wrote and criticised. I think it was not Custer's
habit to add to his fame by disparaging the reputation of others. As he loved praise himself, so he
liked to award it to others whenever it was due.

He had a remarkable memory. He could recall
in its proper order every detail of any action, no
matter how remote, of which he was a participant.
He was rather verbose in writing, and had no gifts
as a speaker; but his writings interested the masses
from their close attention to details, and from his
facility with the pen as with the sword in bringing a
thing to a climax. As he was apt to overdo in action, so he was apt to exaggerate in statement, not
from any willful disregard of the truth, but because
he saw things bigger than they really were. He did
not distort the truth; he magnified it. He was a

ROSE-COLORED VIEWS.

natural optimist. He took rose-colored views of
everything, even of the miserable lands of the Northern Pacific Railroad. He had a historical memory,
but not a historical mind. He was no philosopher;
he could reel off facts from his mind better than he
could analyze or mass them. He was not a student
nor a deep thinker. He loved to take part in events
rather than to brood over them. He was fond of

fun, genial and pleasant in his manner; a loving and
devoted husband.   It was my privilege to spend two
weeks in his family at one time. and I know how
happy he was in his social relations.   His loss will
be felt by those who had learned to know him
through the productions of his pen; by the remnant
of the famous Seventh he had so often led to victory;
but by none more than by those who had won a
place in his affections.

CHAPTER IX.

IN EXILE.

UNFOUNDED RUMORS OF SITTING BULL'S DEATH—HIS RETREAT INTO
CANADA—VISITED THERE BY A GOVERNMENT COMMISSION—HIS DEFI-
ANT REFUSAL TO RETURN HOME—SPEECHES BY THE CHIEFS—SIT-
TING BULL'S OWN WORDS.

It was at first reported and widely believed that
Sitting Bull himself had been killed in that last desperate fight with Custer. While Gen. Terry was
going over the battle-field, an old sergeant, for many
years in the service on the frontier, rode up to the
General and said that, although he had never seen
Sitting Bull, from the description he had heard given
of him he believed that he had found his body, and
took from his saddle a sort of wrapper, made of
three large elk skins sewed together, beautifully
tanned and elegantly ornamented, in which he had
found a body wrapped lying in a ravine near the
village. A large number of ponies had been led up
to the body and their throats cut, a custom observed
by the Sioux when chiefs die. Gen. Terry sent a
number of men with the sergeant to look at the
body, and among them Fred Girard, the interpreter

at Fort Lincoln, who said that he had, on one occasion, seen Sitting Bull. Girard said that it was not
the body of the chief, as one of his legs was shorter
than the other, and consequently he stepped on the
ball of the other foot, and the body found did not
indicate any such deformity. However, there were
others who insisted that the body was that of Sitting
Bull. These parties gave as their reason for supposing it to be his body, that Sitting Bull had lost
two fingers on his left hand, which had been the case
with the chief whose body lay before them, so that
at the time that Col. E. W. Smith, Gen. Terry's
Adjutant, left for Bismarck, it was still a question
whether Sitting Bull had been killed or not.

Upon Col. Smith's arrival at Bismarck, he
learned that there was a gentleman there who had
lived on the Upper Missouri for the past fifteen
years, and who had seen Sitting Bill frequently.
Col. Smith at once sent for this gentleman, a
Mr. Courtney, and asked him what he knew about
the Indian chief.

"I have seen him," replied Mr. Courtney, "five
or six times, and have talked with him through an
interpreter repeatedly. The last time I saw him
was in 1870, at Fort Peck. We were aroused early
one morning by firing outside the stockade, Sitting
Bull having attacked the agency. The agent by
evening succeeded in communicating with that personage, and ascertained that he wanted ammunition.

The agent asked him to come inside the stockade. This he refused to do until the next day, when he, with a few of his men, visited the agency. The agent told him that the Great Father loved him, and that he did not want to fight with his children ; that if he would make peace with the whites they would treat

SITTING BULL'S REPLY.

him kindly. Pointing his finger at the agent, Sitting Bull said: 'You are the chief of liars, and you know there does not live a white man but hates the Indian, nor an Indian who does not hate the white man, and it will always be so as long as the grass grows and the water runs. I did not come here to make peace, but for ammunition, and I am going to have it. I and my men will fight the white men wherever and whenever we can find them.' The agent gave Sitting Bull what ammunition he wanted and a new rifle, with other articles, which he took to his men."

Mr. Courtney further described Sitting Bull's personal appearance with much minuteness, so that Col. Smith was fully convinced that it was that chieftain's corpse that had been found on the Little Big Horn battle-field. Such, however, was not the case. It soon became known that Sitting Bull and

WENT NORTH.

many of his comrades and followers had made their way northward across the border in the British Northwest Territory, and were at Fort Walsh. Thither, accordingly, in the fall of 1876, a commission was sent to negotiate for the return of the Indians to Dakota. The commissioners arrived at the Canadian border on October 15th, and were there met and cordially received by the Dominion mounted police. The next day they arrived at Fort Walsh, where Major Walsh had succeeded in inducing Sitting Bull to wait for them. The journey of the commission was accomplished through numerous delays and no small amount of actual suffering. The result of the mission undertaken is thus briefly summed up in the opening paragraph of the despatch sent by a correspondent who accompanied the commissioners :

RESULTS OF THE MISSION.

"The United States Commission sent out by the Government to find and treat for peace and good will with the Sioux chief Sitting Bull, has at length succeeded in coming face to face with the redoubtable Indian chieftain and have failed to bring him to any terms. In short, the commission has met Sitting Bull and Sitting Bull has dismissed it abruptly and disdainfully. The expedition has failed in its purpose and the Sioux question is as far from a satisfactory solution as when Gen. Terry and his brother commissioners first set out on their long and tedious journey to the Northwest. It is sad to be compelled to thus preface my despatch, but truth compels the admission."

The correspondent, after describing the march of

the commission, the arrival at Fort Walsh, and the reception, says:—

TALK WITH THE INDIANS.

"When, on the next afternoon, the arrangements for the talk between the commission and the Indians were completed, it was found that they were as simple as the most carping critic could desire. The largest room at the post was selected, and tables were placed for the members of the commission and the two press correspondents who accompanied it. On the opposite side of the room buffalo robes were laid for the accommodation of the Indians. The apartment was just large enough for the commission, its guests, and the chiefs. At 9 o'clock Sitting Bull entered, followed by Spotted Eagle and the rest of his train. Now for the first time was visible to white men since the beginning of the late Indian wars the most noted Indian of the period, and now was made real Cooper's often-derided vision of an

SITTING BULL'S APPEARANCE.

Indian's face. Neither ignorance nor cruelty nor savagery as barbarous as any displayed in savage history has detracted in the least from the expression of manhood and womanliness combined in Sitting Bull's physiognomy. Less rude than Satanta's, less sharp than Spotted Tail's, more intelligent than Red Cloud's, his features, like Gœthe's, made music to the senses. He wore a quiet, ironical smile. His black hair streamed down along his beardless and swarthy cheeks, over clean-cut ears, not burdened with ornaments. His red mourning handkerchief was replaced by a wolf-skin cap. His shirt was a black calico, specked with white dots. His blankets wrapped negligently around him revealed below its edge a pair of rich beaded moccasins, the only finery he wore. Silent, stately, and impassive, this model aboriginal leader, this scoundrelly 'medicine man,' this rascally foe and treacherous friend, this model, in sooth, of Machiavelli's own sort, squatted himself on a buffalo robe next the wall and took out his pipe and smoked it, and expressed, with his insolent manner, the following sentiment: 'This commission which has come to interview me can go to the devil.'

SPOTTED EAGLE.

"The war chief, Spotted Eagle, who sat next to the old chief, Sitting Bull, was a far more engaging and brilliant figure to the eye. He was naked to the waist, a belt full of Winchester rifle cartridges was slung over his bronze shoulders, his muscular breast and arms were daubed with white paint, his hair was knotted in front—the knot thrust through with an eagle's feather—he wore a charm around his neck adorned with pendant plumes, he carried a lance with three projecting knife-blades attached to the staff near the top, forming a lance and tomahawk in one. His waist and legs were swathed in a superb buffalo robe of almost silken texture. He fondled his knife. His every movement was graceful, defiant, lofty.

"The commissioners, who had taken their seats behind the table which intervened between them and the Indians, presented a very dignified appear-

GEN. TERRY'S APPEARANCE.

ance. Gen. Terry is one of the noblest looking officers in the service, as he is one of the bravest and most scholarly. There is nothing peculiar, but everything right and manly in his aspect. If any man in United States uniform could have impressed, persuaded, or cajoled his visitors on that occasion, Gen. Terry must have done so. Gen. Lawrence, the civic commissioner, would certainly have seized upon any point of vantage during the dialogue which, at last, was held, if it had been expedient to indulge in dialogue at all.

"Both commissioners entered without ado upon the performance of a task in which they were given no discretion whatever. They were simply to state the case of the United States Government, await Sitting Bull's reply, decide whether to expostulate with him or not, and retire. An excellent stenographer, Mr. Jay Stone, was present. The interpreters, one employed by the commissioners and two by Sitting Bull, sat near. The utmost pains had been taken by the commissioners to secure accuracy by coaching the interpreters before the conference. The address was, therefore, literally transcribed to Sitting Bull. It was read, sentence by sentence, by General Terry, and translated in due order by Baptiste, his interpreter."

Gen. Terry told the savage chief that his was the only Indian band which had not surrendered to the United States. He proposed that the band should return and settle at the agency, giving up their horses and arms, which would be sold and the money invested in cattle for them.

Sitting Bull replied:

"For sixty-four years you have kept me and my people and treated us bad. What have we done that you should want us to stop? We have done nothing. It is all the people on your side that have started us to do all these depredations. We could not go anywhere else, and so we took refuge in this country. It was on this side of the country we learned to shoot, and that is the reason why I came back to it again. I would like to know why you came here. In the first place, I did not give you the country, but you followed me from one place to another, so I had to leave and come over to this country. I was born and raised in this country with the Red River half-breeds, and I intend to stop with them. I was raised hand in hand with the Red River half-breeds, and we are going over to that part of the country, and that is the reason why I have come over here. [Shaking hands with the British officers.] That is the way I was raised, in the hands of these people here, and that is the way I intend to be with them. You have got ears, and you have got eyes to see with them, and you see how I live with these people. You see me? Here

I am! If you think I am a fool, you are a bigger fool than I am. This house is a medicine house. You come here to tell us lies, but we don't want to hear them. I don't wish any such language used to me; that is, to tell me such lies, in my Great Mother's house. Don't you say two more words. Go back home, where you came from. This country

THIS IS MY COUNTRY.

is mine, and I intend to stay here, and to raise this country full of grown people. See these people here? We were raised with them. [Again shaking hands with the British officers.] That is enough; so no more. You see me shaking hands with these people. The part of the country you gave me you ran me out of. I have now come here to stay with these people, and I intend to stay here. I wish to go back, and to ' take it easy ' going back. [Taking a Santee Indian by the hand.] These Santees—I was born and raised with them. He is going to tell you something about them."

"The-one-that-runs-the-Ree," a Santee Indian, said: "Look at me. I was born and raised in this country. These people, away north here, I was raised with—my hands in their own. I have lived in peace with them. For the last sixty-four years we were over in your country, and you treated us badly. We have come over here now, and you want to try and get us back there again. You

YOU TREAT US BADLY.

didn't treat us well, and I don't like you at all.

[Shaking hands with the English officers.] I have been up and down there as often as these people have. I will be at peace with these people as long as I live. You come over here to tell us lies. I will shake hands with men here, and I have been in peace with them. I have come thus far into this country. These are the people that learned me how to shoot the first time. This country is ours. We did not give it to you. You stole it away from us. You have come over here to our country to tell us lies, and I don't propose to talk much, and that is all I have to say. I want you to take it easy going back home. Don't go in a rush."

" Nine," a Yankton Indian, who joined the Santee band that left Minnesota many years ago during the massacre, said, after shaking hands all round:

"I have shaken hands with everybody in the house. I don't wear the same clothes that these

YOU TELL US LIES.

people do. You come over here to tell lies on one another. I want to tell you a few, but you have got more lies than I can say. Sixty-four years ago you got our country, and you promised to take good care of us and keep us. You ran from one place to another, killing us and fighting us, and I was born and raised with these people over here. I have come here to see the council and shake hands with you all. I wanted to tell you what I think of this. There are seven different tribes of us. They live all over the country. You did not treat us right

over there, and part of us you kept on this side.
You did not treat us right over there, so we came
back over here. These people sitting around here,
you promised to take good care of them when you
had them over there, but you did not fulfill your
promises. They have come over here to this side
again, and here we are together. I come in to these
people here, and they give me permission to trade
with the traders ; that is the way I make my living.
Everything I get I buy from the traders. I don't
steal anything. For fourteen years I have not
fought with your people, and that is what I have lost
by waiting in this country. I have come over here
to these people, and these people, if they had a piece
of tobacco, they gave me half; and that is why I

I HAVE POWDER.

live over here. I have a little powder in my pow-
der-horn, and I gave you a little fourteen years ago.
Since then I have been over in this country. [Shak-
ing hands all around and continuing.] We came
over to this country, and I am going to live with
these people here. This country over here is mine.
The bullets I have over here I intend to kill something to eat with; not to kill anybody with them.
That is what these people told me—to kill nothing
but what I wanted to eat with the ammunition they
gave me. I will do so."

A squaw named "The-one-that-speaks-once," wife
of " That-man-that-scatters-the-bear," said :

"I was over in your country ; I wanted to raise my

children over there, but you did not give me any time.
I came over to this country to raise my children and
have a little peace. [Shaking hands with the English officers.]   That is all I have to say to you.   I
want you to go back where you came from.   These
are the people I am going to stay with, and raise my
children with."

The Flying Bird then made a speecn and said:

"These people here, God Almighty raised us to-

WE LOVE ONE ANOTHER.

gether.   We have a little sense and we ought to
love one another.   Sitting Bull here says that whenever you found us out, wherever his country was,
why, you wanted to have it.   It is Sitting Bull's
country, this is.   These people sitting all around
me : what they committed I had nothing to do with.
I was not in it.   The soldiers find out where we live,
and they never think of anything good ; it is always
something bad."   [Again shaking hands with the
British officers.]

The Indians having risen, being apparently about
to leave the room, the interpreter was then directed
to ask the following questions:

"Shall I say to the President that you refuse the
offers that he has made to you ?   Are we to understand from what you have said that you refuse those
offers ?"

Sitting Bull.—"I could tell you more, but that is
all I have to tell you.   If we told you more—why
you would not pay any attention to it.   That is all I

have to say. This part of the country does not belong to your people. You belong to the other side;
this side belongs to us."

The Crow [shaking hands and embracing Colonel
McLeod, and shaking hands with the other British
officers].—"This is the way I will live in this part of
the county. That is the way I like them. [Making
a gesture of embrace.] When we came back from
the other side you wanted to do something—to lie.
You want us to go back to the other side; that is
the reason why you stay here. What do you mean
by coming over here and talking that way to us?
All this country around here, I know, belongs to
these people, and that is the reason why I came
over here when I was driven out of the other coun-

AFRAID OF GOD ALMIGHTY.

try. I am afraid of God Almighty, that is the reason
why I don't want to do anything bad. When I came
over here, I came to live with these people. My
children, myself, and my women, they all live together. These people that don't hide anything, they
are all the people I like. I suppose you wanted to
hear something; that is the reason you came over
here. The people standing around here want to
hear it also. That is the reason they stand around
here. Sixty-four years ago we shook hands
with the soldiers, and ever since that I have
had hardships. I made peace with them, and
ever since that I have had hardships. I made
peace with them, and ever since that I have

been running from one place to another to keep out of their way. I was over across the line and stayed over there, and I thought you people would take good care of me. You did not do so, and these people over here gave me good care. I have waited here three days, and I have got plenty to eat, and everybody respects me. I came from the other side of the line, and I expect to stay here.

GO WHERE YOU WERE BORN.

Going back, you can take it easy. Go to where you were born, and stay there. I came over to this country, and my Great Mother knows all about it. She knows I came back over here, and she don't wish anything of me. We think, and all the women in camp think, we are going to have the country full of people. When I shook hands before, there were lots of people here then. Now I have come back in this part of the country again to have plenty more people ; to live in peace and raise children."

The Indians then inquired whether the commission had anything more to say; and which the commission answered that they had nothing more, and the conference here closed. This commission had to return without accomplishing anything, and so did others that were sent. In May, 1877, the Rev. Abbott Martin went to see the exile chief. Mr. Martin was accompanied by six Sioux Indians and an interpreter, and was joined, while there, by Major Walsh and other Canadian officers from Fort Walsh, some sixty miles away. Sitting Bull was courteous, very hospitable and attentive. He told the same old story of his wrongs in an eloquent and fiery speech.

WOULD NOT RETURN.

The conclusion reached was that Sitting Bull would not return to the United States, but would remain in the British possessions. He could not bear the idea of surrendering his possessions, ponies, arms, etc., besides fear for his personal safety. He appeared thoroughly subdued. The Indians had lost all their lodges, many arms and supplies, while crossing the river that spring, and were in a bad condition to continue the war. There were three hundred and twenty lodges, or about one thousand warriors. The British officers sympathized with them and assured them of protection during good behavior.

Sitting Bull said "he was not raised to be an enemy of the whites. The pale-faces had things that we needed in order to hunt. We needed ammuni-

NEVER SOLD THE LAND.

tion. Our interests were in peace. I never sold that much land. [Here Sitting Bull picked up with his thumb and forefinger a little of the pulverized dirt in the tent, and holding it up let it fall and blow away.] I never made or sold a treaty with the United States. I came in to claim my rights and the rights of my people. I was driven in force from my land and I now come back to claim it for my people. I never made war on the United States Government. I never stood in the white man's country. I never committed any depredations in the white man's country. I never made the white man's heart bleed. The white man came on to my land and followed me. The white men made me fight for my hunting grounds. The white man made me kill him or he would kill my friends, my women, and my children."

THE CUSTER FIGHT.

Speaking of the Custer fight, Sitting Bull said: "There was a Great Spirit who guided and controlled that battle. I could do nothing. I was sustained by the Great Mysterious One (pointing upwards with his forefinger). I am not afraid to talk about that. It all happened—it is passed and gone. I do not lie, but do not want to talk about it. Low Dog says I can't fight until some one lends me a heart. Gall says my heart is no bigger than that (placing one forefinger at the base of the nail of another finger). We have all fought hard. We did not know Custer. When we saw him we threw up our hands, and I cried, 'Follow me and do as I do.' We whipped each other's horses, and it was all over. There was not as many Indians as the white man says. They are all warriors. There was not more than two thousand. I did not want to kill any more men. I did not like that kind

SELF-DEFENSE.

of work. I only defended my camp. When we had killed enough, that was all that was necessary.

"If the Great Father gives me a reservation I do

not want to be confined to any part of it. I want
no restraint. I will keep on the reservation, but
want to go where I please. I don't want a white
man over me. I don't want an agent. I want to
have the white man with me, but not to be my chief.
I ask this because I want to do right by my people,
and can't trust any one else to trade with them or
talk to them. I want interpreters to talk to the
white man for me and transact my business, but I
want it to be seen and known that I have my rights.
I want my people to have light wagons to work
with. They do not know how to handle heavy
wagons with cattle. We want light wagons and
ponies. I don't want to give up game as long as
there is any game. I will be half civilized till the
game is gone. Then I will be all a white man."

CHAPTER X.

THE MIGHTY FALLEN.

SITTING BULL RUINED BY HIS FLIGHT TO CANADA—HIS FOLLOWERS
STARVED INTO MUTINY AGAINST HIM—THE RETURN TO DAKOTA—
THE FATE OF HIS DAUGHTER, SLEEPING WATER—A VAIN APPEAL
—TAKEN TO FORT RANDALL AS A PRISONER OF WAR.

The flight into Canada was, however, ruinous to
Sitting Bull, and from it we must date his decline.
The British Government gave them refuge and protection, but that was all. It gave them no supplies
whatever, and forbade them to make raids across
the United States border. Thus thrown upon their
own resources, they gradually drifted toward starvation. The land around Fort Walsh was barren,
and game was scarce. The locality was in no wise
to be compared with their old home on the Rosebud.
They gave notice once that they proposed returning
to kill and eat the buffalo, but abandoned the under-
taking on Sitting Bull's advice as one fraught with
too much danger. They entered into negotiations
with the Blackfeet; but these diplomats, finding the
impoverished condition of the Sioux, proved treacherous, stole their ponies, and fled to the mountains.

156

During the three or four years that they lived north of the line they suffered terribly for food and clothing. Their women and children died of want, and the braves themselves hunted in vain.

In the meantime Dakota was fast becoming civilized, and the buffalo and other game were disappearing from the old hunting ground of the Sioux. Sitting Bull kept himself fully posted as to the situation, and satisfied himself that he and his followers could not return except as prisoners. The chief could not keep this information to himself, and as a consequence dissatisfaction became widespread. He lost his power of keeping his followers together, and sub-chiefs led hundreds of the savages away in raiding bands; some of them came

DESERTING THE OLD CHIEF.

over the line and others hovered near the boundary. Gall and Crow King were the leaders of those who deserted him. They returned to the United States and surrendered themselves to the authorities They were placed on the reservation, and have ever since been regarded as the foremost men of the Sioux nation. Sitting Bull, however, stubbornly held out, hoping that the Canadian authorities would make terms for him with the Government at Washington. In this he was disappointed, and at last he found himself deserted by all but a few dozen of his old followers. Then a great blow fell upon him, which for the first time bowed his lofty spirit. A messenger brought him word that his favorite

A GREAT GRIEF.

daughter Minnestema (Sleeping Water), a name
conferred upon her by the whites, had run away
with an Indian buck, who had subsequently abandoned her. These tidings well nigh broke Sitting
Bull's heart. With all his faults he was an affectionate father, as most Indians are. Minnestema,
the flower of the tribe, was his idol, and his pride
was stung to the quick because the Indian who had
so shamelessly deserted her was a man whom he
despised. Humbled, despondent, broken in spirit,
Sitting Bull decided to surrender. When he got to
Standing Rock Agency, under the shadow of Fort
Yates, he found his great rival, Gall, had gained
complete ascendancy over the Indians who had followed his fortunes. He had to endure the mortifi-
cation, also, of seeing a number of those who had
heretofore adhered to him go over to his enemy.
His fortunes, indeed, were at a low ebb, and it
seemed that he had lost his rank and authority forever. It was in vain that he resorted to his old arts
as a "medicine man." The people jeered at his
spells and ridiculed his incantations. He tried to
win them back by his oratory, which had of old been
so persuasive, but they would not listen to him.

CHECKING HIS INTRIGUES.

Finally the other chiefs decided to stop his intrigues, fearing that he would incur the displeasure
of the authorities and bring trouble upon the tribe.
So they warned the United States officials of what

Sitting Bull was trying to do, and the officials deter
mined to take a step which would show the fallen
chief that his power was gone forever. So they
ordered that his father, Four Horns, a decrepit and
imbecile old man, should have rule over the camp
in place of Sitting Bull. Then the steamer "General
Sherman" was sent for and Sitting Bull and one hundred and forty-eight of his people, including his two
wives and their children and his two famous fighting
nephews, were placed on board as prisoners of war
and taken to Fort Randall, several miles distant
from the Standing Rock Agency.

A DRAMATIC SCENE.

But before Sitting Bull embarked a dramatic scene
took place. He determined to make one more effort to regain the prestige he had lost. Three thousand Indians were gathered around. It was a large
audience. Sitting Bull drew his knife from its sheath
and offered it, with his tomahawk, to Captain Stowe,
who was in command of the transfer expedition. At
the same time he made a speech, ostensibly intended
for the captain, but really addressed to the assembled Indians, with the purpose of arousing their
feelings. He posed before them as a hero. After
handing the captain his weapons he said that by
these signs he surrendered (he was already a prisoner of war), and, throwing himself prostrate on
the ground, he besought the captain to take his life,
to inflict any torture he pleased upon him, but to
spare his people and deal with them kindly. The

appeal did not elicit the response that Sitting Bull had hoped for. Instead of applauding, most of the Indians laughed at him. As a hero and patriot they had no faith in him. In their eyes he had only rendered himself ridiculous. With the butt ends of the soldiers' muskets he was pushed out of camp into the steamer.

At Fort Randall Sitting Bull sent a message to the government, promising that if he were allowed to go back to the place of his birth, on the Grand

WHITE MEN'S CLOTHES.

River, he would wear white men's clothes, and endeavor to persuade his followers to do the same thing. He said that he had come to the conclusion that there could be no more fighting on the part of his people, and that the next generation of Indians would have to become like the white men around them and learn to till the earth and master the mechanical arts. After awhile Sitting Bull was permitted to return to Standing Rock, and later was allowed to go to the Grand River valley. This valley comprises the traditional sacred hunting grounds of the Sioux Indians. It is the richest of all the Indian possessions in North America. Sitting Bull built for himself a little "shack" on the Grand River, about fifteen miles from the place where he was born. With the exception of a trip which he made to the East, accompanied by some of his people, he has lived at this place ever since.

Down to this time Sitting Bull had always de-

spised the white men and disbelieved in their power.
When Red Cloud and other chiefs who had visited
Washington told him of the greatness of the United
States, he shook his head incredulously, and told them
that they had been deceived by "bad medicine."
But after a time he came on himself to the East and
made a tour of the principal cities, and thus got his
eyes opened. For the time he sunk his aversion to
the white race and professed great love for all, from
the Great Father at Washington down to the most
recently naturalized citizen. At one time he contemplated a European tour, but abandoned the pro-
ject. In 1884 he was placed on exhibition in the
hall of the Young Men's Christian Association in

PRESS ABUSE.

Philadelphia. A local newspaper made an exhaus-
tive attack on him, telling of his atrocities, and not
sparing some peculiarly horrible embellishments.
The agent of the show was delighted, but when
night came and the pious Philadelphians refused to
look upon the moon-faced warrior, he became
annoyed, and spoke to the painted attraction in
severe and blasphemous language. After this tour
he returned to the agency, which had been located
at Standing Rock. For the four or five years previous to the recent ghost dances the Bull lived a
retired life and did little mixing with the whites at
the post. "Jim" Finley, of Kansas City, who was
given the Pine Ridge tradership, said upon his first
trip home after his appointment that Sitting Bull's

10

days of prominence were past. The Sioux had grown to pay much heed to their agent, and the young blood was coming to the front in tribal leadership. Sitting Bull was no longer potent as a leader as in former days, although as a medicine man he was still in high repute.

When the census of Indian tribes was taken in 1881, Sitting Bull was visited by Mr. William Selwyn, a full-blooded Dakota Indian, who was employed by the Government as a census-taker. The chief on that occasion dictated a message to the " Great Father" at Washington, which Mr. Selwyn wrote down in Sioux and afterward translated into English. Sitting Bull's address to Mr. Selwyn and his message to the President were as follows:

MESSAGE TO THE PRESIDENT.

"I am the son of the He-Topa (Four Horns, late a chief of the Unk-pa-pas), and it is said that he was one of your relatives; so, then, you are a younger brother to me (sunkachiye). You are a full-blooded Dakota, but you adopt the ways of the whites, and I hear that you have been employed by the Great Father.

"For the last few years I have been in the North, where there are plenty of buffalo, for the buffalo were my means of living. God made me to live on the flesh of the buffalo, so I thought I would stay out there as long as there were buffalo enough for us. But the Great Father sent for me several times, and although I did not know why he wanted me to come

down, at last I consented to do so. I never, myself, made war against the children of the Great Father, and I never sought a fight with them. While I was looking for buffalo, they would attack and shoot at me, and of course I had to defend myself or else I should die. But all the blame is put on me. I have always thought that the Dakotas were all one body, and I wanted to make an agreement with them to come and settle down. While I have been in the North, here and there, a good many little things have happened, and I have been blamed for them ;

I AM INNOCENT.

but I know that I am innocent. Those men who have made the trouble ought to be blamed. Everybody knows that I was not going to stay at the North any longer, but that when the buffalo disappeared I should make up my mind to come down.

"Although you are a Dakota, you are employed by the Great Father; therefore I want you to let him hear my words. When I first came down, white men came to me almost every day to get some words out of me, but I said: 'No! When I settle down I shall say some words to the Great Father.' I know that some white rascals have dealt with the Dakotas, and by their foolish ways have ruined them. As for myself, I do not want any one to do mischievously or deceitfully. So I do not want to let any ordinary man hear my words. I tell the whites that my words are worth something; and even if they were willing to pay me for it, I never made any reply. But as soon as I saw you I was well pleased. Although you are a Dakota, you have gathered up many good words and put them into my ears. To-day I was wishing that some one would come in and advise me, and as you have done

THIS PEOPLE BELONG TO ME.

so, it pleases me very much. All this people here belong to me and I hope that the Great Father will treat them kindly. I always thought that when we came back, and any of my relatives came to me with good words, I should reply, ' Yes, yes.' To-day you have put good words into my ears, and I have said, ' Yes.' In the future I hope I shall have some good, honest, reliable man with me. Interpreters have come to me often, following me up, and I have said, ' No. I am not a child; if I want to do anything, I shall take time to think it over.' It is said Spotted Tail was killed by getting mixed up with bad men. Oftentimes a man has lost his life by being mixed up with bad men. But I wish that my people may be treated well, so that they may do rightly. I am the last one that has come in from the North, and yet I want to surpass the old agency Dakotas in what is right, and I wish that the Great Father would furnish me with farming implements, so that I can till the ground.

"My brother, I wish you would send this message to the Great Father right away, so that he will help me. Now I have confidence in you that you will be able to send off my message. I am glad that you came to see me. It is a good thing for relatives to see each other. I have no objections to your numbering the people.

"SITTING BULL."

CHAPTER XI.

THE LAST CAMPAIGN.

SITTING BULL INVOLVED IN THE MESSIAH CRAZE—HIS HOPE OF RE-
GAINING HIS OLD POSITION—PLOTS AND DISAFFECTION—VISITED BY
A YOUNG LADY MISSIONARY—AGENT MCLAUGHLIN'S VISIT—THE
GHOST DANCES—SITTING BULL'S REMARKABLE PROPOSITION.

Sitting Bull's camp, in the summer and fall of
1890, was on the Grand River, about forty miles
southwest from the Standing Rock Agency. The
place lies away from lines of travel, and is quiet and
secluded. He was glad there to be hidden from
the world in which he had been such a striking
figure. It was his intention to spend the rest of
his days in seclusion there; but such was not to be
his fate. He came forth from his isolated camp to
die.

The year 1890 was a hard one for the Indians.
In addition to the broken faith of the Government,
the swindling practices of its agents, and the unscrupulous aggressions of the settlers, they had to
bear the burden of bad weather, poor crops, and a

168

scarcity of game. Their complaints were just, and loud, and bitter; but were little heeded. Then there

MESSIAH COMING.

was started, somewhere or other, a rumor that the Messiah was coming—the Messiah whom immemorial tradition had declared would one day come, followed by all the great chiefs and warriors of the past, returned to life, to lead the Indians to victory over their white oppressors. This idea broke forth simultaneously in the minds of many tribes—of the Sioux in Dakota, of the Cherokees in Indian Territory, of the Apaches in Arizona. It spread like an epidemic. It was born of the wretchedness and need of the people, and it found believers everywhere. The Indians began holding religious gatherings, with wild ceremonies, commonly called "ghost dances."

This was to prepare for the Messiah's coming. Some great dances were held at Kicking Bear's camp, near Cheyenne, and were attended by a few of Sitting Bull's men. When these returned home they took Kicking Bear with them. He told Sitting

REVELATIONS OF MESSIAH.

Bull the revelations the Messiah had made to him, and stated that the spirit had deputized Bull to conduct the dances at the agency, finally presenting to him a decorated shirt or mantle of apostleship. Bull at once gathered about him all the bad elements he could to commence the dances. He stopped when ordered to, but soon recommenced with redoubled vigor. In the meanwhile, he sent agents into the hills to spread his wishes among the other clans of the Sioux nation, and to visit the Shoshones, the Blackfeet, the Araphoes, the Gros Ventrias, the

EVIL INFLUENCE OF BULL.

Ogalallas and other tribes. What his influence for evil would have been, his previous career gives abundant suggestion. He now saw, as he supposed, his opportunity to regain his old standing in the Sioux nation, and he tried his best to take advantage of it. Naturally superstitious, the Indians were ready for such an outpouring of their pent-up feelings in the form of a religious dance. Bull had always gained his greatest successes from his ability as a medicine man or diplomat, and he felt that the time for him to get his revenge on the other chiefs and on the Government had arrived. He at the start joined in with the ghost dancers, not shouting and dancing so much as inciting the others to the greatest activity in that line. When the Indians would go dancing around in a circle until they fell to the ground from giddiness and exhaustion, the wily old chief would take his place alongside of the fallen one, and, after a few words with him, would

SPURRING THEM ON.

announce what visions of the Messiah and the coming again of the hunting grounds of the past had been witnessed, and the dance would be resumed with renewed vigor. Soon another would fall in a faint and the same programme would be gone through with.

The Government gave orders that all the ghost dances everywhere should be stopped, but especially those at Sitting Bull's camp. It had become evident that while he was allowed to run around corrupting the weak minds of his tribe and inciting them to outlawry, there could be no quietude. Evidence had been secured that he had arrangements made to gather in a body all the young bucks in the spring and start out on a general raid. The ghost dances, which the young bucks rightly interpreted as war dances, he was keeping up, that their enthusiasm and hatred might not die out, and he urged the excitement on, despite the desires and orders of the authorities. As he was indifferent to advice Gen. Miles concluded it would be a good move to arrest him and isolate him for a time from the scene of his pernicious activity.

Several visits were paid to Sitting Bull by various persons in the hope of persuading him to give up the dances and stop his plotting without harsh steps being taken. One young lady, a missionary and

A LADY'S HEROISM.

teacher, went to see him. She went alone, unarmed, and without any commission from the Government, to remonstrate with this most savage chief. With only an Indian boy to accompany her she went over to Cross Bear's village, and there came in sight of Sitting Bull's people. They had several hundred tepees, and a ghost dance was in progress. When she arrived there the men were dressed in old-time war dress, painted and feathered. The women also were painted, and, what is rather strange in Indian life, every woman had a white feather tied to her hair. The Indians regard feathers as a sign of masculine superiority and prowess, and do not allow women to wear them. There seems to be something about this craze that invests the woman with greater importance, and it is supposed that in case of hostilities the women would fight as the men. The Sioux had a tall centre pole, with all sorts of flags flying on it, and around this pole they formed a ring and were chanting some religious song, all the while gazing fixedly at the sun. Near this pole, outside of the ring, was a tepee, in which old Sitting Bull sat. All who took part in the dance went to this tepee to be painted by the old medicine man. He put blue crescents on their foreheads, cheeks, and chins, and a cross on the nose between the eyes, Even the little Sioux children went into the tepee and were decorated, and coming out went off a little distance and set up a dance of their own.

The young woman went into Sitting Bull's tepee and had an interview with him. He sat opposite the door. His hands and wrists were painted yellow and green, and his face red, green, and white. The zealous young missionary gave him a thorough lecturing in his own language. The old man replied that the other chiefs had ignored him in selling their lands and opening the reservations; that he was determined to be chief, and his only way was by giving the people religious excitement. He did not want his people to become civilized or Christianized,

LOVE OF POWER.

because if they did he would lose his power. The young woman gave Sitting Bull another lecture and retired.

Sitting Bull was also visited at about this time by Mr. James McLaughlin, the agent at Standing Rock, who made to the Commissioner of Indian Affairs the following report of his misison:

"Having just returned from Grand River district, and referring to my former communication regarding the ghost dance craze among the Indians, I have the honor to report that on Saturday evening last I learned that such a dance was in progress in Sitting Bull's camp, and that a large number of Indians of the Grand River settlements were participators. Sitting Bill's camp is on the Grand River, forty miles southwest from the agency, in a section of country outside of the line of travel, only visited by those connected with the Indian service, and was therefore a secluded place for these scenes. I concluded to take them by surprise, and on Saturday morning left for that settlement accompanied by Louis Primeau, arriving there about 3 P. M., and having left the road usually traveled by men visiting the settlement, we got upon them unexpectedly, and found a ghost dance at its height. There were about forty-five men, twenty-five women, twenty-five boys, and ten girls participating, a majority of the latter (boys and girls), until a few weeks ago, pupils of the day schools of the Grand River settlements. Approximately, 200 persons, lookers-on, had come to witness the ceremony, either from curiosity or sympathy, most of whom had their families with them and encamped in the neighborhood.

"I did not attempt to stop the dance then going

CRAZED EXCITEMENT.

on, as in their crazed condition under tne excitement it would have been useless to attempt it, but after remaining some time talking with a number of the spectators, I went on to the house of Henry Bull Head, three miles distant, where I remained over night, and returned to Sitting Bull's house next morning, where I had a long talk with Sitting Bull and a number of his followers. I spoke very plainly to them, pointing out what had been done by the Government for the Sioux people, and how this faction, by their present conduct, were abusing the confidence that had been reposed in them by the Government in its magnanimity in granting them full amnesty for all past offenses, when from destitution and imminent starvation they were compelled to surrender as prisoners of war in 1880 and 1881; and I dwelt at length upon what was being done in the way of education of their children and for their own industrial advancement, and assured them of what this absurd craze would lead to, and the chas-

tisement that would certainly follow if these demoralizing dances and disregard of department orders
were not soon discontinued.

"I spoke with feeling and earnestness, and my
talk was well received, and I am convinced that it
had a good effect. Sitting Bull, while being very
obstinate and at first inclined to assume the rôle of
'Big Chief' before his followers, finally admitted the
truth of my reasoning, and said that he believed me
to be a friend to the Indians as a people, but that I
didn't like him personally, but that when in doubt in
any matter following my advice he had always found
it well, and that he had a proposition to make to me,
which, if I agreed to and would carry out, would
allay all further excitement among the Sioux over
the ghost dance, or else convince me of the truth of
the belief of the Indians in this new doctrine.

HIS PROPOSITION.

"He then stated his proposition, which was that
I should accompany him on a journey to trace from
this agency to each of the other tribes of Indians
through which the story of the Indian Messiah had
been brought, and when they reached the last tribe,
or where it originated, if they could not produce the
man who started the story, and we did not find the
new Messiah, as described, upon the earth, together
with the dead Indians returning to re-inhabit this
country, he would return convinced that they (the
Indians) had been too credulous and imposed upon,
which report from him would satisfy the Sioux, and

all practices of the ghost societies would cease, but that if found to be as professed by the Indians, they be permitted to continue their medicine practices, and organize as they are now endeavoring to do.

"I told him that this proposition was a novel one, but that the attempt to carry it out would be similar to an attempt to catch up the wind that blew last year, but that I wished him to come to my house, where I would give him a whole night or day and night, in which time I thought I could convince him of the absurdity of this foolish craze, and the fact of his making me the proposition that he did was convincing proof that he did not fully believe in what he was professing and endeavoring so hard to make others believe. He didn't, however, promise fully to come into the agency to discuss the matter, but said he would consider my talk and decide after deliberation.

"Desiring to use every reasonable means to bring Sitting Bull and his followers to abandon this dance, and to look upon its practice as detrimental to their individual interests and the welfare of their children,

INVESTIGATING THE CRAZE.

I made the trip herein reported to ascertain the extent of the disaffection and the best means of effecting its discontinuance. From close observation, I am convinced that the dance can be broken up, and after due reflection would respectfully suggest that in case my visit to Sitting Bull fails to bring him in to see me in regard to the matter, as invited to do, all Indians living on Grand River be notified that those wishing to be known as opposed to the ghost doctrine, friendly to the Government, and desiring the support provided in the treaty, must report to the agency for such enrollment, and be required to camp near the agency for a few weeks, and those continuing their medicine practices, in violation of department orders, to remain on Grand River, from whom subsistence will be withheld."

CHAPTER XII.

DEATH OF THE GREAT CHIEF.

GENERAL MILES GAVE THE WORD FOR HIS ARREST.—WAS IT INTENDED
TO KILL HIM, RATHER THAN TAKE HIM ALIVE?—INDIAN POLICE LED
THE WAY.—THE ARREST AND ATTEMPTED RESCUE.—THE FATAL SHOT.
—ANOTHER ACCOUNT OF THE TRAGEDY.—DISPOSITION OF HIS RE-
MAINS.

Persuasion failed, and it became evident that
force must be used to stop the evil influence of Sitting Bull in the Messianic propoganda. Orders
for his arrest were accordingly issued. Colonel W.
F. Cody, " Buffalo Bill," was at first sent to execute
the order, but was recalled. It was realized that a
stronger military force would be needed.

NO AGENCY INDIAN.

" God Almighty made me ; God Almighty did not
make me an agency Indian, and I'll fight and die
fighting before any white man can make me an
agency Indian." This was the declaration made by
Sitting Bull to General Miles on the occasion of
their first meeting. He was now animated by this
same spirit, and serious work was feared. He was
known to be preparing for a rush to the Bad Lands,

where the difficulty of taking him would be vastly increased. Once in the Bad Lands it would be a long time and there would be much hard fighting before any of the hostiles could be taken or starved out. Therefore it seemed necessary to act at once, and orders were given to the police to get ready for action, and they set out during Sunday night for the scene of the next morning's encounter.

A correspondent of *The Chicago Tribune* asserts that there was a quiet understanding between the officers of the Indian and military departments that it would be impossible to bring Sitting Bull to Standing Rock alive, and that if brought in nobody would know precisely what to do with him. Though under arrest he would still be a source of great annoyance, and his followers would continue their dances and threats against the neighboring white settlers. There was, therefore, a complete understanding between the commanding officers and the Indian police that the slightest attempt to rescue the old medicine man should be a signal to send Sitting Bull to the happy hunting ground. That the Government authorities, civil as

HIS DEATH DESIRED.

well as military, from President Harrison and General Miles down, preferred the death of the famous old savage to his capture whole-skinned, few persons in Dakota, Indian or white, had a doubt. It was felt that Sitting Bull's presence anywhere behind iron bars would be the cause of endless troubles, while should he fall a victim to the ready Win-

11

chester the thousands of Messiah-crazed ghost
dancers would rudely realize that his "medicine,"
which was to make them bullet-proof and yet could
not save so great an oracle, must be worthless after
all, and should be forsaken for the paths of peace.

It is conceded that the operation against Sitting
Bull's personality was suggested by the effectual
quelling produced by the removal of Medicine Arrow, the great Cheyenne leader, when the Cheyennes threatened an unprecedented uprising. The
promise to "die fighting," quoted above, had much
to do also in shaping the determination for a sudden,
decisive result, as well as the old chief's oft-ex-
pressed wish to be remembered as the last Indian
on the continent to give up his rifle.

When General Miles set out for Dakota, it was
the beginning of the end. With the General stepping quietly aboard the train at the big railway depot
at Chicago the expedition which had been with equal
quietude under preparation at Fort Yates, which
forms part of the agency, was also ready to move.
Almost at the same moment that General Miles's
car glided out for the Northwest the members of his
little command at the Fort, like so many automatons
guided by his will, silently took their departure and

THE STAGE SETTING.

were quickly lost in the inky darkness that envel-
oped the wilderness stretching to the camp of Sitting Bull on the banks of the Grand River.

The death of Sitting Bull had an appropriate

GENERAL NELSON A. MILES.

stage-setting. The preparations for the tragedy lacked no element of the picturesque and impressive The van was led by men of Sitting Bull's own blood, superbly mounted and accoutered, and every one wearing the bright brazen buttons and showy blue cloth uniforms of Uncle Sam's service. This was no mere coincidence. It was to be part of the great object lesson to the 'ghost dancers and a demonstration of the value of General Miles's new method of solving the Indian problem by turning the Indians by wholesale into soldiers.

On Saturday, December 13, 1890, General Miles sent word to Major McLaughlin and Captain Fechet that the time to strike the blow had come, and on the next morning, Sunday, Troops F and G, Eighth Cavalry, and a company of infantry, preceded by about twenty of the Indian police, started to the southwest to capture the chief of the recalcitrants. The distance was forty-three miles, and the United States troops stopped and consulted with the police about five miles from the tepees on the Grand River. It was agreed at a consultation that the troops should move up to within two or three miles of the Indian camp and station themselves where they could be easily signaled. The Indian police were then to move quietly down to the tepees and proceed immediately to that of Sitting Bull, arriving there just at dawn.

The band of well-fed, warmly clad, copper-faced athletes that led the way for the white soldiers were

in striking contrast with the starving, ragged
wretches that, with such a cunning leader as Sitting

STEALING UPON HIM.

Bull, formed a menace in the Grand River camp.
Close behind the Indians' hardy ponies, but taking a
slower pace on the frozen trail, came Captain Fouchet's cavalry command.   The cavalry were encumbered with two pieces of modern light artillery—
machine guns that are similar to those which so
speedily settled the fate of Louis Riel's half-breed
followers.   To the rear of Fouchet's cavalry, and at
times taking a double-quick step forward, for the
night was bitterly cold, the infantry command of Colonel Drum swung along in the darkness.   A weary,
difficult march it was, too.   The distance, and the
capabilities of the troops to withstand the fatigues of
such a journey, had been figured out nicely, and
when the first faint light of dawn appeared the expedition was within easy distance of its destination.
The broken order of a triple separation of forces
had been carefully preserved, and the Indian police
were the first to sight the huddled cluster of ugly
looking tepees on the river bank.

Despite the early hour all was astir in the village,
where on every hand was evidence that a hurried
exodus was contemplated.   The ponies of the police
were pushed for all they were worth, and before
Sitting Bull's dazed adherents had half a chance to
realize the situation a dozen of the police had pulled
their panting animals up short on all sides of the

chief's abode. Bull Head, lieutenant of police, and Shaved Head, first sergeant, were in command. No time was wasted in ceremony. The proud old medicine man was hustled out, hoisted on a waiting horse,

RAGED AND SPUTTERED.

and in a trice faced toward civilization. He raged and sputtered for a moment, then straightening up shouted hoarsely, not for help, but a command to his followers. Despite the threatening of the police, Winchesters being alternately directed at his head and at those of his kinsmen, the old chief retained his presence of mind, and with a powerful voice, continued to direct his own rescue.

Suddenly there was a puff of smoke beside a tepee and the sharp crack of a Winchester. The policeman at Sitting Bull's right, grasping the chief's bridle, reeled in the saddle, and, toppling over, was trampled under the hoofs of the ponies in the mad helter skelter of retreat from the village. The shot was instantly answered by a volley from the police at their blanketed tribesmen, many of whom were already mounted and in frenzied pursuit. The police volley told with deadly effect, and the firing in a moment was general on both sides. Sitting Bull could be heard in the confusion still attempting, though captive, to direct the fight. Raising his gaunt form, he was beckoning his sons and warriors on, when suddenly his body straightened rigidly, then dropped limp on the hard prairie. The police halted round the corpse, not knowing for a moment but that it was a trick of the wily old chief. The sudden movement and the fall of Sitting Bull disconcerted the pursuers, who, remaining at a distance, fired at intervals toward the police. The latter held their ground, knowing the cavalry under Captain Fouchet would be at hand.

To the surprise of all, however, the hostiles, who had been consulting among themselves, began a movement to close in from all sides. The rattle of Winchesters was now redoubled by both parties, the police using their ponies as protection. It was at this critical juncture that Captain Fouchet's men dashed up, and the machine guns, which had been put in position, opened on the Indians. The latter were too dismayed at this unexpected onslaught to stand for a moment, and all bolted for the river. The cavalry followed only a short distance, deeming it better policy not to drive to desperation the now

A DIFFERENT STORY.

leaderless mob. Among the Sioux killed were two sons of Sitting Bull, named Blackbird and Crow Foot, the latter being only twelve years old.

A different story is told by one of the soldiers, however. According to him "Bull Head, the lieutenant of the Indian police, went to the chief's house with a warrant for his arrest. No one but the old chief and two sons were there. Sitting Bull opened the door, and his son seeing the house surrounded by police gave a cry of alarm. Without hesitating a moment Bull Head fired at Sitting Bull, the ball

striking him in the breast over the left nipple, killing him instantly. While reeling Sitting Bull managed to draw a revolver, which exploded just as he
fell, the ball entering Bull Head's thigh. One of the
Indian policemen lifted Sitting Bull's scalp. The old
chief's face was a sickening sight. An Indian bat-
tered his face into jelly after death with a plank.
The few remaining hairs in his head were clipped
off, and his mocassins and most of his clothing carried away for relics. Among his personal effects
were letters from Mrs. Weldon, of New York, warning him to flee from the agency, as the Government
was about to have him killed."

It should be added that Bull Head was among
those mortally wounded in the affray, and a few
days later his body was interred with military honors
at Fort Yates. His widow stood with his father and
brother at the head of the grave. This poor woman
was at the Cannon Ball River on a visit when she
learned from a runner that her husband had been
kill in arresting Sitting Bull. She started at once
on foot to find him, and walked eighty miles without a rest, falling in a faint when admitted to her
husband's room, which she reached before his death.

Sitting Bull's wives and daughters remained in
their camp, under the charge of an Indian policeman, Gray Eagle. What became of his body is not
yet positively known, "It is learned," said a *Chicago Tribune* correspondent, "that Sitting Bull's
body, when brought in from Grand River, was taken

to the military hospital to be dissected. The Indians at the agency, the police and friendly Indians, would have nothing to do with the remains. It is said the morning they were to be buried a couple of soldiers took the box supposed to contain the remains and dumped it in an isolated grave away from the graves of other Indians and a guard placed around it. It is an open secret that really the box did not contain the remains and that the guard was put on the grave as a blind. It is believed Sitting Bull's body is now in the dissecting-room, and that in time the skeleton will turn up either in the Government museum or some other place."

CHAPTER XIII.

TRIBUTES TO HIS MEMORY.

His Niece's Indignation and Grief—A Senator's Attempt to be Funny Over a Tragedy—"Buffalo Bill's" Tribute—General Schofield's Views—"Adirondack" Murray's Eloquent Protest and Rebuke—Sitting Bull Compared with Webster and with Gladstone.

Thus died Sitting Bull. Thus the world was rid of a troubler. But what made him a troubler? Wrongs, injustice, outrage. There are those who declare that the only good Indian is a dead Indian. But they libel humanity, the humanity that dwells in red skins as well as in white. The real cause of Indian troubles, wars, massacres, is and has been the incredibly and inexpressibly base treatment of the Indians by the white men, in which the Government has often, if not always, been *particeps criminis.* There were those who raised a cry of exultation at the death of Sitting Bull. There were many who regarded it with relief. But the real mind and heart of the American people felt sad and ashamed, with

SAD AND ASHAMED,

a sadness and a shame too deep for words. Perhaps it was necessary to kill him. But the circumstances, a century old, that made it necessary to kill him, that made him a being whom it was necessary to kill, are only to be regarded with national humiliation.

It will be of interest to record here a few of the utterances which this grim tragedy evoked. In the city of Wilmington, Del., there live two nieces of the famous chief. One of them, Mrs. George Leonard, spoke thus:

MRS. LEONARD'S STATEMENT.

"I lived in the Sioux territory during the wars in which my uncle, Sitting Bull, who was my father's younger brother, took part. I left the territory soon after my uncle's return from Canada, where he went after the Custer fight. I went to New York city and thence came here and was married five years ago. My uncle's death has made me very nervous. I understand that my uncle's body will be taken to Washington, and I have written to the Secretary of the Interior to see it. My father's name was Carmock Bull. We can prove our identity by papers which we have in our possession. My uncle, I think, was about 53 years of age."

At this point she became very much agitated, and said through her tears:

"Our people have been robbed, ruined and persecuted by the white people, who have driven us from the lands which were formerly ours, and not content with this robbery they have now killed my uncle in cold blood. This country was wned by our people before any white men came. Now they have killed the chief, and white men now come to his family to look into his history. You shall hear nothing. His history will be published, and then the world will get it.

"You can understand how we feel about this matter. He was killed, you see, without cause or provocation, and it is natural that we should feel strongly. I have two brothers yet living in the Sioux territory. Many others, like myself, left the territory, and are now scattered over the country. It is against the traditions of our race to permit white men to examine our records or pry into any of our secrets."

Senator Sanders, of Montana, who was formerly one of the rough-and-ready, quick-shooting, vigilance committee men of the mining camps, may be quoted as one of those who took the worst possible view of Sitting Bull. He chose to strive to be humorous in talking of the tragedy.

SENATOR SANDER'S DESCRIPTION.

"I am in great distress of mind," said he, "my heart is bowed down with woe, because of the death of my fellow-being, Mr. S. Bull, formerly a resident of my State, but recently a sojourner in a neighboring territory. He has gone the way of all flesh, and there is other copper-colored flesh that would not go far astray if it followed him. S. Bull was a man of some activity in the line of industry which he pursued. His vocal organs were always in good repair ; his larynx never troubled him as much as it did other people. If he ever suffered from any pharyingeal difficulty I was not aware of it, and his stomach was never satisfied.

"In justice to him I should say that most of the work he did was performed by somebody else. (If there's any bull in that it's all right; we're talking Bulls just now). His fighting was universally by proxy, and the domestic labor pertaining to his home was entirely vicarious, as his squaws can testify. He was a newspaper Indian, craving notoriety and deadhead advertising. I knew him as a warrior and can say truthfully that, when he was not taking any risks, he expressed himself fearlessly. Vale, Bull."

Col. W. F. Cody, best known as "Buffalo Bill," said : "I do not know certainly whether I met Sitting

BUFFALO BILLS STATEMENT.

Bull or not during the campaigns of '76. He was not at that time a chief of any note ; in fact, he was not much of a chief, but more of a medicine man. It was General Sheridan who really made him 'a big Indian.' They had to have some name for that war, and I was on the mission at Red Cloud Agency when they were talking about what name to give it. They spoke of Chief Galla, Crazy Horse, and others, all bigger men than Sitting Bull, but finally decided to call it Sitting Bull's war, and that made him seem to be a great man, and his name became known all over the country. The first time I ever saw him to know him was when he joined my show at Buffalo, coming with eight or nine of his chosen people from Grand River. He appeared there before 10,000 people, and was hissed so it was some time before I could talk to the crowd and secure their patience. The same thing occurred at almost every place. He never did more than to appear on horseback at any performance and always refused to talk English, even if he could. At Philadelphia a man asked him if he had no regret at killing Custer and so many whites. He replied: 'I have answered to my people for the Indians slain in that fight. The chief that sent Custer must answer to his people.' That is the only smart thing I ever heard him say. He was a peevish Indian, always saying something bad in council. He was an inveterate beggar. He sold autographs at $1 a piece and during the four months he was with the show picked up a good deal of money."

GENERAL SCHOFIELD'S STATEMENT.

General Schofield, the head of the United States Army, said: " Sitting Bull was a conspicuous man as an Indian. He was not a warrior. He was not a great battle chief. He never in his life wore the 'war bonnet' of the Indian. He was a 'medicine man,' what would be called in our civilization a preacher, a teacher. He was purely an Indian politician, and the effort to get him into our camp and endeavor to dissuade him from his wretched demagogue ghost dance were what led to his death."

Asked as to whether there was any scheme to lure

Sitting Bull into a trap and kill him, General Schofield said: "Certainly not." He said that the Interior Department people felt that old Sitting Bull ought to be brought in and reasoned with. "I did not at all believe in the Buffalo Bill idea," said General Schofield, "and that purpose was quickly abandoned. Major McLauglin of the Standing Rock Agency insisted that old Sitting Bull ought to be apprehended, and on authority of the Interior Department the Indian police were sent on the mission. They did their work well, and that is only another proof that the North American Indian ought to be an important constituent of the United States Army."

"Look at those police," exclaimed the General, "faithful, true, and victorious and glorying in their victory. I believe that the North American Indian, with authorized enlistment, good pay, and good food, would be the finest soldier the world could ever see. Wherever he has been tried he has never failed."

W. H. H. MURRAY'S EULOGY.

An eloquent and impassioned tribute was paid to Sitting Bull in *The New York World* by Mr. W. H. H. Murray, formerly a popular clergyman, but best known as a writer and commonly called "Adirondack" Murray. He spoke for the myriads who saw in Sitting Bull a sacrifice to injustice. Perhaps he was extreme in his expressions, but not more so than those who think the only good Indian the dead

one. Mr. Murray said : " The land grabbers wanted
the Indian lands. The lying, thieving Indian agents
wanted silence touching past thefts and immunity to
continue their thieving. The renegades from their
people among the Indian police wanted an opportunity to show their power over a man who despised
them as renegades, and whom, therefore, they hated.
The public opinion of the frontier—the outgrowth of
ignorance, credulity and selfish greed—more than
assented to a plan to rid the country of one who
while he lived, so great was he in fame and in fact,
must forever stand as a reminder of wars passed
and a threat of war to come. Out of all these and
other causes peculiar to the condition of things there
localized, some accidental and deplorable, others
permanent and infamous, was born, as Milton's
Death was born, from Satan and Sin, the plot to kill
him.

AND SO HE WAS MURDERED.

"I knew this man ; knew him in relation to his
high office among his people and in his elements as
a man. As to his office or rank I honored him. He
filled a station older than human records, as a man
I admired him. He represented in person, in manners, in mind and in the heroism of his spirit the
highest type of a race which in many and rare virtues stands peer among the noblest races of the
world. As to his rank or official station, we whites
called him Medicine Man. It is a name that does
not name. It is and has been from the beginning of

our intercourse with the red race a delusion and the source of delusions among even the scholarly.

"This man Sitting Bull was a prophet, not war chief, to his people. The seer, in the line of seers of a race, beside which, as to antiquity, the Jews are but mushrooms, What was a misnomer, a joke, a term of contempt to us in our ignorance of fact and ancient things, to the red men—for the term Indian as applied to them is also a misnomer and a proof of fourteenth-century ignorance—was a rank above all ranks won or bestowed by the tribe ; an office above all earthly offices, connected with and symbolic of the highest truths and deepest mysteries of their religion.

"Hence, by virtue of his office old as custom and tradition, this man, Sitting Bull, was counsellor of chiefs, the Warwick behind the throne stronger than the throne, the oracle of mysteries and of knowledge hidden from the mass ; hidden even from chiefs, to whose words of advice and authority all listened as to the last and highest expression of wisdom.

"Such was Sitting Bull as to his office, as interpreted and understood from a standpoint of knowledge of the religion, the traditions and the supersti-

FAITHFUL TO HIS OFFICE.

tion of his people. That he was, faithful to his high office all knew. He was in fact, Counsellor of Chiefs, that as Joshua did to Moses, so he in hour of battle upheld their arms till the sun went

down and the battle was lost or won, let all who
fought his tribe declare : that the gods of his race
found in him a high priest faithful to his trust none
may ever deny. He lived and he has died, a red
man true to his office and his race. That leaf of
laurel none can deny to his fame—not even his ren-
egade murderers.

"But no office, however great, is as great as the
man if he fills it greatly, and this man Sitting Bull
was greater as a man than he was even as a prophet. I met him often ; I studied him closely as one
of intelligence studies the type of a race—I may add
of a departing race—and I knew him well. And
this I say of him : He was a Sioux of the Sioux, a
red man of the red men. In him his race, in physique, in manners, in virtues, in faults, stood incar-
nate. In face he was the only man I ever saw who
resembled Gladstone—large featured, thoughtfully
grave, reflective, reposeful when unexcited. In
wrath his countenance was a collection of unex-
ploded or exploding thunder—the awful embodi-
ment of measureless passion and power.

"In conversation he was deliberate, the user of
few words, but suave and low voiced. In moments
of social relaxation he was companionable, receptive

GENTLE IN HIS HOME.

of humor, a genial host, a pleasant guest. In his
family gentle, affectionate and not opposed to merriment. When sitting in council his deportment was
a model ; grave, deliberate, courteous to opponents,

12

patient and kindly to men of lesser mind. I suggest that our Senators copy after him.

"In pride he was equal to his rank and race, a
rank to him level with a Pope's and a race the oldest
and bravest in the world. Of vanity I never saw
one trace in him. I would couple the word with
Gladstone or Webster as quickly as with him. He
was never over-dressed. He wore the insignia of
his office as a king his robes or a judge his gown.
In eating he was temperate ; from spirituous drinks
an abstainer. His word once given was a true bond.
He was a born diplomat, No foe ever fathomed his
thought. I have watched him by the hour when I
knew his heart was hot with wrath, but neither from
eye nor lip nor cheek nor nostril nor sinewy hand
might one get hint of the storm raging within.
There was no surface to him. He was the embodi-
ment of depths.

"Was he eloquent? What is eloquence? Who
may say—who may agree as to it? Men tell me
that Mr. Depew is eloquent, and that New Yorkers
go wild with the glasses in front of them when their
Mr. Choate is speaking. I have read their words.
Their eloquence is not that of the great Sioux
Prophet. Here are some words of his. You can
compare them with your orators' best:

INDIAN ELOQUENCE.

" 'You tell me of the Mohawks. My fathers knew
them. They demanded tribute of them. The Sioux
laughed. They went to meet them : ten thousand

DEATH OF SITTING BULL.

horsemen. The Mohawks saw them coming, made them a feast and returned home! You tell me of the Abenaznis. They are our forefathers and the forefathers of all red men. They were the men of the Dawn. They came from the East. They were born in the morning of the world. The traditions of my people are full of the Abenaznis. They rocked the cradles of our race.'

"And again:

"What treaty that the whites have kept has the red man broken? Not one. What treaty that the whites ever made with us red men have they kept? Not one. When I was a boy the Sioux owned the world. The sun rose and set in their lands. They sent 10,000 horsemen to battle. Where are the warriors to-day? Who slew them? Where are our lands? Who owns them? What white man can say I ever stole his lands or a penny of his money? Yet they say I am a thief. What white woman, however lonely, was ever when a captive insulted by me? Yet they say I am a bad Indian. What white man has ever seen me drunk? Who has ever come to me hungry and gone unfed? Who has ever seen me beat my wives or abuse my children? What law have I broken? Is it wrong for me to love my own? Is it wicked in me because my skin is red; because I am a Sioux; because I was born where my fathers lived; because I would die for my people and my country?'

"And again:

"They tell you I murdered Custer. It is a lie. I am not a war chief. I was not in the battle that day. His eyes were blinded that he could not see. He was a fool and he rode to his death. He made the fight, not I. Whoever tells you I killed the Yellow Hair is a liar.'

DO WE LOVE JUSTICE?

"But why tell more of this man? Does this generation love justice enough to ask that it be shown to the red men? Have we not as a people fixed the brutal maxim in our language, 'That the only good Indian is a dead Indian?' We laugh at the saying now as a good jest, but the cheeks of our descendants will redden with shame when they read the coarse brutality of our wit. I read that the great Sioux was dead, that he was set upon in the midst of his family, with his wives and children and relatives around him, that he had committed no overt act of war; that he was simply—so far as aught is known—moving himself, his kith and kin from the midst of cold, hunger and peril, and that while doing this, a company of Indians—yclept Indian police—many of them despised renegades from his own tribe and enemies of his under cover of the United States flag and backed by a company of United States cavalry—placed suspiciously handy to see that the renegades from his tribe should not fail in killing him—they went to kill—had killed him, and I said—understanding the conditions and circumstances better than some—I said: 'That is murder.' And then

I read in a great journal that ' everybody is well satisfied with his death.' And I cried out against the
saying as I had against the deed.

" I read that they have buried his body like a dog's
' —without funeral rites, without tribal wail, with no
solemn song or act. That is the deed of to-day.
That is the best that this generation has to give to
this noble historic character, this man who in his
person ends the line of aboriginal sanctities older
than the religion of Christian or Jew. Very well.
So let it stand for the present. But there is a generation coming that shall reverse this judgment of

RECORD OF HISTORY.

ours. Our children shall build monuments to those
whom we stoned, and the great aboriginals whom
we killed will be counted by the future American as
among the historic characters of the Continent.
Moreover, I ask *The World* to send out through all
the land this request of mine that the spot where
this great character was buried—buried like a dog
—be carefully marked—marked beyond questioning
or doubt, for as the Lord liveth and my soul liveth
a monument shall be builded on that spot before
many years—if I live—inscribed to the memory of
the last great Prophet of the Sioux, and of the noble
characteristics of the red race, whose virtues, like
his own, were many, and whose fate was pathetic."

CHAPTER XIV.

THE SIOUX NATION.

The aboriginal inhabitants of the territory now comprised within the United States were divided into various nations, which might almost be called races, so widely did they differ from each other in physical and intellectual characteristics. The early settlers from Europe came into contact with the Iroquois and Algonquins and their numerous sub-tribes in the North, and with the Choctaws, Creeks, and Seminoles in the South. But in later years, pushing westward, the new masters of the land became aware of the existence of another still more numerous and powerful Indian nation, occupying the country west of the Mississippi River and north of the Arkansas. These Indians were known in their own tongue as La-ko-tas, which the whites soon transformed into Dakotas. By their traditional enemies, the Chippewas, greatest of the

Algonquin tribes and the only Indians able to contend with them in war, they were contemptuously called Nadowessioux, which name the whites abbreviated into Sioux. Longfellow, in his immortal "Song of Hiawatha," makes his heroine, the beauteous Minnehaha, a Sioux, whom Hiawatha found and wooed and won

> "In the land of the Dakotas,
> Where the Falls of Minnehaha
> Flash and gleam among the oak-trees,
> Leap and laugh into the valley."

The Sioux also call themselves Oceti Sakowin, or the Seven Council Fires; having a tradition that they once all belonged to one council, but afterward, through intestine strife, separated into seven. These seven councils or tribes are as follows: 1. The Inde-wa-kan-ton-wan, or Village of the Holy Lake; 2, the Wah-pe-ku-te, or Leaf Shooters; 3, the Wah-pe-ton-wan, or Village in the Leaves, commonly known as the Wahpeton Sioux; 4, the Sis-se-ton-wan, or Village in the Marsh, called the Sisseton Sioux; 5, the I-hank-ton-wan-na, or Upper End Village, known as the Upper Yanktonnais; 6, the I-hank-ton-wan, or End Village, known as the Lower Yanktonnais; and, 7, the Te-ton-wan, or Prairie Village, best known as the Teton Sioux. The first four of these tribes are called I-san-ti, or Santee.

THE TETONS.

At the present time we have most to do, how-

ever, with the last and greatest of the Seven Councils, namely, the Tetons. This tribe is subdivided
into seven great families, known as (1) the Si-can-
gu, Brule, or Burnt Thighs; (2) the I-taz-ip-co, Sans
Arcs, or No Bows; (3) the Si-ha-sa-pa, or Blackfeet;
(4) the Mi-ni-kan-ye, or Those Who Plant by the
Water; (5) the Oo-hen-on-pa, or Two Kettles; (6)
the O-gal-lal-las, or Wanderers in the Mountains;
and (7) the Unk-pa-pas, or Those Who Dwell by
Themselves. It was to this last that Sitting Bull
belonged—an Unk-pa-pa, Teton, Sioux. The original home of the four Santee tribes was in Minnesota
and Eastern Dakota; that of the Yanktonnais, east
of the Missouri, from Sioux City to the Northern
Pacific Railroad; and that of the Tetons, from the
Missouri to the Rocky Mountains, north of the
Platte River.

The early history of the Sioux is little known.
They were always a notably brave and warlike race,
possessed of magnificent physique. They were
seldom attacked by other Indians, save by the
famous Chippewas, who rivalled them in strength
and daring, and who for many generations were
their implacable foes. Catlin, writing some fifty
years ago from the mouth of the Teton River, spoke
as follows of the Sioux Nation:

" This tribe is one of the most numerous in North
America, and also one of the most vigorous and
warlike tribes to be found, numbering some forty or
fifty thousand, and able undoubtedly to muster, if

the tribe could be moved simultaneously, at least eight or ten thousand warriors, well mounted and well armed. This tribe takes vast numbers of the wild horses on the plains toward the Rocky Mountains, and many of them have been supplied with guns; but the greater part of them hunt with their bows and arrows and long lances, killing their game from their horses' backs while at full speed. The

FINE APPEARANCE.

personal appearance of these people is very fine and prepossessing, their persons tall and straight, and their movements elastic and graceful. Their stature is considerably above that of the Mandans and Riccarees, or Blackfeet; but about equal to that of the Crows, Assinneboins, and Minatarees, furnishing at least one-half of their warriors of six feet or more in height. The great family of Sioux, who occupy so vast a tract of country, extending from the banks of the Mississippi River to the base of the Rocky Mountains, are everywhere a migratory or roaming tribe, divided into forty-two bands or families, each having a chief, who all acknowledge a superior or head chief, to whom they all are held subordinate.

"There is no tribe on the continent, perhaps, of

HANDSOME HUNTERS.

finer looking men than the Sioux; and few tribes who are better or more comfortably clad, and supplied with the necessaries of life. There are no parts of the great plains of America which are more abundantly stocked with buffaloes and wild horses, nor any people more bold in destroying the one for food, and appropriating the other to their use. There has gone abroad, from the many histories which have been written of these people, an opinion which is too current in the world that the Indian is necessarily a poor, drunken, murderous wretch; which account is certainly unjust as regards the savage, and doing less than justice to the world for whom such histories have been prepared. I have traveled several years already amongst these people and I have not had my scalp taken, nor a blow struck at me; nor had occasion to raise my hand against an Indian; nor has my property been stolen as yet, to my knowledge, to the value of a shilling; and that in a country where no man is punishable by law for

WHITE MEN STEAL.

the crime of stealing; still some of them steal, and murder too; and if white men did not do the same, and that in defiance of the laws of God and man, I might take satisfaction in stigmatizing the Indian character as thievish and murderous. That the Indians in their native state are drunken is false; for they are the only temperance people, literally speaking, that ever I saw in my travels, or ever expect to see. If the civilized world are startled at this, it is the fact that they must battle with, not with me; for these people manufacture no spirituous liquors themselves, and know nothing of it until it is brought into their country and tendered to them by Christians. That the people are naked is equally untrue, and is easily disproved; for I am sure that with the paintings I have made amongst the Mandans and Crows, and other tribes; and with their beautiful costumes, which I have procured and shall bring home, I shall be able to establish the fact that many of these people dress, not only with clothes comfortable for any latitude, but that they also dress with some considerable taste and elegance. Nor am I quite sure that they are entitled to the name of poor, who live in a boundless country of green fields, with good horses to ride; where they are all joint tenants of the soil, together; where the Great Spirit has supplied them with an abundance of food to eat—where they are all indulging in the pleasures and amusements of a lifetime of idleness and ease, with no business hours to attend to, or professions

NO DEBTS TO PAY.

to learn—where they have no notes in bank or other debts to pay—no taxes, no tithes, no rents, nor beggars to touch and tax the sympathy of their souls at every step they go."

Such was the account of the Sioux given by this accomplished and impartial observer, half a century ago. Let us quote by way of contrast the words of a recent writer who was imbued with ineradicable hatred of all red men:

"Of all the Indians on the continent the northern Sioux are the finest men, the best hunters, and the fiercest warriors. They have never confined themselves to the agencies, and they hated the other Indians who did. Their principal chief, Sitting Bull, would never treat honestly with the government, and used all his ability to prevent the other tribes from doing so. From the beginning they have been

CONTEMPT OF THE WHITES.

hostile to the whites, and have rejected with contempt all the overtures of the Peace Commission to submit themselves to their policy. For fifteen years they have made constant cruel war upon the whites, murdering them by wholesale in Iowa and Minnesota, previous to crossing the Missouri. After that time, and since 1865, they have been the terror of the frontier. Under the command of Sitting Bull and Crazy Horse, they have been constantly employed attacking emigrant trains on the plains and boats on the river, fighting soldiers and harassing the forts and stations. Not content with making war on the whites, the Sioux also regarded all Indians friendly to the whites as their enemies, and attacked their villages, slew their warriors, and carried off their women and children whenever they got a chance. With the booty obtained by killing and robbing miners and emigrants, they purchased arms and ammunition of the white and half-breed traders, until, with what they captured, they are now

WELL EQUIPPED.

armed with the best weapons and abundantly supplied with ammunition. Their number was originally about 7,000, and, although some were induced to go into the agencies, that number is probably still kept up by the additions to the band from other tribes ; for all dissatisfied, turbulent, and unruly Indians, and all who were afraid for any cause, as the commission of crime, to remain with their own tribes, or, at the agencies, sought the band of Sitting Bull.

"The Peace Commission, failing to accomplish anything with these Sioux, desired to turn over their case for management to the War Department, as it was necessary to reduce them to submission, lest their example should demoralize all the other Indians and make incalculable trouble. In 1875 the War Department assumed the control of them. A consultation was held in Washington between the President, the General of the Army, the Secretary of War and Gen. Crook in regard to what was the best course to pursue, and it was resolved to send an expedition against them. It was in pursuance of this resolution that the Custer expedition was organized.

"The bloody career of Sitting Bull shows him to be a bold and skillful warrior, and the relentless foe

INVINCIBLE.

of the whites. He refuses to believe he can be beaten, and declares that if all the Indians would unite under him he would be able to drive the whites back into the sea whence they came. The result of Custer's expedition will, of course, strengthen this belief, and will also give Sitting

Bull great prestige and influence with the Indians. He will be regarded as a great warrior, and his glory will be all the more splendid on account of the respect and dread felt by the Indians for Crook, whom he defeated, and Custer, whom he slew with all his command.

"Still, it is not possible to doubt what the end will be. The war may be prolonged and many brave lives lost before Sitting Bull is slain and his tribe dispersed ; but the power of the United States cannot be resisted and will prevail. Sitting Bull will either meet the fate of Capt. Jack or die in battle, and the sanguinary Sioux will scatter and be lost to history. It is not likely their fate will excite much sympathy. They were the Ishmaelites of the plains, and their hands were turned against Indians and whites alike. To murder, to commit nameless crimes without pity or compunction, to burn and steal, was the habit of their lives. When they perish they will not be regretted."

CHAPTER XV.

THE INDIAN HOLY LAND, THE MOUNTAINS OF THE PRAIRIES—THE SIOUX STORY OF THE FLOOD—ORIGIN OF THE RED PIPE STONE—INDIAN LOVE OF THE MYSTERIOUS—THEIR IDEAS OF THE FUTURE LIFE—THEIR CODE OF WORLDLY ETHICS VINDICATED.

The Holy Land of the Indians is the Coteau du Prairie, the Mountain of the Prairie, the Red Pipe Stone country. Longfellow pictures the Great Spirit descending and appearing to the tribes at that place:

> " On the Mountains of the Prairie,
> On the great Red Pipe Stone Quarry,
> Gitche Manito, the mighty,
> He, the Master of Life, descending,
> On the red crags of the quarry
> Stood erect, and called the nations,
> Called the tribes of men together."

Accordingly there was a gathering of all the Indian tribes:

> " Down the rivers, o'er the prairies,
> Came the warriors of the nations,
> Came the Delawares and Mohawks,
> Came the Choctaws and Comanches,
> Came the Shoshonies and Blackfe
> Came the Pawnees and Omahas,

Came the Mandans and Dakotas,
Came the Hurons and Ojibways,
All the warriors drawn together
By the signal of the peace-pipe,
To the Mountains of the Prairie,
To the great Red Pipe Stone Quarry."

As they stand there, glaring at each other with ancestral hatred, Gitche Manito addresses them, bids them lay aside their feuds, and promises to send them Hiawatha, the Teacher. This sacred region was long recognized as common ground, belonging to all Indians, where all must meet in peace and fellowship. But it lay within the country of the Dakotas, or Sioux, and those mighty warriors eventually drove out and shut out all rival tribes, and made the Mountain of the Prairies their own exclusively. Around this legendary spot linger many traditions, and much of the religious lore of these people. Here is one legend which was told to Catlin by a Dakota chief:

"In the time of the great freshet, which took place many centuries ago, and destroyed all the nations of the earth, all the tribes of the red men assembled on the Coteau du Prairie to get out of the way of the waters. After they had all gathered here from all parts, the water continued to rise, until at length it covered them all in a mass, and their flesh was converted into red pipe stone. Therefore it has always been considered neutral ground—it belonged to all tribes alike, and all were allowed to get it and smoke it together.

"While they were all drowning in a mass, a young woman, K-wap-tah-w (a virgin), caught hold of the foot of a very large bird that was flying over, and was carried to the top of a high cliff, not far off, that was above the water. Here she had twins, and their father was the war-eagle, and her children have since peopled the earth.

"The pipe stone, which is the flesh of their ancestors, is smoked by them as the symbol of peace, and the eagle's quill decorates the head of the brave."

Here is another tradition of the Sioux:

ORIGIN OF MAN.

"Before the creation of man the Great Spirit (whose tracks are yet to be seen on the stones, at the Red Pipe, in form of the tracks of a large bird) used to slay the buffaloes and eat them on the ledge of the Red Rocks, on the top of the Coteau des Prairies, and their blood running on to the rocks turned them red. One day when a large snake had crawled into the nest of the bird to eat his eggs, one of the eggs hatched out in a clap of thunder, and the Great Spirit, catching hold of a piece of the pipe stone to throw at the snake, molded it into a man. This man's feet grew fast in the ground where he stood for many ages like a great tree, and, therefore, he grew very old. He was older than a hundred men at the present day, and at last another tree grew up by the side of him, when a large snake ate them both off at the roots, and they wandered off together. From these have sprung all the people that now inhabit the earth."

Amongst the Sioux of the Mississippi, who live in the region of the Red Pipe Stone Quarry, Catlin found the following not less strange tradition on the same subject:

ANOTHER TRADITION.

"Many ages after the red men were made, when all the different tribes were at war, the Great Spirit sent runners and called them all together at the 'Red Pipe.' He stood on the top of the rocks, and the red people were assembled in infinite numbers on the plains below. He took out of the rock a piece of the red stone and made a large pipe. He smoked it over them all; told them that it was part of their flesh; that, though they were at war, they must meet at this place as friends; that it belonged to them all; that they must make their calumets from it and smoke them to him whenever they wished to appease him or get his good will. The smoke from his big pipe rolled over them all, and he disappeared in its cloud. At the last whiff of his pipe a blaze of fire rolled over the rocks and melted their surface. At that moment two squaws went in a blaze of fire under the two medicine rocks, where they remain to this day, and must be consulted and propitiated whenever the pipe stone is to be taken away." This is the legend which forms a part of the basis of "Hiawatha."

LOVE OF LEGENDS.

A love of legends and of mysteries is characteristic of all Indians, and particularly of the Sioux. This trait comprises equally their admiration of the

STANDING HOLLY.—Daughter of Sitting Bull.

thunder-storm and their childish wonder and awe at petty tricks of legerdemain. Says Capt. Bourke, U. S. A., a high authority on the subject:

"The Indians are very superstitious. They believe in the supernatural, and an adroit sleight-of-hand performer can have a great influence over them. One way to beat them is to fight them with their own fire by sending first-class American jugglers out to them. When the medicine men of their tribe do their wonders, let these jugglers perform their tricks, and the power of the medicine men will wane. This was the method I pursued in my work with them. I never discredited the power of any of the medicine men. I only told them that my medicine was better than their medicine, and that I could do a great deal more than they could.

ELECTRIC PUZZLE.

"I had once an old electric battery with me when I visited a big camp of these Sioux. There was some excitement at the time, and the medicine men were boasting what they could do. I arranged my battery, and took a silver dollar and placed it in a pan of water, and told their best medicine men that I would give the one who could pull it out five dollars, provided he took hold of the brass handle of the battery with one hand and picked the coin out with the other.

"There were, perhaps, one thousand Indians looking at us, and they conceived a deep reverence for me, as they had seen the most famous of their medicine men attempt to do this and fail, being almost thrown into convulsions in the attempt. At last one of the strongest Indians in the West came

BROKE THE MACHINE.

up to make the trial. He seized the battery and made a grab for the dollar. The electricity went through him like a shot, and he kicked the battery all to pieces. He wanted to try it again and we patched the battery up, and he finally succeeded in getting the dollar, owing to the weakness of the broken battery. He was twisted out of shape almost by the effort, and the Indians of that camp looked upon me for the time as a great medicine man.

"At another time I was at a sun-dance of one of the Sioux Indian tribes, and an American juggler, who was quite a sleight-of-hand performer, begged to be allowed to go along with me. I thought he might do some good and took him. I shall not forget how he astonished the Indians.

" He went up to one of the chiefs, and without a warning gave him a slap on the cheek, nearly knocking him over. Then with his other hand he got hold of the other cheek and apparently pulled a twenty-dollar gold piece out of it, while the rest of the Indians looked on with open-mouthed won-

A CUTE TRICK.

der. He went up to another chief, who rejoiced in the title of Little Big Man, and grabbing him by the nose pulled a twenty-dollar gold piece out of his nose, much to the chief's surprise. I saw him a number of times afterward, and when he thought I was not looking would pull his blanket up over his nose and feel the end of it to see if there were not some more twenty-dollar gold pieces where the other one had come from.

" I remember another medicine man, a big Apache, who called upon me in the surgeon's office of one of the stations. I was very anxious to see his medicine charm, which he carried carefully concealed under his shirt, and which not even the other Indians ever saw. I told him I knew he was a great medicine man, but that I believed that my medicine was better than his medicine, and with that I picked up a bottle of nitric acid. It was not much bigger than your thumb

ASTONISHED.

" I said : ' I will put a drop of this on your tongue and in one minute I will burn a hole clear through it.' He opened his eyes, but when I again asked him to stick out his tongue he said he believed I could do it, and that he would not test my skill. I then picked up a bottle of chloroform and said : ' Here is more of my medicine. If you smell this I can put you to sleep, and no one can wake you until I want to wake you, and with this,' picking up another bottle, ' I can strike you dead.' By this time he was thoroughly scared, and he showed the wonderful talisman by which he performed his tricks. It was a chamois bag covered with mysterious char-

acters.   He wore it over his chest and it never left
him, night or day."

The religious beliefs of the Sioux, however, are
of a noble and exalted character, comparing favor-
ably in their sublime simplicity with the great myths

A FUTURE STATE.

of other races.   Their ideas of a future state have
been thus stated by one of their foremost prophets:

"Our people all believe that the spirit lives in a
future state—that it has a great distance to travel
after death toward the West—that it has to cross
a dreadful deep and rapid stream, which is hemmed
in on both sides by high and rugged hills—over this
stream, from hill to hill, there lies a long and slippery
pine-log, with the bark peeled off, over which the
dead have to pass to the delightful hunting-grounds.
On the other side of the stream there are six persons of the good hunting-grounds, with rocks in
their hands, which they throw at them all when they
are on the middle of the log.   The good walk on
safely, to the good hunting-grounds, where there is
one continual day—where the trees are always
green—where the sky has no clouds—where there
are continual fine and cooling breezes—where there
is one continual scene of feasting, dancing, and

ETERNAL LIFE AND HAPPINESS.

rejoicing—where there is no pain or trouble, and
people never grow old, but forever live young and
enjoy the youthful pleasures.

"The wicked see the stones coming, and try to

dodge, by which they fall from the log, and go down thousands of feet to the water, which is dashing over the rocks, and is stinking with dead fish and animals, where they are carried around and brought continually back to the same place in whirlpools—where the trees are all dead, and the waters are full of toads and lizards, and snakes—where the dead are always hungry, and have nothing to eat—are always sick, and never die—where the sun never shines, and where the wicked are continually climbing up by thousands on the sides of a high rock from which they can overlook the beautiful country of the good hunting-grounds, the place of the happy, but never can reach it."

The worldly ethics of the Sioux were also inquired into by Catlin, who found much to admire in them, and little to condemn, in comparison with the codes of civilized people. On an occasion when he had interrogated a Sioux chief, on the Upper Missouri about their government—their punishments and tortures of prisoners, for which he had freely condemned them for the cruelty of the practice, the

INQUIRIES.

Indian took occasion, when Catlin had got through, to ask some questions relative to modes in the civilized world, which, with his comments upon them, were nearly as follows:

"Among white people, nobody ever take your wife—take your children—take your mother—cut off nose—cut eyes out—burn to death? No! Then you no cut off nose—you no cut out eyes—you no burn to death—very good."

Then the Indian went on to say that he had often heard that white people hung their criminals by the neck and choked them to death like dogs, and those their own people; to which Catlin answered, "Yes." He then said he had learned that they shut each other up in prisons, where they keep them a great part of their lives because they can't pay money! Catlin replied in the affirmative to this, which occasioned great surprise and excessive laughter, even

CRUELTY AMONG PALE-FACES.

amongst the women. The Indian said that he had been to the fort at Council Bluffs, where there were a great many warriors and braves, and he saw three of them taken out on the prairies and tied to a post and whipped almost to death, and he had been told that they submit to all this to get a little money. "Yes." He said he had been told that when all the white people were born, their white medicine men had to stand by and look on—that in the Indian country the women would not allow that—they would be ashamed; that he had been along the Frontier, and a good deal amongst the white people, and he had seen them whip their little children—a thing that is very cruel. He had heard, also, from several white medicine men that the Great Spirit of the white people was the child of a white woman, and that he was at last put to death by the white people! This seemed to be a thing that he had not been

able to comprehend, and he concluded by saying:

GREAT SPIRIT NEVER DIE.

" The Indians' Great Spirit got no mother—the Indians no kill him—he never die." He put to Catlin
a chapter of other questions, as to the trespasses
of the white people on their lands—their continual
corruption of the morals of their women, and dig-
ging open the Indians' graves to get their bones,
etc.—to all of which the traveler was compelled to
reply in the affirmative, and quite glad to close his
note-book and quietly to escape from the throng
that had collected around him, saying (though to
himself and silently) that these and an hundred other
vices belong to the civilized world, and are practiced
upon (but certainly, in no instance, reciprocated by)
the " cruel and relentless savage."

"I fearlessly assert to the world," said Catlin,
" (and I defy contradiction) that the North American
Indian is everywhere, in his native state, a highly
moral and religious being, endowed by his Maker
with an intuitive knowledge of some great Author
of his being and the universe; in dread of whose
displeasure he constantly lives, with the apprehension before him of a future state, where he expects
to be rewarded or punished according to the merits
he has gained or forfeited in this world."

CHAPTER XVI.

IN PEACE AND WAR.

THE SIOUX LANGUAGE—AN INDIAN'S SENSE OF HUMOR—"OLD HUN-
DRED," "COME TO JESUS" AND THE LORD'S PRAYER IN SIOUX—
WAR PAINT OF THE BRAVES—A BATTLE WITH THE PAWNEES—THE
VALUE OF A SCALP—A LEISURELY INTERVIEW WITH A BUSY SEC-
RETARY.

The languages of Indian tribes differ much from
each other, and many of them have become considerably modified by the assimilation of English,
French, and Spanish words. The Sioux language is
one of the most elaborate and sonorous of them all,
and its grammar and rhetoric, as well as its euphony,
entitle it to serious consideration among the many
tongues of mankind. "In entering the Sioux country," says a writer in the *Inter-Ocean*, "one no
longer hears the familiar words of the pale-face, 'Ah,
there,' and 'I say, old boy;' but it is 'How Rola,'
and 'Lila Washte,' everywhere. To become a master of the Sioux language is tne task of years. For
the brightest mind to become acquainted with the
peculiar construction of the Dakota sentence, the
idiomatic expressions, and any proportion of their
20.000 words would require months of toil; but for

226

the purposes of trade or social intercourse a few weeks will give one a very fair start. In fact, the whole stock in trade of many so-called interpreters consists only in knowing a score or two of words, a dozen or two verbs, a slight acquaintance with the sign language, some native wit, and the ability to lie without changing color. The great difficulty is, like the French, in placing the accent. This is generally on the second syllable, but, alas, where one least expects it the accent belongs on the first.

"I tried to find out, the other day, how many acres one of the scamps cultivated, and asked : 'How many acres of field have you?' Alas for me, 'maga' with the accent strong on the first syllable, means field, but the same word with accent on the second syllable means 'goose.'

FULL OF HUMOR.

"The Indian has a fine sense of humor, and he howled and yelled when I asked how many acres of goose he had. The letters of the alphabet are the same as in English, and are pronounced the same, except the following : C is like ch in chin, e as a, j as z in azure, g like an explosive k, u as oo in ooze, while g has a rough, gutteral sound unlike anything in English, and h is a laughing h not found in any other language. In constructing the sentence they state first the subject, then its qualifying words, next the object with its adjectives, and then the verb followed by its qualifiers."

For example: The white soldier is afraid of the noble red man, would be "soldier white, Indian brave, afraid heap," "akicita ska ikcewicasta wakokipa pahi." Or, for another example, dog is "sunka," a large dog is "sunka tanka," a large yellow dog would be "sunka tanka yawa," to eat is "yuta," good is "washte," very is "lila." So that if one wishes to sympathize with his dusky brother and change the conversation from the weather by observing that a large yellow dog is very good to eat, he should say, "Sunka tanka yawa yuta lila washte." Such a remark would place you on good terms with the family and be greeted with deep grunts of approval.

All Indian books have been abolished in the schools, and neither teacher or pupil are allowed under strictly imposed penalties to use a word of Dakota under any circumstances. In all of the shops notices dignified with the signature of the agent are posted forbidding an Indian word to be used. In their churches and Sunday-schools, however, the native language is used, and one may hear all the familiar songs given in the Sioux. "Old Hundred" has a majestic sound even when pronounced:

"Wakantanka yatan miye,
Cinhintku kin makata hi,
Wicaceji yatanpi kte,
Qa Woniya Wakan kici."

And the children's voices have the fresh, sweet melody of youth when they sing "Come to Jesus" in their native tongue:

"Jesus en u, Jesus en u, Jesus en u wanna,
U wo, Jesus en u, Jesus en u wanna."

To attend their churches and to learn that they are human beings, with human hearts and souls, and in spite of all prejudice of all memory of frontier horrors, one comes back realizing that there is a meaning that cannot be ignored in the words the fatherhood of God and the brotherhood of man, when he has seen a room-full of Indians with heads bowed repeating

THE LORD'S PRAYER.

Ateunyanpi Mahpiya ekta nanke cin,
Nicaje wankandapi kte; Nitokiconze u kte.
Nitiwacin maka akan econpi nunwe; mahpiya ekta iyececa.
Anpetu kinde ampetu woyute ungu po.
Qa waunhtanipi unkicicajuju miye, tona sicaya ecaunkicoupi wicunkicicajujupi
    kin iyececa,
Qu taku wawiyutan en unkayapi sni ye; tuka taku sice cin etanhan eunyaku
    po.
Wokicsnse kin he Fiye nitawa, ga
Wowasake kin, ga wowitan kin, owihanke wanica. Amen.

The war-customs of the Sioux have also their own peculiarities. When the braves go on the war-path, they black their faces from the eyes down, the forehead being colored a bright red. When in mourning, and very eager to revenge the death of friends or relations, they cut their hair short and daub their faces with white earth. Their feats of horsemanship are wonderful. They consider the greatest act of valor to be the striking of their enemy with some hand instrument while alive, and, whether live or dead, it is the first one that strikes the fallen foe that "counts the coup," and not the one that shoots him. They do not always scalp. Their object in scalping is to furnish a proof of their deed, and give them to their women to dance over. They always attack in a sweeping, circling line, eagle-like, give a volley, pass on, circle, and return on a different angle. When they kill one of the enemy there is always a rush to get the first crack at him, so as to "count the coup," and then some Indian who was disappointed in getting a cut at the victim while alive, scalps him. The Sioux always camp with tepes (lodges) in a circle, making, as it were, a stockade, and when on dangerous ground they picket their ponies in the centre.

A story characteristic of Indian battle superstition is related by Miss Rheta Louise Childe, who lived for some years among the Sioux and witnessed many of their doings in both peace and war.

"On the fourth day's march from the Missouri River," she says, "the troops reached the Pawnee Reservation. The Pawnees and the Sioux have been at war from time immemorial, and these Indians were hourly expecting an attack from their old and inveterate foes. Within an hour of the arrival of the troops yells of alarm and firing of

guns were followed by bugle-calls of 'boots and
saddles' and the 'assembly.' The Pawnee videttes
came in on a desperate run, and met the Pawnee
braves going to their rescue, only to be driven back
pell-mell into the village by vastly superior numbers
of Sioux, who killed and scalped all who were
unable to escape. Although the fight was entirely
between the two tribes of Indians, the troops, as in
duty bound, rushed to the defense of the Government buildings, in which were quartered several
teachers and missionaries. They were not a minute
too soon; for at the next instant the victorious
Sioux, under the already famous Rain-in-the-Face,
swept into the yard of the mission.

CHARACTERISTIC INCIDENT.

"And here occurred an incident characteristic of
Indian superstition. A young squaw, fleeing from
the advancing Sioux, reached the inclosure, pursued
by half a score of painted devils, their hands already
reeking with Pawnee gore. Seeing escape impossible, she fell flat on the ground and pulled her
blanket over her head to lose sight of the descending blow. It came from a tomahawk that glanced
off her skull without penetrating it. The whites
were within a few rods, firing as they ran, and one
of the Sioux braves fell, shot dead, beside the prostrate woman. Another, however, jerked the blanket
from her bleeding head, and, with haste born of
fear, cut around and cruelly lifted her scalp, she
conscious all the time, but never uttering a sound,

The savage fled with his bloody trophy to rejoin his comrades. The troops came to the rescue of the sadly outnumbered Pawnees, and together they succeeded in putting the Sioux to rout. When the panic subsided, the wounded squaw was borne into the mission hospital and her injuries dressed. In spite of the scalping, she bade fair to recover. Strange to relate, however, her friends showed great reluctance to her receiving medical treatment, claiming that, according to all Indian precept and example, a scalped person should be dead, and her recovery would only bring 'bad medicine' to her tribe. The woman acquiesced in this opinion, and expressed perfect willingness to be sacrificed to the ancient customs. The next morning the squaw's cot was empty, and the patient nowhere to be found.

RESCUE OF THE SQUAW.

"Two days later, some troopers hunting a stray horse on the river bank, miles away, were startled to hear groans coming from a neighboring thicket. Thinking that some wounded Sioux had been abandoned to die, they cautiously approached. There, buried all but her face in the drifting sand, was the scalped squaw, still alive and conscious. They dug her out and brought her back to the mission, thoroughly cured of her willingness to die. She told how she had been stolen from the hospital by her own family and buried by the river bank. She now wanted to live, and a close watch was kept to prevent her being again offered as a victim to savage superstition. Once afterward, when walking in the yard, she was spirited away by the Pawnees and hidden in a tepee, that, when night fell, she might be buried more securely. Again she was restored to the mission, and upon strong threats of military vengeance should anything occur to her in future, the poor creature was allowed by her tribe to live out the remainder of her days."

Swift as is the Indian in the hunt and on the war-path, he is a lover of leisure, and he is most persistent in that love. This trait is to be observed in his pow-wows or diplomatic interviews with Government officials. He insists upon taking full time to think things over. During the administration of President Cleveland, it is told, a party of Sioux chiefs went to Washington to see Mr. Vilas, the Secretary of the Interior, who had supreme charge of the In-

VILAS OUTWITTED.

dian Department. When they reached Washington, says Mr. L. E. Quigg, who tells the story, Mr. Vilas arranged to see them. Vilas is one of those nervous, bustling men who never have the tenth part of a second to spare. The Indians are, above all things, deliberative in ceremonial matters. When they were ushered into the Secretary's room, he wheeled around in his chair and said he was the Great Father's Secretary, and would hear what they wished to say. His brusque manner greatly offended the Sioux. There was a long pause, broken at last by the Secretary, who urged them to go ahead, speak their speech and get done. Finally, one old fellow arose and delivered himself as follows: "We are glad to see the Great Father's chief. We are glad to hear his voice. We are his friends. We have come a long way in the Great Father's carriage that says 'chu! chu!' (imitating the puffs of a steam engine), and that rolls and bounces—so! (imitating the motion of the car). We are tired. We will see the white chief on Monday."

Mr. Vilas was much disgusted. He said he didn't do business that way. If they wanted to talk they must do it now. Another long pause, and then a second chief arose.

"We are glad to see the Great Father's chief," said he. "We are glad to hear his voice. We are his friends. We have come a long way in the Great Father's carriage that says 'chu! chu!' and that rolls and bounces—so! We are tired. We will see the white chief on Monday."

GUESSED MONDAY WOULD DO.

Again the Secretary remonstrated. He said he was a busy man. He could not see them again. They must talk now or not at all. A third pause, more prolonged than ever. Then the third chief slowly got up and said: "We are glad to see the Great Father's chief. We are glad to hear his voice. We are his friends. We have come a long way in the Great Father's carriage that says 'chu! chu!' and that rolls and bounces—so! We are tired. We will see the white chief on Monday."

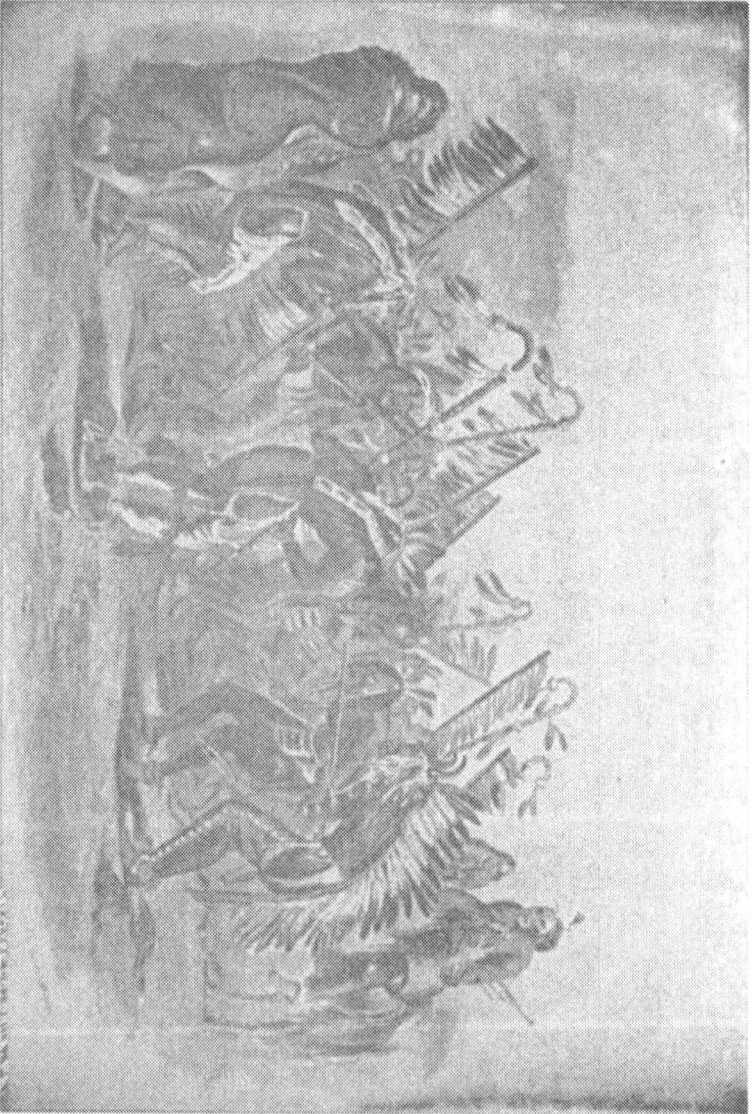

WILD GRASS DANCE.

Poor Mr. Vilas was becoming as tired as the weary Injun. But he tried it once more, this time appealingly. The fourth chief, after waiting fully five minutes in silence, responded: "We are glad to see the Great Father's chief. We are glad to hear his voice. We are his friends. We have come a long way in the Great Father's carriage that says 'chu! chu!' and that rolls and bounces— so! We are tired. We will see the white chief on Monday."

Mr. Vilas gave it up. He meekly replied that he guessed Monday would suit him as well as any other day.

XVII.

FEASTING AND DANCING.

Conspicuous Features of Indian Public Life—A Grand Festival in the Olden Time—The Speech of Welcome—Stewed Dog the Leading Dish—The Grass Dance of the Two Kettles, and its Accompanying Feast of Dog—Dancing Extraordinary—The Bear Dance, Beggar's Dance, Scalp Dance and Sun Dance.

Among the public ceremonies of the Indians feasting and dancing occupy a conspicuous place. Thus they entertain distinguished visitors. Thus they manifest their religious enthusiasm. Thus they prepare for the warpath, and thus they celebrate their triumphant return therefrom. When Catlin and his white comrades visited the Sioux, when that nation was at the zenith of its power, they were entertained at a great festival. The chiefs and braves formed, says the artist-historian, a huge semicircle. "In the centre was erected a flag-staff, on which was waving a white flag, and to which also was tied the calumet, both expressive of their friendly feeling to ward us. Near the foot of the flag-staff were placed, in a row on the ground, six or eight kettles with iron covers on them, shutting them tight, in which were

238

prepared the viands for our voluptuous feast. Near the kettles, and on the ground also, bottomside upward, were a number of wooden bowls in which the meat was to be served out. And in front, two or three men, who were there placed as waiters, to light the pipes for smoking and also to deal out the food.

"In these positions things stood, and all sat, with thousands climbing and crowding around for a peep

THE ONE HORN.

at the grand pageant, when at length Ha-wan-je-tah (The One Horn), head chief of the nation, rose in front of the Indian Agent in a very handsome costume, and addressed him thus: 'My father, I am glad to see you here to-day—my heart is always glad to see my father when he comes—our Great Father who sends him here is very rich, and we are poor. Our friend Mr. M'Kenzie, who is here, we are also glad to see; we know him well, and we shall be sorry when he is gone. Our friend who is on your right hand we all know is very rich, and we have heard that he owns the great medicine-canoe. He is a good man, and a friend to the red men. Our friend the White Medicine, who sits with you, we did not know—he came amongst us a stranger, and he has made me very well—all the women know it and think it very good. He has done many curious things, and we have all been pleased with him—he has made us much amusement—and we know he is great medicine.

" ' My father, I hope you will have pity on us, we are very poor. We offer you to-day not the best that we have got, for we have a plenty of good buffalo

WE OFFER OUR HEARTS.

hump and marrow, but we give you our hearts in this feast. We have killed our faithful dogs to feed you, and the Great Spirit will seal our friendship. I have no more to say.'   .

"After these words he took off his beautiful war-eagle head-dress, his shirt and leggings, his neck-lace of grizzly bears' claws and his moccasins, and tying them together laid them gracefully down at the feet of the agent as a present; and, laying a hand-some pipe on top of them, he walked around into an adjoining lodge, where he got a buffalo robe to cover his shoulders, and returned to the feast, taking the seat which he had before occupied.

"Major Sanford then rose and made a short speech in reply, thanking him for the valuable present which he had made him, and for the very polite and impres-sive manner in which it had been done; and sent to the steamer for a quantity of tobacco and other presents, which were given to him in return. After this, and after several others of the chiefs had addressed him in a similar manner and, like the first, disrobed themselves and thrown their beautiful costumes at his feet, one of the three men in front deliberately

SMOKING THE PIPE.

lit a handsome pipe and brought it to Ha-wan-je-tah to smoke. He took it, and after presenting the stem to the North, to the South, to the East and the West, and then to the sun that was over his head, and pronouncing the words 'How–how–how!' drew a whiff or two of smoke through it; and holding the bowl of it in one hand and its stem in the other, he then held it to each of our mouths, as we successively smoked it; after which it was passed around through the whole group, who all smoked through it, or as far as its contents lasted, when another of the three waiters was ready with a second, and at length a third one in the same way, which lasted through the hands of the whole number of guests. This smoking was conducted with the strictest adherence to exact and established form, and the feast the whole way, to the most positive silence. After the pipe is charged and is being lit, until the time that the chief has drawn the smoke through it, it is considered an evil omen for any one to speak; and if any one break silence in that time, even in a whisper, the pipe is in-

SUPERSTITION.

stantly dropped by the chief, and their superstition is such that they would not dare to use it on this occasion, but another is called for and used in its stead. If there is no accident of the kind during the smoking, the waiters then proceed to distribute the meat, which is soon devoured in the feast.

"In this case the lids were raised from the kettles, which were all filled with dogs' meat alone. It being well cooked and made into a sort of a stew, sent forth a very savory and pleasing smell, promising to be an

DOG FEAST.

acceptable and palatable food. Each of us civilized guests had a large wooden bowl placed before us, with a huge quantity of dogs' flesh floating in a profusion of soup or rich gravy, with a large spoon resting in the dish, made of the buffalo's horn. In this most difficult and painful dilemma we sat, all of us knowing the solemnity and good feeling in which it was given, and the absolute necessity of falling to and devouring a little of it. We all tasted it a few times and resigned our dishes, which were quite willingly taken and passed around with others to every part of the group, who all ate heartily of the delicious viands, which were soon dipped out of the kettles and entirely devoured; after which each one arose as he felt disposed and walked off without uttering a word. In this way the feast ended, and all retired silently and gradually until the ground was left vacant to the charge of the waiters or officers, who seemed to have charge of it during the whole occasion.

"This feast was unquestionably given to us as the most undoubted evidence they could give us of their

EVIDENCE OF FRIENDSHIP.

friendship; and we, who knew the spirit and feeling in which it was given, could not but treat it respectfully, and receive it as a very high and marked compliment.

"Since I witnessed it on this occasion I have been honored with numerous entertainments of the kind amongst the other tribes which I have visited toward the source of the Missouri, and all conducted in the same solemn and impressive manner; from which I feel authorized to pronounce the dog-feast a truly religious ceremony, wherein the poor Indian sees fit to sacrifice his faithful companion to bear testimony to the sacredness of his vows of friendship, and invite his friend to partake of its flesh to remind him forcibly of the reality of the sacrifice and the solemnity of his professions."

GRASS DANCE.

Resembling this is the "Grass Dance" of the Two Kettle Sioux, which is much practiced by them in their fallen estate at the present day. These Two Kettle Sioux have never attracted the attention of the military in a professional way. They are a thoroughly peaceable set of people, and even during the recent tumult of religious enthusiasm have manifested no interest in the expected advent of the Red Man's Messiah. They inhabit the muddy gumbo hills around Fort Pierre, S. D., and have so attached themselves to that unbeautiful region that they prefer the lesser evil of civilization to the calamity of seeking another, and peradventure a better, dwelling-place. Most of them speak English; they till the soil and are daily seen in the markets of Fort Pierre, exchanging the fruits of their labor for such luxuries as coffee, sugar and tobacco. Their horses, cattle, clothing and farming implements are furnished by the Government, according to the industry and worth of the individual, or, to be more literal, according to the estimation in which he is held by John Holland, head farmer and general superintendent of the tribe. For instance, if a Two Kettle wants an axe or a spade he has to apply to John Holland, who audits the claim and awards or withholds the tool as his superior judgment dictates.

The "Grass Dance," says Miss Childe, is supposed to propitiate the spirits who have charge of the growth of grass and increase of game. The visitor to the festival sees a curiously picturesque gathering. Twenty teepees, red and yellow in the sunset light, surround a large log-house, thatched

DESCRIPTION.

and chinked with mud—the dance-house. In the foreground two lithe Indian boys, almost naked, are racing. A mob of Two Kettles look on with noisy interest. An aged Indian crosses the middle distance, leading a large and very dejected dog. The animal is about one-third staghound and the rest yellow cur. The two disappear in one of the teepees, a pistol shot is heard and the poor dog has gone to the "happy land of canine."

Why this sacrifice? At the risk of offending your sensibilities—this is a barbecue. The dog is placed on a bed of coals and thoroughly singed. A squaw deftly runs a knife over him and removes the entrails—delicacies reserved for chiefs and dignitaries present. He is now cut up into small bits and flung into the pot in the presence of an enthusiastic rabble of Two Kettles, whose mouths water at the sight. There are other dogs, of course, since one would not suffice to feed such a multitude, but this big fellow is the *piece de resistance.* If your nostrils are delicate you will leave the kitchen and wander among the other teepees. Dirt, squaws, dogs, children and braves adorn the interiors.

Presently a leather-lunged crier announces the beginning of the dance in vernacular Two Kettle. The summons of " John-Hunts-the-Enemy," who, as a town-crier is a glittering success, whatever he may be as a farmer, is not unheeded. The band assembles in the large log-house, men on one side, women on the other. Dogs, fleas, children and dirt *ad lib.* A huge kettledrum, on which six virtuosos

INDIAN CHANT.

perform, occupies one corner. Then is raised that universal Indian chant, " Hi-yah, hi-yah, hi-yah, hi-yah," beginning in a low guttural key and increasing both in volume and pitch until the participants reach a state of frenzy and breathlessness. Then, after a brief pause, some one recovers wind enough to start up a hoarse " Hi-yah, hi-yah !" and in a moment the whole crew are yelling for dear life. The object of the "music" is a double one. It serves to mark time and to excite the dancers. One by one they fall into the ring to dance and whoop.

The costumes are many and varied. One gentleman is attired principally in a plug hat, another in a
sort of a Grecian bend made of turkey feathers,
another in two yards of red flannel that drags behind
like the tail of the Irishman's coat at Donnybrook
Fair. David Smoking Bear has arrayed his person
in a generous coat of gray gumbo mud. All are
more or less painted. One Indian wears a blue
breech clout. His head, even before it was smashed
in on the left side, was not handsome. Now he has
adorned the smashed portion with red and green
paint. The vicissitudes of an eventful life have
cropped off both legs below the knees and crippled
his left hand for him. All of which, while it is not
his fault, has served to decrease his popularity among
the fair sex. He is a good dancer, notwithstanding

INDIAN ATTIRE.

his infirmities, and is as graceful as any of his friends.
His body is smeared with yellow, and his hair is
stuck full of turkey feathers and porcupine quills.
He dances, yells and bounces around in a frenzy
which strikes you as ridiculous or sickening, according to your sense of humor or lack of it. He has a
wild fascination for me, either in the mazes of the
dance or in the pursuit of his business, which is
horse-breaking. When he wraps those stumps of
his around the lean hide of a broncho, that noble
animal may as well make up his mind first as last,
that those stumps are there to stay.

Now the dog soup is brought in to regale the nostrils of the dancers. The pungent odor fills the air and whets the appetite of the famished crowd, but the dance goes on. One huge brave plucks a bunch of grass from the ceiling, thrusts it into the fire and lights it. Another seizes his Grecian bend and holds it in the smoke, chanting and moaning meanwhile. In the pauses of the dance the old warriors recount thrilling tales of their prowess and daring in battles with the Paleface. Assent and ap-

HOWLS OF APPROVAL.

proval are evinced by loud and prolonged howls and beating of the kettle-drums. Finally the souls of the company are deemed sufficiently purified, and the soup is cool enough to eat. Several of the old fellows dance around the pot and make passes at it, keeping time with the orchestra. Several rounds of this, then more dancing. One seizes a handful of tin cups and distributes them. Again the dancers circulate around the pot. The ceremonies seem endless and the waiting grows very wearisome. But at last the cups are brought forth and filled with soup, a dainty *morceau* of dog is placed in each, and the banquet is begun. The dog soup being disposed of, all but the odor, which "hangs 'round you still" for several days, the assemblage breaks up, and that Grass Dance is over.

There are many other different dances among the Sioux, who are the greatest dancers of all Indians.

Some of these were witnessed by Catlin, and thus described :

"Instead of the 'giddy maze' of the quadrille or the country dance, enlivened by the cheering smiles and graces of silkened beauty, the Indian performs his rounds with jumps and starts and yells, much to the satisfaction of his own exclusive self and infinite amusement of the gentler sex, who are always lookers on, but seldom allowed so great a pleasure,

BUCKS ONLY.

or so signal an honor, as that of joining with their lords in this or any other entertainment. Whilst staying with these people on my way up the river, I was repeatedly honored with the dance, and I as often hired them to give them, or went to overlook where they were performing them at their own pleasure, in pursuance of their peculiar customs, or for their own amusement, that I might study and correctly herald them to future ages. I saw so many of their different varieties of dances amongst the Sioux, that I should almost be disposed to denominate them the 'dancing Indians.' It would actually seem as if they had dances for everything. And in so large a village there was scarcely an hour in any day or night but what the beat of the drum could somewhere be heard. These dances are almost as various and different in their character as they are numerous—some of them so exceedingly grotesque and laughable as to keep the bystanders

in an irresistible roar of laughter—others are calculated to excite his pity, and forcibly appeal to his
sympathies, whilst others disgust, and yet others
terrify and alarm him with their frightful threats and
contortions.

BEAR DANCE.

"All the world has heard of the 'Bear Dance,'
though I doubt whether more than a very small proportion has ever seen it. Here it is. The Sioux,
like all the others of these Western tribes, are fond
of bear's meat, and must have good stores of the
bear's grease laid in, to oil their long and glossy
locks as well as the surface of their bodies. And
they all like the fine pleasure of a bear hunt, and
also a participation in the Bear Dance, which is given
several days in succession, previous to their starting
out, and in which they all join in a song to the Bear
Spirit, which they think holds somewhere an invisible existence and must be consulted and conciliated
before they can enter upon their excursion with any
prospect of success. For this grotesque and amusing scene, one of the chief medicine-men placed over
his body the entire skin of a bear, with a war-eagle's
quill on his head, taking the lead in the dance, and

MASQUE OF BEAR SKIN.

looking through the skin which formed a masque
that hung over his face. Many others in the dance
wore masques on their faces, made of the skin from
the bear's head; and all, with the motions of their

hands, closely imitated the movements of that animal; some representing its motion in running, and others the peculiar attitude and hanging of the paws when it is sitting up on its hind feet and looking out for the approach of an enemy. This grotesque and amusing masquerade oftentimes is continued at intervals for several days previous to the starting of a party on the bear hunt, who would scarcely count upon a tolerable prospect of success without a strict adherence to this most important and indispensable form!

"Dancing is done here too, as it is oftentimes

BEGGAR'S DANCE.

done in the enlightened world, to get favors—to buy the world's goods—and in both countries danced with about equal merit, except that the Indian has surpassed us in honesty by christening it in his own country the 'Beggar's Dance.' This spirited dance was given, not by a set of beggars though, literally speaking, but by the first and most independent young men in the tribe, beautifully dressed (*i. e.*, not dressed at all, except with their breech clouts or kilts, made of eagles' and ravens' quills), with their lances and pipes and rattles in their hands, and a medicine-man beating the drum and joining in the song at the highest key of his voice. In this dance every one sings as loud as he can halloo, uniting his voice with the others in an appeal to the Great Spirit to open the hearts of the bystanders to give to the poor, and not to themselves ; assuring them that the Great Spirit will be kind to those who are kind to the helpless and poor.

SCALP DANCE.

"The Scalp Dance is given as a celebration of a victory; and amongst this tribe, as I learned whilst residing with them, danced in the night, by the light of their torches, and just before retiring to bed. When a war party returns from a war excursion, bringing home with them the scalps of their enemies, they generally dance them for fifteen nights in succession, vaunting forth the most extravagant boasts of their wonderful prowess in war, whilst they brandish their war weapons in their hands. A number of young women are selected to aid (though they do not actually join in the dance), by stepping into the centre of the ring, and holding up the scalps that have been recently taken, whilst the warriors dance or rather jump, around in a circle, brandishing their weapons and barking and yelping in the most frightful manner, all jumping on both feet at a time, with a simultaneous stamp, and blow and thrust of their weapons, with which it would seem as if they were actually cutting and carving each other to pieces. During these frantic leaps, and

BATTLE YELPS.

yelps, and thrusts, every man distorts his face to the utmost of his muscles, darting about his glaring eyeballs and snapping his teeth, as if he were in the

heat (and actually breathing through his inflated
nostrils the very hissing death) of battle! No description that can be written could ever convey more
than a feeble outline of the frightful effects of these
scenes enacted in the dead and darkness of night,
under the glaring light of their blazing flambeaux;
nor could all the years allotted to mortal man in the
least obliterate or deface the vivid impress that one
scene of this kind would leave upon his memory."

SUN DANCE.

The barbarous "Sun Dance," now happily abolished, was witnessed by Catlin, also. On the bank
of the Teton River he found a group of fifteen or
twenty lodges, watching a man "looking at the sun."
"We found him naked, except his breech-cloth, with
splints or skewers run through the flesh on both
breasts, leaning back and hanging with the weight
of his body to the top of a pole which was fastened
in the ground, and to the upper end of which he was
fastened by a cord which was tied to the splints. In
this position he was leaning back, with nearly the
whole weight of his body hanging to the pole, the
top of which was bent forward, allowing his body to
sink about half-way to the ground. His feet were
still upon the ground, supporting a small part of his
weight; and he held in his left hand his favorite bow,
and in his right, with a desperate grip, his medicine-
bag. In this condition, with the blood trickling
down over his body, which was covered with white

STANDING BUFFALO.

AT HIS INCANTATIONS.

and yellow clay, and amidst a great crowd who were looking on, sympathizing with and encouraging him, he was hanging and 'looking at the sun,' without paying the least attention to any one about him.

MYSTERY MEN.

In the group that was reclining around him were several mystery men, beating their drums and shaking their rattles, and singing as loud as they could yell, to encourage him and strengthen his heart to stand and look at the sun, from its rising in the morning till its setting at night; at which time, if his heart and his strength have not failed him, he is cut down, receives the liberal donation of presents (which have been thrown into a pile before him during the day) and also the name and the style of a doctor, or medicine-man, which lasts him, and ensures him respect, through life.

"This most ordinary and cruel custom I never heard of amongst any other tribe, and never saw an instance of it before or after the one I have just named. It is a sort of worship, or penance, of great

OF RARE OCCURRENCE.

cruelty, disgusting and painful to behold, with only one palliating circumstance about it, which is, that it is a voluntary torture and of very rare occurrence. The poor and ignorant, misguided and superstitious man who undertakes it puts his everlasting reputation at stake upon the issue; for when he takes his stand he expects to face the sun and gradually turn his body in listless silence till he sees it go down at night; and if he faints and falls, of which there is imminent danger, he loses his reputation as a brave or mystery man, and suffers a signal disgrace in the estimation of the tribe, like all men who have the presumption to set themselves up for braves or mystery men and fail justly to sustain the character."

CHAPTER XVIII.

THE GHOST DANCES.

A Memorable Season in Indian History—Prophecies of the Coming of the Messiah—The Ghost Dances Intended to Prepare for his Advent, and to bring the People into Communication with him —Porcupine's Story of the Messiah and his Command for the Dance.

The fall of 1890 and the winter of 1890–91 will

GHOST DANCES

long be remembered in Indian history for the practice of "Ghost Dances" and the attendant circumstances. For a long time the Sioux and other tribes had suffered much at the hand of the whites, and from natural causes. Starvation menaced them, and aid and justice seemed too far away to reach them. Under these circumstances they turned to their medicine-men for supernatural comfort. They were ready to grasp, like a drowning man, at any straw of hope that might be offered. Great, therefore, was their excitement when some of their prophets declared that their Messiah was about to appear. From time immemorial they had looked forward to the coming of a superhuman leader, sent, like Hiawatha, by the Great Spirit. He was to call from

CALL THE DEAD TO LIFE.

the dead all the great warriors of the past and lead them against the palefaces, who would be scattered before his wrath like dead leaves before the northwest hurricane. He would restore the Indians to their old supremacy throughout the land, bring back the countless herds of buffalo, and give the world a foretaste of the Happy Hunting Grounds of the Kingdom of Ponemah, the Hereafter. This Messiah, too, was to come just when he was most needed, just when the Indians were most afflicted and most oppressed.

It may be judged, then, with what eagerness his advent was hailed by the unhappy red men in the fall of 1890, and with what zeal they entered into the "Ghost Dances" which were to make preparation for his coming. From tribe to tribe and nation to nation the wild excitement spread. Dances were organized everywhere, until from Alaska to Mexico there was scarcely an Indian settlement that did not await with savage rites his promised coming.

Among the Sioux in South Dakota the mania was strongest. Not many whites were permitted to witness the dances ; but some were. Among them was

MRS. FINLEY'S ACCOUNT.

Mrs. J. A. Finley, wife of the postmaster and post-trader at the Pine Ridge Agency. She went out to see the dances, after they had been in progress for some time. One Ghost Dance that she saw was participated in by 480 Indians. "In preparing for the dance they cut the tallest tree that they can find, and having dragged it to a level piece of prairie set it up in the ground. Under this tree four of the head men stand. Others form in a circle, and begin to go around and around the tree. They begin the dance on Friday afternoon. It is kept up Saturday and Sunday until sundown. During all this time they do not eat or drink. They keep going round in one direction until they become so dizzy that they can scarcely stand, then turn and go in the other direction, and keep it up till they swoon from exhaustion. This is what they strive to do, for while they are in swoon they think they see and talk with the Messiah. When they regain consciousness they tell their experiences to the four wise men under the tree. All their tales end with the same story about the two mountains that are to belch forth mud and bury the white man, and the return of good Indian

LOSE ALL THEIR SENSES.

times. They lose all of their senses in the dance. They think they are animals. Some get down on all fours and bob about like a buffalo. When they cannot lose their senses from exhaustion they

BUTT THEIR HEADS TOGETHER,

beat them upon the ground, and do anything to become insensible, so that they may be ushered into the presence of the Messiah One poor Indian when he recovered his senses said that the Messiah had told him he must return to earth because he had not brought with him his wife and child. His child had died two years before, and the way the poor fellow cried was the most heart-rending thing I ever saw. At the end of the dance they have a grand feast, the revel lasting all Sunday night. They kill several steers and eat them raw, drink, and gorge themselves to make up for their fast.

"At one dance one of the braves was to go into a trance and remain in this condition four days. At the close of this period he was to come to life as a buffalo—he would still have the form of a man, but he would be a buffalo. They were then to kill the buffalo, and every Indian who did not eat a piece of him would become a dog. The man who was to turn into a buffalo was perfectly willing. If the Government just lets them alone there will be no need of troops; they will kill themselves dancing. Seven or eight of them died as the result of one dance near Wounded Knee."

Mrs. Finley said: "Every Indian had about four war clubs made out of round stones twisted in rawhide. They threw these around during the dance, strewed the ground with them and beat their heads against them."

Lieutenant Gaston, of the Eighth U. S. Cavalry, was one of the army officers who sought to check this craze and to restrain the Indians from the madness into which it was leading them. He held a conference with them at Tongue River, Montana, at which there were present Spotted Wolf, Old Crow, White Elk, Badger, Porcupine and a number of other Cheyenne Sioux, and Fire Crow, an Ogallalla Sioux.

THE CONFERENCE.

When the conference came together Lieut. Gaston stated the precise position of affairs in their section of the country, and further said that he had learned that the Indians thought Gen. Miles was no longer their friend, and that he had gone away and forgotten them. The lieutenant assured them that this was not so, and that the General was still their friend, although he had ordered into their posts a number of soldiers, with instructions to remain friends with the Indians and keep them out of trouble, and at the same time the lieutenant told them that he had left his soldiers behind and had come to the agency unarmed to act as their friend.

Porcupine then arose, and, evidently with a conception that he was a most majestic power, said:

"I will answer your question and talk a little more. To-day I have heard something good. I have been told something I wanted to hear. When Gen. Miles held his council we were downhearted for fear we would be moved, but to-day I feel better, for I see that they have sent from Washington to find out, and I have hope; I don't think you are telling us lies. All who live along the river are cattle-men, and when they meet the Cheyennes and their children we are cursed and they wish the Cheyennes to be far away. We are afraid that those people who are living around here will fight and whip us. I heard about Gen. Miles' council, but I was not here at that time. Gen. Miles, as I understood it, told the Cheyennes he would be their friend until he had white hair, white beard and was bent double with age. The Cheyennes never lost these words, and we remember that he would love us and help us. We will remember this, and we don't mind the ill-treatment of the cowboys when we have Gen. Miles' words to rely upon.

BAD COWBOYS.

"The country is overcrowded with cattle-men who love their cattle, and when these men treat us in a bad way we are not angry. If Gen. Miles would arrange it so that the cowboys would be moved, then it would be nice and there would be no trouble. The Cheyennes carry no guns, but when the white men go around they carry revolvers. We told Gen. Miles we would give up Tongue River if we got the Little Horn on the Crow reservation. The chiefs were all glad to do this. To-day I am very glad about the good news for my home for the future. To-day I am very glad because I was told that those who had houses could not have their land stolen by the whites. When we started to make fences the white people told us not to, for it is of no use, for we will be sent away. We are in a poor condition.

"It is getting cold. The Indians are shivering. They would like to get their blankets now, not next summer. If I talk all I want to it will be morning before I stop, but I will only tell a little (referring

THE NEW GOD.

to the new God), and I want the soldiers and all ot the people to listen well to what I have to say. I went to Washington myself some time back. I saw the Great Father and came back and told my people what I saw. When I was in Washington the Great Father told me I must not fight, but must love the people here. Now this same thing has been told me again. I did not see at first, but after being told these things I went around among the people and told them and thought then I would settle down. When Upshaw went away I asked him for a pass, and Upshaw was crazy: he would not give it to me. I was told about this new God by the Arapahoes. It was the Shoshones and Arapahoes that went over to this place and saw this God. They saw a holy man and he talked nice words. The Arapahoes told me that if we would listen to this new God he would take away all the bad things and give us the nice things.

"Up to this time I did not see the new God, but now I have traveled and the snow was very deep. If this God tells the Indians not to fight with the whites they will not do so. I went on the train, traveled a long distance, and now I will tell you what the God said when we got there. I have told the soldiers many times, and I don't see why they don't know.

"I am going to tell about the dance. When this new God first saw me he called us all to come to him.

GOD'S SPEECH.

"He said: 'My children, I want you to listen well to it.' The God was glad that I came to see him. When the Indians were created they were made bad, but that badness is to be thrown off and they are to be made good. If they listen to him he will change all their condition and make them good. Everything is now very old and there are now very few Indians. Our dances were bad and the God has given us a new dance. We must not get tired dancing. Every one must dance—the young and the old, the men and the women, the boys and the girls. Four nights in succession we must dance, and then on the fifth day we must dance when the moon is just round. When we are through dancing we must go to our homes. If we dance this way we will never get tired. If we dance our gardens will grow nice and we will never get sick or crazy. We cannot quarrel or scold each other. We must not hate each other. We must love all the world. The new God said, 'My children, listen to me well. The one that does not listen to me will die. If the whites or Indians do not listen those will die.' That is what he said. If any

one asks me I must tell what the God said. I must
not tell lies. The lies are not good. The God hears
everything that is said about him. If the soldiers

WE MUST DANCE.

won't let us dance we must dance anyhow. We
must dance even if the soldiers beat us for it. We
must not let the soldiers see the dance. First God
made the white man and he was nice ; after that
God went to Heaven, and after awhile came down
on earth and talked with the white man. The white
man was afraid of him. He saw him and abused
the God, and he did not do anything to the white
man or get angry, and then they nailed him on a
cross and cut him in his heart and abused him.
Then the God said he was going up to Heaven
again. All this was concerning the white man. The
whites work six days, and on the seventh they must
tell about this God. This God said if we live
good lives we would not become poor. When this
was finished he went up into Heaven. Before he
went up into Heaven he said he would come back
for the Indians. The Indians must not abuse him
when he comes as the whites did. That is what he
said. When I came home I was glad and called all
the Indians and told them these things. I told them
just what I have told here. I told all the Indians
that they must listen, the young men and the old
men, the young and the old women, all must listen
well. Then we danced four nights and the fifth day.

We must work if the whites ask us to work. We must say yes and not no. It will please the God if we say yes. He told the Indians that they must not quarrel with the whites or kill them. We must dance. If we do not dance we will get crazy and poor."

CHAPTER XIX.

THE INDIAN MESSIAH.

THERE is no doubt that the majority of the Indians were sincere in their belief in their Messiah. Even the well-educated Sioux believed in him. One of them, Masse Hadjo, or John Daylight, wrote thus to the editor of The Chicago *Tribune* in reply to some rather harsh criticisms of the mania:

"You say, 'If the United States army would kill a thousand or so of the dancing Indians there would be no more trouble.' I judge by the above language you are a 'Christian,' and are disposed to do all in your power to advance the cause of Christ. You are doubtless a worshiper of the white man's Saviour, but are unwilling that the Indians should have a 'Messiah' of their own. The Indians have never taken kindly to the Christian religion as preached and practiced by the whites. Do you know why this

267

is the case? Because the Good Father of all has given us a better religion—a religion that is all good and no bad, a religion that is adapted to our wants. You say if we are good, obey the Ten Commandments and never sin any more, we may be permitted eventually to sit upon a white rock and sing praises to God forevermore, and look down upon our heathen fathers, mothers, brothers and sisters who are howling in hell. It won't do. The code of

WHITE CODE OF MORALS.

morals as practiced by the white race will not compare with the morals of the Indians. We pay no lawyers or preachers, but we have not one-tenth part of the crime that you do. If our Messiah does come we shall not try to force you into our belief. We will never burn innocent women at the stake or pull men to pieces with horses because they refuse to join in our ghost dances. You white people had a Messiah, and if history is to be believed nearly every nation has had one. You had twelve Apostles; we have only eleven, and some of those are already in the military guard-house. We also had a Virgin Mary and she is in the guard-house. You are anxious to get hold of our Messiah, so you can put him in irons. This you may do—in fact, you may crucify him as you did that other one, but you cannot convert the Indians to the Christian religion until you contaminate them with the blood of the white man. The white man's heaven is repulsive to the Indian nature, and if the white man's hell suits you, why, you keep it. I think there will be white rogues enough to fill it."

The most circumstantial account of the alleged Messiah was made by Porcupine, the chief quoted in the preceding chapter, to Lieutenant Robertson, of the First U. S. Cavalry. Lieutenant Robertson made the following report of it to General Miles:

PORCUPINE'S ACCOUNT.

"On my arrival at the agency I put myself in immediate communication with Porcupine, the apostle of the new religion among the Cheyennes, and with Big Beaver, who accompanied him on his visit to the new Christ at Walker Lake, Nev., in 1890. Bear Ridge, the third Cheyenne who made this trip, is now a scout at Keogh. When questioned as to the identity of the 'fifteen or sixteen tribes' who were at the Walker Lake meeting in 1890, Porcupine said that they included Cheyennes, Sioux, Arapahoes, Gros Ventres, Utes, Navajoes, Sheep Eater Bannocks, and some other tribes whose names he did not know. He says all of the Utah Indians had been there and had left before his arrival. He is sure there were no tribes from Indian Territory represented and thinks the Sioux were the most eastern Indian present.

"He says that he first heard of this new Christ at the Arapahoe (Shoshone) Agency, Wyoming, where he and twelve other Cheyennes went on a visit in

1890. An Arapahoe Indian named Sage, who had been to the southwestern country in 1888, told them that there was a new Christ arisen for the Indians; told where he could be found and explained his doctrine to them. Sage's story related, Porcupine says, to the man he himself afterward saw near Walker Lake. Porcupine goes on to say that he and the other Cheyennes were much interested and determined to see this Messiah; but, as all couldn't

TO SEE THE MESSIAH.

go so far, nine of the Cheyennes were sent back to the Tongue River Reservation to tell the people what they had heard. Porcupine and the other Cheyennes went on. When they got to Utah they received large accessions to their caravan, Indians joining them in groups at different points en route, so that when the final meeting took place at Walker Lake to hear the new Christ speak, there were, as near as Porcupine could estimate, several hundred Indians present, including women and children.

"The rest of the story accorded minutely with that of last summer. He especially insists that the teachings of the new Christ were in the interest of peace, good order and industry on the part of the Indians. I asked him if he could explain how it was, then, that certain Indian tribes had made this new doctrine a basis for neglecting their crops, indulging in demoralizing dances, and even in disorder, as had been the case on certain reservations. His answer

THE INDIAN MESSIAH CRAZE.

is so shrewd and touches so nearly the probable explanation of these facts that I recorded it. He said that the Indians who had gone to hear this new Christ with him had gone hoping to hear him preach some incendiary doctrine, and that they were disappointed at hearing that the new creed required them simply to work and behave themselves; that, being known by their people to have visited this new Messiah, they concluded on their return home not

ONLY TELL PART.

to relate strictly what this man had told them, but to put into his mouth doctrines more agreeable to the Indians. 'These men,' said Porcupine, 'are all liars, and they are responsible for any trouble that occurs—not the new Messiah.'

" Porcupine says also that the Indians do not follow the new Messiah's advice, ' to dance only four days at the beginning of each new moon,' but that, on the contrary, they dance without moderation and lose their heads with excitement.

"From Henry Reed, the Arapahoe interpreter, information was obtained which, if true, would establish the identity of the so-called new Messiah. Reed says this ' new Messiah' is a Pah-Ute Indian named John Johnson. He says Johnson is very intelligent, but not educated, that he dresses in white men's clothes and wears his hair somewhat short, though not nearly so short as a white man. He is quite wealthy in cattle and horses. This man lives on the Walker Lake (Pah-Ute) Reservation, where Reed says there ought to be no difficulty

MESSIAH DESCRIBED.

about finding him. Reed claims to know this man personally. He says he is elderly, and has as a distinguishing mark both wrists tattooed. There is, he says, another man named John Johnson in the same country, but this second Johnson is a half-breed, is well educated, is considerably younger, and could not be mistaken for the other one, who is a pure blood Pah-Ute. Reed seems to be positive as to the identity of this man with the new Christ. As a test of this I asked Porcupine afterward if the new Christ had any especial marks about him that he could recognize. He immediately answered that as the new Christ sat in the circle he noticed (pointing to both wrists) that he was tattooed on the wrists and arms."

Porcupine, in his statement of his visit to the new Messiah at Walker Lake in November, 1890, says :

" I and my people have been living in ignorance until I went and found out the truth. All the whites and Indians are brothers, I was told there. I never knew this before.

" The fish-eaters near Pyramid Lake told me that Christ had appeared on earth again. They said Christ knew he was coming; that eleven of his children were also coming from a far land. It appeared that Christ had sent for me to go there, and that was why, unconsciously, I took my journey; it had heen fore-ordained. Christ had summoned myself and others from all heathen tribes, two, three, or four from each of fifteen or sixteen different tribes.

COUNCIL CALLED.

The people assembled, called a council, and the chiefs' sons went to see the Great Father, who sent word to us to remain fourteen days in that camp, and that then he would come to see us. He sent us a small package of something white to eat that I didn't know the name of. There were a great many people in the council, and this white food was divided among them. The food was a big white nut. Then I went to the agency at Walker Lake, and they told us Christ would be there in two days. At the end of two days, on the third morning, hundreds of people gathered at this place. They cleared a place near the agency in the form of a circus ring, and we all gathered there. This space was perfectly cleared of grass, etc. We waited there till late in the evening, anxious to see Christ. Just before sundown I saw a great many people (mostly Indians) coming, dressed in white men's clothes. The Christ was with them. They all formed in this ring. They put up sheets all around the circle, as they had no tents. Just after dark some of the Indians told me that Christ had arrived. I looked around to find him, and finally saw him sitting on one side of the ring. They all started toward him to see him; they made a big fire to throw light on him; I never looked around, but went forward, and when I saw him I bent my head. I had always thought the Great Father was a white man, but this man looked like an Indian. He sat there a long time and nobody went up to speak

MESSIAH'S TALK.

to him. He sat with his head bowed all the time. After a while he arose and said he was very glad to see his children. 'I have sent for you and am glad to see you. I am going to talk to you after a while about our relatives who are dead and gone. My children, I want you to listen to all I have to say. I will teach you, too, how to dance a dance, and I want you to dance it. Get ready for your dance, and then when the dance is over I will talk to you.' He was dressed in a white coat with stripes; the rest of his dress was a white man's except that he had on a pair of moccasins.

"Then we commenced our dance—everybody joining in—the Christ singing while we danced. We danced till late in the night, when he told us we had danced enough. The next morning after breakfast was over we went into the circle and spread grass over it on the ground, the Christ standing in the midst of us. He told us he was going away that day, but would be back the next morning and talk to us.

"In the night when I first saw him I thought he was an Indian, but the next day, when I could see better, he looked different. He was not so dark as

an Indian, nor so light as a white man; he had no
beard or whiskers, but very heavy eyebrows; he was
a good-looking man. We were crowded up very
close. We had been told that nobody was to talk,
and even if we whispered the Christ would know it.
I had heard that Christ had been crucified, and I
looked to see, and I saw a scar on his wrist and one
on his face, and he seemed to be the man; I could
not see his feet. He would talk to us all day. That
evening we all assembled again to see him depart.
When we were assembled he began to sing, and he
commenced to tremble all over violently for a while,
and then sat down. We danced all that night, the

APPARENTLY DEAD.

Christ lying down beside us apparently dead. The
next morning when we went to eat breakfast the
Christ was with us. After breakfast four heralds
went around and called out that the Christ was back
with us, and wanted to talk with us. The circle was
prepared again, the people assembled, and Christ
came among us and sat down. He said he wanted
to talk to us again and for us to listen.

"He said: 'I am the man who made everything
you see around you. I am not lying to you, my children. I made this earth and everything on it. I
have been to Heaven and seen your dead friends
and have seen my own father and mother. In the
beginning, after God made the earth, they sent me
back to teach the people, and when I came back on

earth the people were afraid of me and treated me badly. This is what they did to me (showing his scars). I did not try to defend myself. I found my children were bad, so went back to Heaven and left them. I told them that in so many hundred years I would come back to see my children. At the end of this time I was sent back to try to teach them. My father told me the earth was getting old and worn out, and the people getting bad, and that I was to renew everything as it used to be and make it better.' He told us that all our dead were to be resurrected; that they were all to come back to earth, and that as the earth was too small for them and us he would do away with Heaven and make the earth itself large enough to contain us all; that we must tell all the people we met about these things. He spoke to us about fighting, and said that was bad,

MUST ALL BE GOOD.

and we must keep from it; that the earth was to be all good hereafter, that we must be friends with one another! He said that in the fall of the year the youth of all the good people would be renewed, so that nobody would be more than forty years old, and that if they behaved themselves well after this the youth of every one would be renewed in the spring. He said if we were all good he would send people among us who could heal all our wounds and sickness by mere touch, and that we would live forever."

This Johnson, the alleged Messiah, has been for some time a notorious character among the Indians. In 1878 the Ute tribe, of which he was a petty chief, was located at White River Agency, in Grand County, Colorado. The head chiefs were Douglas and Jack, while the head chief of all the Ute tribes was Ouray, who lived at Los Pinas Agency, some distance from White River. There was a strong feeling in Colorado that the Utes must go. The miners and ranchmen were clamoring for the rich mineral deposits supposed to be slumbering in the mountains and the grand valleys and parks where the Indians fished, hunted, picked the luscious wild fruit and grazed their ponies. It was the same old story. The Indians are a thriftless lot anyhow; they have no use for this grand country. In May, 1878, N. C. Meeker, who had founded the town of Greeley, Col., under the patronage of Horace Greeley, and was well known as a correspondent for the New York *Tribune* over the signature of N. C. M., was put in charge of White River Agency.

MEEKER WAS HONEST.

That Meeker was an honest man no one doubted who knew him, but he wholly misunderstood Indian character and had Utopian ideas of the management of Indian affairs that ended disastrously to himself. He precipitated the bloodiest massacre ever perpetrated west of the Missouri, in which he lost his life and the lives of all whites connected with his agency except those of his wife, daughter and a Mrs. Price. These three ladies were made prisoners and suffered a fate of outrage and indignity to which death were preferable. The "Messiah," who in 1890 was promising a millennium to such old cut-throats as Sitting Bull, Geronimo, Jack, Diah, Colo-row, Sa-rap-sah-patch, Porcupine and Big Beaver, was prominent in the White River massacre.

Another account of the "Messiah" was given by Mr. J. S. Mayhugh, lately a census agent among the Nevada Indians. Writing in November, 1890, he said:

"The prophet resides in Mason Valley, Esmeralda County, Nev., close to the Walker River Reserva-tion. His name is Jack Wilson, known among all Indians by the Indian name of We Vo Kar and also Ko We Jo, an intelligent, fine-looking gentleman of about 35 years of age, who goes into trances, or seemingly so, for twelve to fourteen hours in the presence of large numbers of Indians upon invitation of a prophet. Upon his recovery he relates to them what he has seen.

BEEN TO HEAVEN.

"He tells them he has been to heaven, and that the Messiah is coming to the earth and will put the Indians in possession of this country; that he has seen in heaven a heap of Indians, some of whom are dressed in white men's clothes. He counsels the Indians not to disturb the white folks, saying that the blanket or rabbit skin that was put over the moon by the Indians long ago would soon fall off, and then the moon, which is now afire, will destroy the whites. The "Messiah" is to appear on Mount Grant, which is a very large mountain and is about sixteen miles south of the White River Agency buildings and on the west side of the lake. Here is where the first Indians appeared according to their belief.

"I visited this mountain last September in performance of my duty as special census agent of the Indians. This mountain is held as a sacred mountain to the Indians, and on the top they allege they

MOUNT GRANT.

can see footprints of their first father, Numerna. If I may be permitted to suggest, I would recommend that all the Indians be permitted to visit this mountain, as I am satisfied they will only send delegations from each tribe for the purpose of ascertaining the truth of the prophecy. The Indians of Nevada expect delegations from most of the tribes north and northwest, and Sitting Bull is expected. The only fear the Nevada Indians have is that the Government will interfere with troops. I think if the Indians are left alone at the various reservations the whole thing will die. All of the Indians here do not believe in the prophet, although Josephus, the chief at Walter Lake, believes it to be so."

CHAPTER XX.

INDIAN WARS

A Shameful Record—A Thousand Dollars Spent for Every Indian in the Country—The Long Catalogue of Conflicts and Expenses—Fearful Cost in Life and Limb as well as Money and National Honor.

The story of our dealing with the Indians is a story of wars, and the story of these wars is a story of expense, of barbarity and of shame. The sum total of cost of life and treasure is appalling. Not long ago a writer in *St. Louis Globe-Democrat* reckoned that the Government had been put to an

ONE THOUSAND DOLLARS AN INDIAN.

expense of $1,000 for every Indian that was in the country when the Pilgrims landed at Plymouth. The statement seemed extravagant; but was really borne out by facts. There were not, probably, more than a million Indians in the whole country in 1620; and down to 1886 very nearly a thousand million dollars had been spent on them.

Mr. Donaldson, a Goverment census agent, has shown by actual records that from July 4th, 1776, to June 30th, 1886, the Indians had cost the Government $929,239,284.02. It is safe to say that the four years added to the record since Mr. Donaldson's researches will bring the figures close up to one thousand millions. This enormous sum is

ASTOUNDING FIGURES.

about one-third of what the War of the Rebellion cost. One-third of the one thousand millions has been spent in pacifying and civilizing Indians. Two-thirds of the one thousand millions have been absorbed in fighting Indians. Here is the account :

Total cost of the Indians to the United States :
Indian Department proper, from
July 7, 1776, to June 30, 1886, $232,900,006.34
Expended by War Department for
Indian wars and incidental thereto, from July 4. 1776, to June, 1886, 696,339,277.68
_____

Grand Total cost of Indians, $929.239,284.02
These figures are not too large. They probably underestimate the cost to the Government of the Indian wars. In March, 1882, the Senate called on the Secretary of War for the cost of the Indian wars for ten years. The period covered was from 1872 to 1882. The Secretary reported that it was

COST OF WAR.

$202,994,506. Wars come high. They come higher of late years than they did forty or fifty years ago. The United States fought England from 1812 to 1815, and spent only $66,614,912.34. The cost of the Mexican war, 1845-1849, was $73,941,735.12.

These two foreign wars were carried through with an expenditure of $140,000,000. But ten years of Indian fighting, from 1872 to 1882, cost $202.994,-506. It appears that Indian wars come highest of all.

Senator Doolittle, of Wisconsin, once ventilated this Indian war business. He was in the Senate when it was proposed to negotiate a peace with the Navajoes. Several other Senators demurred to the cost of the proposed treaty. Mr. Doolittle told them something about the cost of Indian Wars. At the same time he gave some interesting facts about the origin of these Indian wars. What is known as the great Sioux war started in 1852. At that time there was perfect peace on the plains. Some Mormons were driving their cattle toward Salt Lake. Near Fort Laramie was a gathering of Indians. The military post was there, and the Indians were camped near it. One of the Sioux killed a cow be-

TWENTY SOLDIERS FOR A COW.

longing to a Mormon. The emigrant complained. The officer in command at the post sent out a subordinate with twenty men. This little force went to the Indian camp and demanded the surrender of the Sioux who had killed the cow. The alternative was that the camp would be fired upon. The Indians replied to the demand: "We are willing to pay for this animal; we will pay you in buffalo robes or buffalo skins." The army officer declined. He repeated his demand for the immediate surrender.

The Indians refused. The officer gave the order to fire. The twenty men obeyed. In twenty minutes the soldiers were killed and scalped. That was the beginning of the Sioux war of 1852. The war lasted three or four years. It cost the United States between $15,000,000 and $20,000,000.

The Navajo was another which Senator Doolittle told about. For many years after this Government acquired the territory in which the Navajoes lived there was no trouble. One day a Navajo Indian was visiting the fort where the troops were. He got into a quar-

TWENTY MILLION DOLLARS FOR A NEGRO.

rel with a negro boy belonging to one of the officers. The supposition was that the negro insulted the Indian. The latter drew his bow and put an arrow into the negro, killing him. Then he fled to his tribe. The officer sent a demand for the surrender of the Indian. The tribe refused to give him up. Without any delay the troops were marched out and war was begun. Three campaigns were made against the Navajoes on this provocation. The United States troops were beaten in each of them. This Navajo war cost the Government nearly $20,000,-000.

One more illustration was furnished by the Senator. He told how the Cheyenne and Arapahoe war began. Some cattle had been stolen. It was supposed that the Indians had taken them. A Lieutenant was sent out with a detachment from the post. His instructions were peculiar. He was ordered to follow the Indians and disarm them—not to demand the cattle or reparation, but to take the arms of the Indians. The little command was to start without any interpreter. The Lieutenant overtook the Indians. He had no means of communication but signs. He tried to take away from them their bows and arrows. What was the result? A fight, of course; and so the bloody Cheyenne and Arapahoe war began.

THE BIGGEST WAR,

The biggest of all recent Indian wars was the one about which least was published. It occurred during the Civil War. There was so much fighting going on between white men that the campaign against the Sioux in the Northwest was only a side show. This war began in 1862. It had its origin in a comparatively insignificant matter. A contractor for furnishing Indian supplies sent to the Sioux agencies what was supposed to be prime mess pork. The consignment was found to consist largely of heads of hogs. The Indians went back on such rations and took the warpath instead of the souse. Generals Sibley and Sully conducted the campaign. They had 15,000 troops under them. It was in this Sioux war that the "Galvanized Yankees," as they were called, made their appearance. There were several regiments of these "Galvanized Yankees," and they did good service against the Sioux. It may be explained that "Galvanized Yankees" were Confederate prisoners who took the oath of allegiance and enlisted in these regiments to fight Indians in preference to remaining in Northern prisons.

Not being hampered by the humanitarians and the philanthropists, General Sibley adopted a very vig-

HUNG THEM.

orous Indian policy. As he made prisoners he selected the worst and hung them. As many as thirty braves were made "good Indians" by the rope route in one day.

There is "a record of engagements with hostile Indians within the military division of the Missouri from 1868 to 1882." In the recapitulation of this record it is stated that "more than 1,000 officers and soldiers were killed or wounded" in the Indian fighting of that period. Four hundred battles and skirmishes were fought with Indians in the fourteen years.

In 1886 the Senate sent a resolution to the Secretary of War, asking: "What has been the cost to the Government during the last ten years of so much of the army as has been engaged in the observation or control of Indians, or whose presence has been rendered necessary as a protection from danger of Indian hostilities?

COST IN TEN YEARS.

The Secretary replied that the total cost of the troops in the Indian country from 1876 to 1886 has been $223,891,264,50.

In 1868 and 1869 there was a lively Indian war

in what is now the Indian Territory and Oklahoma. Between 1862 and 1868 there had been murdered by the Indians 800 settlers in the Southwest. On the 2d of March, 1868, this war to punish the Cheyennes, Arapahoes and Commanches began. It ended on the 9th of February following. Three hundred and fifty-three officers, soldiers and citizens were killed, wounded or captured in the eleven months' campaign. The Indian loss was 319 killed, 289 wounded and 52 captured. The actual field operations during the eleven months cost $1,057,515.57.

The Modoc war in the lava-beds cost the army 111 soldiers killed or wounded. The chief incident of this campaign was the assassination of General Canby. Seventeen citizens were killed or wounded. The record which was sent to the Senate by the War Department says : " No Indians reported killed."

INDIAN LOSSES.

So far as losses were concerned the Indians usually had the best of it. In the record of 1868-1882 an explanation of the comparatively small number of Indians killed was offered by the War Department. This explanation was that the Indians carried off their dead and wounded whenever that was possible, and so concealed the number. This may be so. But the conclusion of Senator Doolittle was that Indian wars were not only enormously expensive, but also very unprofitable when the small number of dead Indians was considered.

From Photographs taken on the spot by the Philadelphia *Press* Artist.

JOHNSON, THE ALLEGED MESSIAH.

The Apache campaign of 1873 was one in which the army made a good score. The loss of soldiers was only 4; 84 Indians were reported killed.

In 1874 a campaign was carried on against the Kiowas, Commanches, and Cheyennes in the South-west. The net results were 24 killed or wounded soldiers and 84 dead Indians.

THE SIOUX WAR OF 1876.

The Sioux war of 1876 cost, for the actual field expenses, $2,312.531. But the campaign was chiefly notable for the Custer massacre. The army loss was 283 killed and 125 wounded. The Indian loss was only 85. Had Sibley's policy toward the Sioux been continued Sitting Bull and other Sioux leaders would have ornamented gallow-trees and there would have been no ghost-dancing in 1890. The Custer massacre was never atoned for. The guns which the Indians took from the soldiers are still in their possession

The Nez Perces war of 1877 lasted three months. It cost according to the report made by the Quarter master General, the snug sum of $931,329.52. That was a good deal more than $1,000 apiece for the Indian braves engaged in it. This was the campaign which General Sherman described in his report as "one of the most extraordinary Indian wars of which there is any record."

The Nez Perces lived in a valley in Eastern Oregon. They occupied land which, from its extraordinary fertility and adaptability for irrigation, is now worth from $50 to $75 an acre, That ought to be

a sufficient explanation of the way hostilities came
about. Two bad white men killed a good Indian.
Two bad Indians killed a good white man. Troops
were sent to the Nez Perces camp and were whipped
with a loss of a Lieutenant and thirty-three soldiers.
Then followed the Nez Perces war. Chief Joseph
commanded the tribe. General Howard took the field
in person with the army. The opening engagement
already referred to, was fought June 17th. The
Indians were encumbered with their women and
children. The troops had the resources of the Government to draw upon. Yet for three months the
chief baffled and outwitted the General.

"The Indians throughout," said General Sherman
in his report, "displayed a courage and skill that
elicited universal praise. They abstained from
scalping, let captive women go free, did not commit
indiscriminate murder of peaceful families, which is
usual, and fought with almost scientific skill, using
advance and rear guards, skirmish lines, and real
fortifications."

The campaign began in Eastern Oregon. It
moved by a zigzag across Idaho into Montana and
crossed the Missouri River two or three times. The

marching and countermarching extended from the
National Park almost to the Dominion line.

After Howard had been in the field for about six

weeks he telegraphed Sherman that his troops were worn out. He suggested that he go back to the country from which he had started and that the Generals east of the mountains try their hands on wily Chief Joseph. General Sherman was at Helena. He replied:

" I don't want to give orders, as that may confuse Sheridan and Terry. But that force of yours should pursue the Nez Perces to the death, lead where they may."

Howard resumed active operations. He followed the Nez Perces over 1,400 miles and then failed to be in at " the death." Miles, who had been attending to the Sioux, fell on Chief Joseph, and his band in the vicinity of the National Park. He killed six chiefs and a lot warriors and captured all of the others. The wind-up was on the 30th of September.

In that campaign 241 officers and soldiers were killed and wounded. Twelve citizens were killed. The Indians loss was 158.

The Bannock war of 1878 was a small affair. It cost only $556,636.19, When it was ended the record showed a loss of twenty-four to the army, thirty citizens murdered, and seventy-four Indians killed.

The Northern Cheyenne outbreak of 1879 entailed a loss on the army of thirty-two killed and wounded. No Indians were reported killed.

Since 1882, down to 1890, the only Indian fighting

was with the little squads of Apaches in Arizona and New Mexico. For every Apache run down and killed or captured the Government is said to have spent $100.000.

CHAPTER XXI.

THE FIRST SIOUX WAR.

PROVOKED BY WHITE MEN—NARRATIVE OF ONE WHO WAS THERE—
INDESCRIBABLE OUTRAGES PERPETRATED BY THE SAVAGES UPON
WOMEN AND CHILDREN—A CITY OF DEATH—GENERAL SIBLEY'S
CAMPAIGN—SENTENCES OF THE RINGLEADERS.

It was in August, 1862, that the first great trouble with the Sioux Indians occurred, and it was one of the ghastliest episodes in the whole history of savage warfare. A detailed narrative of it has been given by Isaac V. D. Heard, who was a member of the expedition that was sent to quell the uprising, but there is much of it that cannot be repeated here. The story is too horrible, the nameless crimes committed too frightful, to record in print.

The outbreak was provoked, as about all others have been, by the infamous injustice of the whites The four Indians to whom the beginning of the bloodshed is credited by Heard were belonging to Shakopee's village, at the mouth of Rice Creek. They were on their way to Acton when they attacked and killed two men named Baker and Webster, a Mr. Jones and wife, and a Miss Wilson.

Having accomplished these murders, they hastened to Shakopee's village and informed the rest of the tribe what they had done. A general massacre of the whites was immediately resolved upon, and messengers were sent to the bands of Wabashaw, Waconta, and Red Legs. The Shakopee band then proceeded to the agency under Little Crow, their chief. The village was entered in small parties, and the houses and stores surrounded. The discharge of a gun was to be the signal for simultaneous attack. This given, the hideous, painted savages, with mad shouts and wild shrieks, began the slaughter and plunder. Age, sex, former friendships or kindnesses availed nothing. Every building but two at the agency was burned. The massacre extended down the river on both sides, below the fort, to within six miles of New Ulm, and up the river to Yellow Medicine. Large numbers perished at Beaver and Sacred Heart Creeks. Parties of men, women, and children were intercepted in their flight and mercilessly slaughtered and mutilated.

SAVAGE BRUTALITY.

Near New Ulm, a father and his two sons were stacking wheat, when twelve Indians approached unseen and killed the three. Then they entered the farmer's house and killed two of his young children in the presence of their mother, who was ill with consumption, and dragged the mother and a daughter, aged thirteen years, miles away to their camp. There, in the presence of her dying mother, they tortured the girl with indescribable brutalities, until death came to her relief.

One Indian went into a house where a woman was making bread. Her small child was in the cradle. He split the mother's head open with his tomahawk, and placed the babe in the hot oven until it was almost dead, when he beat its brains out against the wall.

Children were nailed living to tables and doors, and knives and tomahawks thrown at them until they were dead. Cut-Nose, one of the chiefs, when brought to trial, acknowledged several of his atrocities, among which was the following: A

TERRIFIC BUTCHERY.

party of settlers were gathered together for flight; the helpless and defenseless women and children being huddled together in wagons. The men having been killed, Cut-Nose, while two other Indians held the horses, leaped into one of the wagons, and in cold blood tomahawked them all—cleft open the head of each, while the others, stupefied with horror and powerless with fright, as they heard the heavy, dull blows crash and tear through flesh and bones, awaited their turn. Taking an infant from its mother's arms, before her eyes, with a bolt from one of the wagons, the Indians riveted it through its writhing little body to the fence, and left it there to die in agony. The mother was kept alive and made to witness this agonizing spectacle, after which they chopped off her arms and legs, and left her to bleed to death. Thus Cut-Nose and his band ruthlessly butchered twenty-five persons within a quarter of an acre, and then kicking the bodies out of the wagons, they filled them with plunder from the burning houses and pushed on for more adventures.

An old Indian, shriveled almost to a mummy, when placed on trial, was confronted by two little boys, his accusers. Looking at him a moment, one of them said, "I saw that Indian shoot a man while he was on his knees at prayer;" and the other boy said, "I saw him shoot my mother."

The hands, feet, and heads of the victims were, in many cases, cut off, their hearts ripped out, and other disgusting mutilations inflicted. Whole families were burned alive in their homes.

OVER 700 MURDERS IN A WEEK.

The outrages for the first few days were confined to the vicinity of New Ulm and Fort Ridgely, but soon the depredations extended throughout the whole Western frontier of Minnesota, and into Iowa and Dakota. Over 700 persons perished in about a week, and more than 200 were made captives, and in every case the women were brutally treated.

One little girl, only ten years old, who had received several wounds at the hands of the savages, was treated with the most repulsive bestiality from day to day until she was nearly lifeless. Another little girl, aged nine, was treated still more brutally, her person being shamefully mutilated by the savages. Imagination cannot depict the enormities perpetrated upon these poor women. Shooting arrows into defenseless women and children constituted a favorite amusement of the younger warriors. In the Norwegian Grove back of Henderson, one of their grossest and most wanton outrages was committed. Stripping a captive naked, they fastened her arms and legs to the ground by tying them to stakes. They subjected her for hours to indescribable outrages, and then, when she was fainting from her exhaustion, they sharpened a rail and drove it through her body, leaving her to die in most horrible and excrutiating torments.

SAVAGE FURY.

The bold frontiersmen made many determined stands for their homes and lives, but with little avail. The savage fury and overwhelming numbers of the Sioux carried everything before them, and the pale-face found hope only by taking to the brush, where many of them died of starvation. White men then fought under very great disadvantage. They were few, resolute, and bold; but there is something so fiendish in the Indians' yells and terrifying in their wild appearance in battle, that it takes a good deal of time to overcome the unpleasant sensation it inspires. There is a snake-like stealth in all their movements that excites distrust and uncertainty, and which unsteadies the nerves at first.

Finally the news of the horrible outrages reached

St. Paul, and troops were raised and sent out
against the Indians, with Col. Sibley in command of
the expedition.   The forces under Sibley amounted
to 1,400 men, and in their upward march through

STREAM OF FUGITIVES.

the valley they met a stream of fugitives far out-
numbering those who were going to their relief.
Shakopee, Belle Plain, Henderson, and St. Peter's
were filled with fugitives from the scenes of massacre, and each of these villages in momentary expectation of an attack from the savages.   Oxen were
killed in the streets of the latter place, and hastily
prepared over fires on the ground.   The grist mills
were surrendered to the public use.   All thought of
property was abandoned, women hung upon each
other's necks weeping, and the surviving terror-
stricken children were crying piteously around their
knees.   Houses and stables alike were occupied,
and hundreds were without any shelter.   Belle Plain
was crowded, too, so was Mankato, so was Shakopee.   Panic existed throughout the whole valley.
And the safety of those towns, with the thousands
of lives within, depended upon Col. Sibley's success.

SICKENING SIGHTS.

Detachments of mounted and foot soldiers were
dispatched to New Ulm and Fort Ridgely, the principal centres of the slaughter.   The New Ulm detachment cautiously approached the town, expecting
to cut their way through the beleaguering Indians,
and to be received with the cheers and hospitality

of the people; but no sound greeted their ears. Soon they saw, thickly scattered around, vast swollen carcases of cows and oxen and horses, perforated with bullets. Presently they came upon the blackened remains of burnt buildings. Across the principal street lay the naked, headless body of a man, swollen like the cattle, and blackened in the sun, the head cut off and scalped, and tumbled some distance from the trunk. Off the street were new-made graves. The doors of standing houses were ajar. Every place was silence, every place the confusion of a hasty departure. With drawn swords and pistols the soldiers rushed up and down the streets of the deserted city. Friend and foe had departed.

The Lake Shelek settlement, about seventy miles west of Mankato, and numbering some forty-five persons in all, was attacked by the bands of Lean Bear, White Lodge, and Sleepy Eyes. Three women and six children were shot down by one Indian who had been the recipient of frequent charities from the very persons he so cruelly murdered. Only twenty persons escaped, ten or eleven being taken prisoners and the remainder killed.

SURROUNDED BY INDIANS.

A detachment of soldiers under Major Brown were surprised and surrounded by the Indians, and when relieved by Col. Sibley they had been thirty-one hours without food or water, and with but thirty rounds of ammunition. The camp, when rescued, was surrounded by the dead bodies of the horses, over ninety in number. The tents were riddled with bullets, as many as 104 being found in a single one. Ditches were dug between the tents and the dead horses, and the dirt piled on the latter to form a breastwork. Thirteen dead and many wounded soldiers were found in the ditch. A few feet distant were found more dead bodies, twenty-three having been killed in all, and forty-five wounded.

Sibley was compelled to remain inactive for many days at the fort, owing to the want of ammunition and supplies, and during this time correspondence was carried on with the Indians for the delivery of captives and a cessation of hostilities. Nothing was accomplished in either direction.

At the battle of Wood Lake, on the 18th of September, Sibley lost four men, and had about fifty wounded. The Indian loss was fifteen killed, all of whom were scalped by the soldiers.

CAPTIVES RELEASED.

On September 26th, the Indian camp opposite the mouth of the Chippewa was taken, and the white captives released, Little Crow and some two hundred warriors having hurriedly fled. This virtually ended the Sioux war. A military commission of inquiry was appointed to ascertain the guilty parties, and thirty or forty arrested. Many Indians gave themselves up and others were surprised in the night. The prisoners were linked together in pairs by chains forged to their ankles. On the 21st

of October other prisoners were brought in from
Wild Goose Neck Lake, and on the 23d more were
captured at the Yellow Medicine Agency. The
prisoners were taken to Fort Snelling, where over
four hundred of them were tried. Of these three
hundred and three were sentenced to death and
eighteen to imprisonment.

The records of the testimony and sentences of
the Indians were sent to the President, but no
action was taken for several weeks. Finally, thirty-
eight of them were ordered to be executed at
Mankato, on Friday, the 26th day of February, 1863.
The sentence was carried into effect on the appointed
day, and the remainder were taken down the Mississippi to Davenport and confined.

CHAPTER XXII.

CAUSES OF THE LAST WAR.

WHAT THE INDIANS SAY—FATHER JULE'S INTERVIEW WITH THE CHIEFS—
THE CENSUS—BROKEN FAITH AND DIMINISHED SUPPLIES—LETTER
FROM AMERICAN HORSE—THE INDIANS' STORIES CONFIRMED BY
GOVERNMENT REPORTS.

The Indian war of 1890–91 had its inciting causes
in a long train of events. There has been much
discussion of it; many statements and counter-
statements have been made. But from all the mass
of testimony, one conclusion only can be reached,
that through mismanagement by Government officials, and dishonesty, too, on the part of some
agents, the Sioux were brought into a condition of
great privation and distress. Many of them were
actually starving. Under these circumstances they
became desperate, and determined, since there was
no help in man, to seek help from their " Messiah,"
and, since they must die, to die fighting their pale-
faced foes.

Conspicuous among those who, after the hostilities had begun, went with their lives in their hands

FATHER JULE'S EFFORT.

to the Indians and tried to make peace was Father

Jule, a Catholic priest. Gen. Brooke asked him, early in December, 1890, to go from the Pine Ridge Agency to the camp of the hostiles, and he unhesitatingly did so. He was accompanied by Jack Red Cloud, the respected son of the famous chief, who went more as a guide than with the belief that he would be of any use in making the mission a success. The story of the visit gives the best possible idea of the feeling of the Indians, their grievances, and the impulses that moved them to their desperate course.

There were present at the council Two Strike, the head chief; Turning Bear, Short Bull, High Hawk, Crow Dog, Kicking Bear, Eagle Pipe, Big Turkey, and High Pipe. The pipe of peace was conspicuous by its absence.

Father Jule opened the council by asking the chiefs to state the particular cause of the grievance that had led them to assume their war-like attitude. The replies were substantially as follows:

THE INDIANS REPLY.

"We object to the recent census returns made by Mr. Lee. His enumeration, as he is now making it, would not give food sufficient for us to live on. Lee puts us down many less for each tepee than the tepee contains. We are to receive food according to that enumeration. We shall starve; we know we shall starve if the Great Father chooses to lay a trap to cheat us. We will have one big eat before the starving time comes. After that we

shall fight our last fight, and the white man shall
see more blood, more dead by us from our guns
than ever before.   Then we shall go to the last
hunting-ground happy.   If the white men did not
mean to cheat us out of food, the Great Father
would never have sent soldiers.   There is no need
of soldiers if the Great Father intended to be fair
with us.   We know he intends cheating us by the
way the census man is now putting down figures
that lie, and by which we are to be fed.   The Great
Father has done another wrong, he put a new
boundary line between Rosebud and Pine Ridge
Agency, that makes many of us leave our homes
and give them to others.

"The Great Father broke the old treaty when he
did this.   We can no longer believe the Great
Father.   He says to us : 'Children, you shall never
be moved again unless you want to move,' and then
he goes right away and moves us.   We are done
with promises, and now we make a promise that we
will fight, and the Great Father will find that we
will not break our promise.   We will now be very
plain with you, Christian Father, and tell you
another thing, something of which you may have
already thought.   It is this : We are not coming in
now and will not lay down our rifles, because we
are afraid of the consequences.   We have done
wrong ; we know it.   If we stop now we will be
punished.   The Great Father will send many of us
to his big iron house to stay many moons.   We

TEPEE OF SITTING BULL

would die. No, we will not go and give up. We know the Great Father better than he knows us, or cares to know us."

After a long pause, Crow Dog said that they might come in if the soldiers were taken away.

Father Jule then urged them with much fervor to give up their designs of war and be peaceable. He explained that the soldiers were not present to harm the Indians, but to protect the agency; that rations had been increased at the agency, and that, if they came, Gen. Brooke would telegraph to Washington and get permission for them to stay on this agency, as they desired. So far as depredations were concerned, the priest told them they had better stop committing them, and they would be

URGING PEACE.

more easily forgiven. Finally he urged the chiefs that they all come back with him. To this some of the older ones made favorable answers, but the young ones, who were heavily in the majority, said no; but the old men finally agreed that they would come on horseback to Father Jule's house, which is about four miles northwest of the agency, this morning, and there meet Gen. Brooke, and tell them in person just what they had told Father Jule. This brought on a renewal of bitter opposition from the majority, which came near ending in a row. Finally the young chiefs cooled down, and Two Strike, addressing Father Jule, said:

"Hold your hands up to the Great Spirit, and

tell us, as though you were about to start on a journey to the last hunting-ground of the red man, whether what you say to us from Gen. Brooke be true, and that we will not be harmed if we come in simply to talk to Gen. Brooke."

Father Jule says he complied with the request. All the chiefs then extended their hands toward the heavens, and with great solemnity promised they would come. This ended the council, and Father Jule and young Red Cloud withdrew, the former telling the chiefs that, if they broke their word to him, he would never again believe an Indian.

A petition and statement of grievances was, in November, 1890, drawn up and signed by Hollow Horn Bear and fifty-two other representative men of the different Sioux families. They wrote as follows to the President:

LETTER TO THE PRESIDENT.

"Great Father: This day we will write you a letter with a good heart.

"When we gave up the Black Hills, you told us in that treaty that a man would get three pounds of beef a day. The meaning was three pounds for one man. Beside, you said we could get food just like the soldiers. You did not give it to us at this rate. We are starving, and beg you to give to us just so as you have promised. Thirty men of us get for eighteen days only one cow to eat. That is why we mention it, and if you do not understand it send money, and Hollow Horn Bear and five men will come to you. Great Father, if you do not want to do so, then please let us have a soldier for our agent."

The Sioux Indians signed the last agreement under the express understanding that rations would not be reduced. Within one month after signing the beef supply was reduced 2,000,000 pounds for the first time in years. Those signing the agreement felt imposed upon; those not signing, who then became the leaders in the outbreak, blamed the signers and pointed to the reduction in the beef supply as the result.

American Horse, a leading chief at Pine Ridge, wrote to a friend in Cincinnati, on December 22d, 1890:

"I have been hunting for my cattle, but found only thirteen; therefore, they (the soldiers) must have killed 156, although it is barely possible that I may find one or two more. We found all my ponies except two; that is, we found them at the 'hostiles'' camp, and it is likely that I shall get them back. The things that these white men and the Indians together have unwarrantably destroyed amounted to $196.

HESITATING.

"This evening a Sioux, one of the returned 'hostiles,' told me that almost half the Indians in the Bad Lands would come away, but the other half threaten them so they could not come, but there is a delegation of 167 men of the friendly Indians who have gone there to persuade them to come in. My own son and thirty of my young men are among the delegation trying to get them to come back and stand a little while longer the mean treatment without making trouble. They are there by this afternoon. I am thoroughly informed of the state of things immediately surrounding these agencies that I could not for a moment think of taking up arm. against the whites. But you must understand what we friendly Indians have to endure, losing all our cattle, and thus cutting off all subsistence outside of the poor and small rations, which I can tell you are very meagre, indeed, and thus hardly are fit for any human appetite for food. It has been getting worse and worse and less and less from ration-day to another. Among the things they have come and taken away from my house was my overcoat that you gave me. I am sorry that I did not take this coat with me when I came to the agency. Now, my dear friend, there is one thing I would like

KEEP MY BOY AWAY.

you very much to favor me with. I have a boy at Carlisle School, in Pennsylvania, but at present he is at Dolington, Bucks County, Pa., working. He wishes to come home, but I want him to stay there until this trouble is over, and learn all he can. I wish you would write to him and encourage him as much as you can. Tell him my position in this trouble. You can tell it to him better than I can through my interpreter.

"When this trouble is over and the people are quiet, I would like to remind the Government, or rather request it, to make good the losses of the friendly Indians. Can you use your influence, either directly or indirectly, in our behalf? I thought, perhaps, you may have some friends at Washington who may say a good word for us. This is all I have to say."

To confirm these stories of bad faith, privation, and unjust dealing, it is only necessary to turn to the Government's own reports. As early as the spring of 1890 trouble was foreseen, and the causes that were inevitably leading to it were clearly set forth. Mr. F. C. Armstrong, an Indian inspector, wrote, on April 7th from Pine Ridge, to the Secretary of the Interior as follows:

STERN FACTS.

"In former years this agency was allowed 5,000,000 pounds of beef. This year it has been reduced to 4,000,000 pounds. These Indians were not prepared for this change. No instructions had been given the agent that 1,000,000 pounds of beef would be cut off from the Indians this year. Consequently, issues were made from the beginning of the fiscal year—July 1st, 1889—until the date of the final delivery of beef, about October 15th, 1889, on the basis of 5,000,000 pounds for the year. This necessitated a large reduction in the beef issue afterward to catch up with the amount, and came just at the worst season of the year. The Indians were kept at the agency between three and four weeks in the farming season of 1889, when they should have been at home attending to their corn.

"Their enforced absence attending the Sioux Commission caused them to lose all they had planted by the stock breaking in on their farms and destroying everything they had. They have been compelled to kill their private stock during the winter to keep from starving, and in some cases have been depredating upon the stock of white people living near the line of the reservation.

BAD FEELING GROWING.

"A bad feeling is growing among the Indians out of this, and may lead to trouble between the settlers and the Indians. The killing of a hog made the Nez Perces war, with Indians far more advanced than these people. The full allowance of beef should be given them. They complain and with good grounds, that they were told by the Sioux Commissioners that their rations, etc., should not be reduced; that while this very talk was going on the Department in Washington was fixing to cut off one-fifth of their meat supply, but did not let them know it, nor did the agent know it, until they had signed the Sioux Bill. They had a good start in cattle, but have had to kill over three times as many of their own cattle, old and young, as they did the year before that they have been deceived in doing what they did by the Government, and that they don't get as much now as they did before.

"I think cutting off this 1,000,000 pounds of beef and thereby forcing them to kill their own young cattle, has put them back two years or more in raising stock, and has created a feeling of distrust, which, unless something is done to repair it, will

KILLING THEIR OWN CATTLE.

lead to trouble and bad conduct. They have now killed many of their own cattle and will next commence to kill range cattle. Already hides and other evidences of this are being found on the reservation borders.

"Men will take desperate remedies sooner than suffer from hunger. Not much work can be expected with the present feeling. The Indians who advocated signing are now laughed at and blamed for being fooled. They don't get even their former rations, and ask where are all the promises that were made. The Government must keep faith as well as the Indians.

SERIOUS DISSATISFACTION.

"The attention of the Department has frequently been called to the condition of the Cheyenne Indians at this agency, their dissatisfaction and determination to do nothing to better their condition. They now openly say they will leave there this spring, and therefore have no intention of putting in crops or doing any work.

"They may be held here by force, but it is questionable if it is a good policy to keep them at Pine Ridge Agency any longer. The nine hundred Cheyennes at Tongue River, Montana, and these five hundred Cheyennes of the same band here, should be concentrated at one agency. The Sioux don't want them here, and they don't want to stay. They should not be kept as prisoners only. The Tongue River reservation is, I know, wanted by cattlemen. They should be a secondary consideration. These Indians should be concentrated there, and a reservation obtained for them from the Crows, and the Cheyennes should be moved to it. They will then be satisfied, settle down, and go to work. No good can ever come to the Cheyennes if the course pursued toward them during the last six years is continued, and much bad may result.

"Why should Indians be forced to stay where they never located through choice? Put them where they want to live and can make a living, and let them stay there and do it. Without some prompt action regarding this beef matter, and also in the Cheyenne matter, on this reservation, the Department may, this summer or fall, expect trouble. I have thought this of sufficient importance to lay it before the Department, and to go in person to ask that some action be taken. I have seen this Cheyenne matter brewing for two years, and I see now the Sioux put back in the principal industry on which they have to depend. With prompt action in this matter, and a proper arrangement of districts for the issuing of rations, a plan for which I will submit, these people will go ahead. If not, they will go backward, which to them is the easier road."

But this warning was unheeded, and these wise recommendations were ignored.

CHAPTER XXIII.

EFFORTS FOR PEACE.

Mrs. Weldon's Remarkable Mission to the Camp of Sitting Bull—Her Desire to Confront the Prophet of the Messiah—Forced to Flee for Safety—Her Views of the Situation—Her Life in Dakota.

Of all white people who ever had any dealings with him, the one who best knew Sitting Bull, and had most influence with him, was Mrs. Caroline Weldon, formerly of New York City. On account of some disappointments in her early life, she went to the Northwest and devoted herself for many years to work among the Indians and to study of Indian character and history. She spent much time at Sitting Bull's camp, and indeed considered it her home. And she did much to bring about a better understanding between the Indians and the whites, and exposed and corrected many of the abuses practiced by the Indian agents.

Mrs. Weldon spent some time in New York in 1889, but in the spring of 1890 she settled all her affairs there, and went to Dakota to spend the rest of her life, intending, if possible, to avert the serious troubles which were then already threatened. She went at once to Sitting Bull's camp, but was soon filled with dismay at the ominous symptoms she

GRIEVANCES EVERYWHERE.

beheld. Grievances were suffered everywhere. Discontent was everywhere. Rumors of the Messiah were extant. The ghost dances were begun. The Indians became suspicious and regarded her as a spy. When she tried to stop the dances, they turned upon her to drive her from the camp. Sitting Bull and his wives were her only friends. They protected her, but when she asked to be allowed to confront Mat-o-wan-a-ti-ta-ka, the prophet of the Messiah, they refused. Then she gave up all hope of maintaining peace, and went to Fort Yates to see the agent there. But her mission was unavailing. She could not inspire the agent with that confidence in and sympathy with the Indians which she herself felt. Then her ten-year-old boy died, and she was quite broken-hearted. On September 15th she wrote:

MRS. WELDON'S LETTER.

"Back again at Cannon Ball. Sitting Bull and Hohesikana have gone away. I hasten away, for there appears to be trouble. They want to go hunting. An Indian rode into camp and told Sitting Bull that Major McLaughlin had forbidden them to go to a certain place to hunt, and that if they persisted in their preparations to go, he would take away all their guns and ponies. This caused great

consternation, and half the night Sitting Bull talked
to them to quiet them.   He says he does not want
war, and will do all he can to prevent it.   He does
not want to fight against the whites.   Sitting Bull
hastened to the Major to find out if the report was
true, and to remonstrate with him.   Sitting Bull,
who loves his people, resents injustice done to them,
and yet he wants peace with the white people.   He
said he would be glad if the soldiers would kill him
so his heart would find rest.   I told them what
would be the result of a war, and that it would
hasten their destruction."

Matters went from bad to worse, and she saw
that war was inevitable.   On November 4th she
wrote again a longer letter in which she discussed
the situation in detail.

"I have been to the Grand River again," she
said; "this time alone.   I went down to denounce
and pursue Matowanatitaka, a prophet who came
from Cheyenne, and is making all the Indians crazy
with his teachings.   I expected him to be an Indian
of another tribe, but when I arrived at the camp I
found that he was Sitting Bull's wife's sister's son,
whose mother is dead.   This made matters worse.
But I could not alter my intention when I was told
that Sitting Bull had not come up, but had remained
at home with Matowanatitaka.   If it had not been
for the latter he would have come up to Cannon
Ball.   He had planned the trip.   Hohesikana was
far away, hunting, so I called for Circling Bear.

When he came I asked him to call the chiefs and men together, as I had something important to tell them. I had already worked against the prophet—who is a young fellow, by the way—down to Cannon Ball, enlightening the Indians in exposing him. I had prepared a long speech for the Indians, and when I delivered it I found that I met with opposition from the elder people. The young people listened with interest and apparent belief. Circling Bear appeared the most obstinate, but never forgot his dignity, while I grew warm and used harsh language. In the first place, this prophet claims to have seen and spoken to Christ, who is now again upon the world, and has come to help the Indians once more to become a powerful people, and that all the white people are to be driven out of the land or transformed into beasts. All the dead are to come to life again and never grow old. All the game is to come back, and buffaloes never to give out, for the hoofs, head, and tail are to be saved, and when your back is turned they become new buffaloes. All the Indians, Sioux, Utes, Shoshones, and many others believe in this great Messiah who will do all this for them. He will visit their living relatives and tell them to fight and become victorious once more. In fact, an Indian war is on the programme.

"I think the Mormons are at the bottom of this, for the Indians leave by tramping, by railroad, and then go south, making the journey in thirty-five days

by horseback, and pass the Sapanicaota (Utes).
Here they see Christ and he speaks to them. Next
spring Christ and the dead will come this way to
help the Indians. To refute this and take their
blindness from them and confound the medicine
men and prophets, I went down. When I learned
that Sitting Bull had not come up I determined to
go down to Grand River and remonstrate with him.
All the Indians say that he did not believe in Matowanatitaka, who strikes one dead by a look. They
say a halo of light is seen around his head in the
dark, and there is a star above his head, and that
those who scorn him he transforms into dogs or
THE FALSE CHRIST.
anything else. It is my opinion that Matowanatitaka himself is the false Christ, and to confound
him I desired to face him. I denounced him as a
liar and a cheat at the camp, and they sent Crowfoot
on horseback to announce my coming. I expected
that Sitting Bull would be displeased and would treat
me coldly, but when the wagon stopped he shook
hands with me and told me how glad he was to see
me; but in spite of his smile he looked sad and
troubled, and seemed to have aged considerably
since I saw him a month before. In the house the
dishes were set for dinner. My plate was, with
several others, on the table, and on the floor was a
white cloth with eight plates for Matowanatitaka
and his followers. His followers came to eat, but
Matowanatitaka and one of his disciples stayed

away, and I did not see him that day. I never got a good look at his face. He always had his blanket drawn over his head, and when he looked at me it generally was from behind a couple of chairs or some other piece of furniture. Instead of coming around and asking for an explanation he avoided me and seemed afraid. The next day the Major sent some policemen to arrest Matowanatitaka and Sitting Bull. The majority of the police stayed four miles above Sitting Bull's residence, and the chief and Catka were brave enough to come to the house and deliver their message. Of course, Matowanatitaka and Sitting Bull declined to accommodate the Indian policemen. Matowanatitaka lay flat on his back kicking his feet in the air in the most ridiculous manner, while Sitting Bull was delivering a speech to the policemen and Indians. I expected a fight every minute, for every man carried a gun and looked desperate, and the room was filled with them. Catka recognized me, as he met me a year before. He bent down and whispered to Matowanatitaka. Sitting Bull had already left the room and Matowanatitaka followed, and then one by one every one left; Sitting Bull's wife and myself were the only occupants in the room with the exception of the chief. Catka and I chatted pleasantly about different things, he admiring Sitting Bull's full-length portrait which I had given to him. After a while the chief men came in and shook hands with the policemen, all but Sitting Bull and Matowanatitaka.

"The next day I was told that Matowanatitaka had left, but I doubted it, although his arms were not there, and subsequently I proved to be in the right. He had taken up his quarters somewhere else, for later on he was my traveling companion with Sitting Bull on my return to Yates. Circling Bear poisoned Sitting Bull's ears. He told him that the attempt to arrest was my doings; that I was Sitting Bull's enemy; and that I was planning the destruction of both. He also called Sitting Bull's attention to a look which passed between me and Catka. Evidence was against me, for I had said that I would pursue Matowanatitaka, and Sitting Bull told me he knew that I was his enemy, and wanted him to be in prison. I simply laughed when he told me. There I had been working for his interest and the interest of the Indians for years; was ready to share all the dangers, and he was foolish enough to believe me his enemy. That night they continued their wacekiyaps (dances and songs), which sounded awful in the stillness of the night, and they kept it up until I could stand it no longer, so I arose and went through the crowd. It was dark, and there was the width of a street between me and Sitting Bull's house. I told Sitting Bull I would go away at daylight if he did not stop it, and he did. The next morning I asked him to have no more dances, as the troops would come and there would be a battle. He said it was not his doings, but the chiefs', and he would be glad if

CHIEF BIG JOSEPH.

the soldiers would kill him, for he wanted to die. 'If you want to die, kill yourself, and do not bring other people into trouble,' I said. He had the post removed to the foot of the hill, where it would not annoy me, but he acted as high priest, for I watched him. He expected the soldiers and battle every hour. You can imagine how pleasant it was for me.

"Miss Carrigan and One Bull came to take me to Yates, but Sitting Bull made me promise to stay five days longer, as the Major had seized some messengers, and so I did not go, but sent some money I had to Major McLaughlin, begging him to keep it for me until I should reclaim it. Not that I distrusted the Indians, for not a pin was ever taken from me, but I feared the battle, and if I was killed no one would get the benefit of it. A few days later I met Gall, a chief, who was going to take me to Yates, but Sitting Bull was not on good terms with him, and I feared Sitting Bull would think I might betray some secrets of the council, for I had always been present, so I stayed until Sitting Bull took me himself. He said:

"'Do as your heart dictates. If you want to go with Gall, go; but if your heart says stay, remain, and I will take you to Yates myself, and perhaps to Cannon Ball.'

SITTING BULL'S FRIENDSHIP.

"Sitting Bull and family were very good to me, and always treated me well, although I did denounce Matowanatitaka and their dances. Some of the

Indians felt very bitter, for they blamed me for the agent's actions. I think this was done to make a rupture between us, and to deprive Sitting Bull of my protection, which was affecting the National Indian Defense Committee in Washington. I could write a whole book of my experience at the camp near Yates. Circling Bear, who formerly befriended me, is now my enemy. He cast the robe he gave me up to me, and I threw it at his feet, and told him I wanted no presents from him. He did not take it back all the same. I had many unpleasant words with them because I opposed their dances which I thought destroyed their reason for days. They said I did not understand it, but that whatever disease they had was thrown off during these paroxysms. These dances occurred once a year, and lasted eight days. The hymns are nice, and I know six or seven of them."

A few days later she wrote concerning various slanders which had been circulated against her by the enemies of the Indians, some of them to the effect that she had become one of Sitting Bull's wives.

"I reached Yates Thursday. Sitting Bull went a few minutes ahead of the team. He dressed as if for burial, wearing the black cloth about his head, which means he is ready to die at any moment. He expected to be seized, and was determined to

SITTING BULL READY FOR DEATH.

defend himself and sell his life dearly. His followers were at the Grand River; he was brave to go alone. On the contrary, the officers treated him well and shook hands with him. I had the chance to go to Cannon Ball in a Government team. He thought I would remain there from Thursday until Monday. The Utes when I left felt sorry. They seemed to realize they had lost one of their best friends forever. Now I have gone, I fear that the last link between the white people and Sitting Bull is severed. The Utes, as well as other tribes, are ready to fight, and I cannot blame them. When one has seen how they are continually cheated, allowances can be made. I read an article about myself in a Washington paper which was sent me. All papers print the most dangerous lies, and I blame Major McLaughlin for allowing it. If he had not started these stories, they would not have been published, although he positively knows they are untrue, for I had sent several notes to him from the Grand River, and when I informed him of the unpleasantness between me and the Sioux on account of my opposition to their songs and dances, he knew I was trying to prevent war, and that my life had been in danger on that account, and yet he allowed these untruths to be told, and stated also the latter to the Secretary of the Interior. If you read romances, do not believe them. I would like to see these articles, for they interest me, and I know they are his doings."

And again she wrote of her life in Dakota:

"No one in the world was as happy as I, and I wish that all might have shared that happiness. A city seems a prison to me. One must work hard to get along in the city, and I enjoyed the freedom of the wilderness. I enjoyed the trees, and the hills, and the clouds. The flowers and the birds make me happy. I love the solitude, with its songs and its scenery, and I was loath to leave it. But I had to go, as my life was in danger. Those who had been my friends were now my enemies, and I left against the wishes of the Sioux. They wanted me to remain for the winter, as I knew too much. I had been at every council and was acquainted with all their plans. They needed an interpreter and a secretary, and they wanted me to so act for them. I feel that I have escaped with my life, and I laugh to think how I have outwitted that cunning Sitting Bull. After I left I was informed that Sitting Bull rode through Yates at night, singing his war songs, which were awful to listen to. If the Indians can

INDIANS STARVING.

gain anything, I say fight, for they are starving. As it turns out, they get only one-fifth of what the Government allows them. If I could only live, and had power enough to see the agents exposed and brought to justice, I should like it, for I know they are stealing goods intended for the Indians. I al-

ways urged them not to fight, for they would get
the worst of it. I feared the leaders would suffer,
and all their ponies and arms be taken, and that
would be awful, but it would be what I have said all
the time. I often wonder if they remember my
words, and things are turning out different from
what they anticipated."

CHAPTER XXIV.

THE SEAT OF WAR.

PINE RIDGE RESERVATION AND AGENCY—THE GARDENS AND THE BUILDINGS—DR. MCGILLICUDDY'S ADMINISTRATION—THE CATHOLIC MISSION SCHOOL—SOME ACCOUNT OF THE BAD LANDS—A TRULY HORRIBLE REGION.

The Pine Ridge Agency is one of the most important of all the Indian posts. Under its care and control lie the bulk of the Sioux Nation—all that is left of it. The agency is situated in the western part of South Dakota and occupies a tract of table land bordering on White Clay Creek, a never-failing stream of clear spring water. When the agency buildings were placed here in 1879 it was thought that the boundary line between Dakota and Nebraska was distant twelve miles to the south. But it was afterward found that it was only two miles away, and this circumstance gave unprincipled persons a chance to reach and corrupt the Indians without entering the reservation. So very soon a large free-for-all dance-house, gambling den, and grog shop was running full blast, day and night, Sundays as well, only two miles from the agency. The bad

332

effect of this made it necessary to set apart for the use of the reservation a tract of land five by ten miles in size in Nebraska immediately south of the agency, thus driving objectionable characters further away.

The Pine Ridge Reservation, of which the agency is the capital, contains about 2,000,000 acres, or about 360 acres for each Indian. Strictly speaking, the land cannot be called arable, although portions

THE PINE RIDGE AGENCY.

of it along the streams have in favorable seasons produced pretty good crops. But the seasons are short and dry, and as yet no general system of irrigation has been found practicable. The majority

SIOUX ANXIOUS TO FARM.

of the Indians here are the very flower of the Sioux race and are anxious to own land in severalty and to earn their living as farmers and cattle raisers.

When this agency was established in 1879 it was

put in charge of the now famous Indian agent, Dr.
V. T. McGillicuddy. Up to the time of his appointment Red Cloud had been the leader in all kinds of
disturbances, and openly defied every agent. It has
become well-known history to every one on the
frontier how the Doctor first taught the Sioux the
meaning of the words obedience and discipline.
He is one of the few men who know no fear, and
innumerable stories of his courage are current to-
day, and no one tells them with keener enjoyment
than the Indians themselves. The noble red man
has a child's mind in a man's body, and no class of
people respect and yield to courage, firmness, and
kindness than they. An Indian police numbering
fifty picked men was organized, given comfortable
quarters, a complete equipment, and were soon as
thoroughly drilled as any body in an Eastern city.
With this small force over 6,500 Indians, including
1,800 of the best fighters who have ever held our
army at bay, were completely controlled. The
Indians were disarmed, the famous torture or sun

WONDERFUL PROSPERITY UNDER DR. M'GILLICUDDY.

dance was broken up never to be revived, schools,
workshops, and a thorough system of farming under
a boss farmer, were established. Every one visiting
the agency is surprised at the substantial, neat, yet
inexpensive character of the buildings, which are
arranged something on the plan of the common
frontier forts. The principal buildings are the
agent's headquarters, the school-house, police quar-

ters, supply houses where rations are issued, two post-trading establishments, Catholic and Episcopal Churches, blacksmith, harness, wagon, and carpenter shops. Around these are clustered the houses of the various employees and assistants. The place bears more resemblance to a well-kept country village than a famous Indian agency. There are no fortifications of any kind, not even a stockade or a strong house to retreat to in case of trouble. The most formidable barriers in the way of a hostile are the picket-fences and the wire screens over the windows.

During the Cleveland Administration, Dr. McGillicuddy, being a Republican, was removed from the agency, and a Mr. Gallagher appointed in his

BAD RESULTS OF CHANGING AGENTS.

place. The results of the change were soon visible. The average Indian will size up a man as quickly as an unruly boy, and tries him in every way so as to find how far he can transgress the established rules. It is the same spirit that is manifested in every unruly school-room, only these dusky pupils of the nation are full grown physically, full of superstition, with fierce, cruel, and uncontrolled tempers and appetites, and many of them have tasted of the pleasures of hunting that most fascinating of all large game—that is, human beings. In a short time they began leaving the reserve in bands and family bunches to visit their friends in Wyoming and Montana without stopping to ask permission,

as the regulations called for; and many a cattleman in Wyoming still quotes freely from profane
history as he recalls their manifested love for roast
beef rare as they crossed his range. In a few
months it was found that they were well supplied
again with arms and ammunition, which they had
purchased during their excursions.

Mr. Gallagher did not remain at the agency long
enough to enjoy all the fruits of his work. In the
summer of 1890 he was succeeded by Mr. Royer,
who took hold of the tangled affairs with a firm and
judicious hand. But he came too late to avert the
catastrophe.

The Pine Ridge Catholic Mission School, which
was recently destroyed by the hostile Indians, was
situated on White Clay Creek, about four miles
from the agency, in one of the most picturesque
spots on the whole reservation. It consisted of a
substantial three-story brick building, about two
hundred feet long by one hundred feet wide, in-
closing two courts or play-grounds for the children.
Around the buildings were extensive gardens, which,
being watered from the creek, were exceedingly
fertile and productive. On a hill near by was a
large tank and windmill, giving the whole place an
excellent water supply. The school was opened in
1887, its object being to educate the Indian children
in the Roman Catholic faith. The south half of the
buildings was occupied by the nuns and girl students, and the north half by the priests and the

boys, each part being a complete institution by itself. In the centre was a handsome chapel. The head of the school was Father John Jutz, a Franciscan monk from Austria. He was assisted by two fathers, six lay brothers, and ten sisters, all Germans. All teaching, however, was in English, as required by the law.

THE BAD LANDS.

The Bad Lands, as they are fittingly called by both whites and Indians, comprise one of the most extraordinary, fantastic, repelling, and desolate regions in the world. Riding over the plains, one comes suddenly to the edge of a precipice from 200 to 500 feet in depth. He may travel for miles along this edge before finding a break that will permit him to descend to the region below. The region before him was once the bottom of a vast inland lake or sea, 110 miles long from northeast to southeast, and from fifteen to forty miles wide from east to west. The bottom of the lake has been the play-ground of the forces of nature for ages; rain, wind, and frost have carved the whole region into more fantastic, weird forms than human brains could conceive. Standing on the edge of the precipice, one feels that a magic pen is needed to describe the scene. Below and beyond is a chaos of hills, buttes, valleys, cañons, dizzy altitudes, blackened, precipitous cliffs, and gloomy gorges. It is a map of the mighty convulsions and pranks of nature in her most rebellious or sportive moods; a fascinating terra-incognita whose edges only have been explored by a few daring white men, and whose interior is known only to the skulking savage. One sees hills, cut in all directions by deep, twisting ravines, displaying along their sides marvelous architectural forms. One sees what is apparently an old dismantled fortress, near by is the wreck of a city, on the right stands a huge castle, on the left the remnants of a village, all stone, all deception, for no human beings have ever called this region home. It is all death and desolation, there is no animal life, and vegetation shuns the ground as though it were plague-stricken. There is no crystal sheen of rivers emerging from graceful groves of richest green; the river beds are dry, and contain only huge boulders scattered around as though some giants had been waking the echoes pelting each other with them.

WONDERS AND DESOLATION OF THE BAD LANDS.

Here and there are plainly seen old high-water marks, with the washed up débris left by the floods of ages ago; but no bubbling brooks or cool spring is left to quench the thirst of the explorer whose nostrils and eyes smart and sting from the thick alkali dust raised in clouds at every step. The absence of life in any form is terrible, oppressive. There is no chirping of insects, no humming of wings to give signs of animation—nothing but silence profound and forbidding. Even the lazy waving of the rare tufts of prairie grass is a relief to the absolute lifelessness. It is a region of terrors, of shivers, and undefined dread. To the scientist the region is one of indescribable fascination. Accustomed to hear the Black Hills described as the mineral wonderland of the world, he is not surprised to find in the bottom of the old sea, that once dashed its waves against the rocky shores of the island of the Hills, a perfect museum of the ancient wonders of this land. The geologist finds himself in what has been a wonderland from the first dawning of life on the globe. The rocky layers, now carved into marvelous imitation of the work of human hands, were once ooze at the bottom of the sea, and are now the richest treasure-houses in the whole world of the well-preserved forms of ancient animal life from which such men as Professors Cope, Marsh, and Leidy have dug out some of the most strange and wonderful freaks of animal life. To read their reports is more romantic and weird than the *Arabian Nights* and their facts seem as strange as the tales of Munchausen. In turn this region has been the

WONDERLAND OF ANCIENT ANIMAL LIFE.

home of such land and water animals of such gigantic size as have never been discovered elsewhere in the deposits of any geological age. Lizard-like forms over 100 feet in length and thirty feet high crawled wearily over the plains; reptiles more hideous than the standard sea serpent bathed their fifty-foot bodies in this inland sea, stretching their necks twenty feet in the air; flying reptiles, with a twenty-foot spread of leathery wings, disputed possession of the air with gigantic birds whose vast jaws were armed with teeth ; two, three, and four-toed horses, from the size of a fox to those larger than any of to-day, in turn sought their food in this labyrinthian wilderness. Tropical climates followed the drying up of the sea, and palms grew, and crocodiles, rhinocerus, tapirs, elephants, mastodons, and even camels lived and died within these boundaries. Everywhere their fossil bones abound, mingled with petrified shells of turtles six feet long, mammoth shells of the ammonite, with the pearl as perfect as the day when it spread its fleshy sails to the cretaceous breeze ; huge masses of fossil oysters awaken longings for the comforts of the East.

THE BAD LANDS THE INDIANS' SECURE RETREAT.

Only the Indian knows the dire and perilous trails that lead in and out of this most terrible of labyrinths. Their light ponies can go where the heavy cavalry horse cannot follow. Hidden in the depths of this wilderness are a few oases where grass and springs are found. In these spots the Indian will hide. The largest oasis is known as Grass Basin, at the foot of Butte Cache. It contains about 2,000 acres, and is surrounded by the most formidable portion of the Bad Lands. The difficulties and horrors of warfare in such a region may be imagined but not described. The battle-ground of the Wilderness was a parade ground compared with the Bad Lands.

CHAPTER XXV.

LIFE AT PINE RIDGE.

EXPERIENCE OF THE WAR CORRESPONDENTS—TRYING TO TAKE A PIC
TURE—THE SQUAW DANCES—"HAVE YOU GOT CHRIST IN THE
GUARD-HOUSE?"—FIRE-WATER WITH A VENGEANCE—THE INDIAN
BOYS—MARRIED LIFE.

Among the six newspaper correspondents who
remained at the Pine Ridge Agency all through the
troubles was Mr. Warren K. Moorehead, who thus
described in *The Philadelphia Press* some of his
experiences and observations:

"Some of the men spent many hours in the
tepees by the ruddy glow of the little fires, which
sent a dense smoke curling upward toward the
aperture at the top. The hours thus spent were
profitable ones, for with a good interpreter and
plenty of cigarettes and smoking tobacco, it was
not at all difficult to engage the Sioux in conversation. As the warrior related anecdotes of the chase,
or recounted his exploits in war, his face would light
up with animation, and he would pour into the ears
of his listeners stories of adventure that rivalled
even the dime novel hero. And when he showed

341

us scars here and there upon his body, proofs of his bravery, of which, by the way, he was very proud, we believed that he spoke the truth.

"One night we were in Keeps-the-Battle's lodge. There were present four women, three children, Interpreter Bartlett, and myself. The old chief, after considerable urging and the gift of two sacks of tobacco, related the following story:

"'When the ghost dance was at its height there suddenly appeared a runner from the agency at our camp on White Clay Creek with the startling news that the "walk-with-guns" (infantry) were coming. We held a big council all the next day to determine what should be done, and at the conclusion of our talk a large number of the people moved into the Bad Lands.

"'It was during the midst of a stormy debate between Red Cloud and Little Wound that a "heap-much-dress-young-man," who had arrived with the soldiers a few hours before, came riding into our

A CARLISLE STUDENT SPOILS A KODAK.

camp alone. Few white men had seen us dance the ghost dance, and, as our hearts *were bad*, we were in no humor to entertain strangers. This heap-much-dress-youth came into the centre of our grave circle, and, taking a small brown box from under his arm, pointed a little hole in the end of it toward the leading Sioux men. A slight click was heard, and the youth opened his box and started to draw out a thin board.

By permission of the *Illustrated American.*

OFFICERS IN THE FIELD AT FORT KEOGH.

" ' All of a sudden a boy who had been to Carlisle to school, sprang to his feet and cried: "Etoape wachee!" (he takes picture). Instantly several men drew clubs, and, running toward the heap-much-dress-lad, struck the box from his trembling hands and smashed it to fragments on the ground. Meanwhile the white boy ran to his horse, mounted in hot haste, and rode away for dear life, his hair standing on end with fright. The Sioux forgot the council and whooped and yelled with merriment.

" ' The white picture-taker dropped a letter from his pocket as he mounted. One of our educated boys read it to us. It said something about getting articles and pictures concerning the ghost dancers, and was signed by some New York man. Our people were very glad the young man did not secure a picture of us. I have done.'

" Many of the Sioux object to being photographed, as they are convinced no good can come of having

BAD MEDICINE.

their likeness in a white man's possession. They say that it is 'bad medicine,' and that the white man will work evil against the person whose picture he secures. Those of us who had kodaks resorted to strategy. We offered a sack of tobacco or cigarette to a blanketed man or woman, and as the Indian uncovered his or her face to light the cigarette we 'pressed the button.'

"One of the most interesting sights to the soldiers, and those unaccustomed to Indians, is the squaw dance. In the Omaha and green corn dances none but the men participate; but, as the women love dancing just as passionately as do the men, there has been, as long as the oldest Sioux can remember, at stated intervals, an opportunity afforded the squaws to dance.

"The several squaw gatherings, as viewed by myself, were held twice a week. Fifty or a hundred women (married) form a circle and seat themselves. Eight or ten others, armed with short sticks, gather about a large bass drum, and at a given signal strike up a monotonous tune, keeping time meanwhile with the instrument. The dancers arise in their places and elevate themselves upon their toes, dropping back upon their heels with each stroke upon the drum (the drummers strike in unison). There is no jumping about or moving from place to place as in the Omaha dance. Of course, this rapid motion of heels and toes soon tires the women; therefore the dance discontinues every five or ten minutes for a short space of time.

"After all have satisfied themselves, the delicacy of the season is served from several large kettles. It is almost needless to add that these kettles contain dog soup. All the Indian families keep from six to eight dogs. There is no distinction made between a fine Newfoundland or a hound, for one makes just as good soup as another. Out of each litter of pups several are selected and carefully fed for three or four weeks to fatten them well. Then the poor doggies are struck on the head and killed, and after being hastily washed in the creek and singed to remove the hair, are thrown in the pot. Blood, brains, and entrails, bones and meat, all combine to make a stew, palatable alone to the Sioux, disgusting to white men.

"One day the residents and visitors at Pine Ridge

RATIONS ISSUED AT PINE RIDGE AGENCY.

were startled by the arrival of a humbug Messiah. Many jokes were cracked at the expense of enterprising reporters, who rushed pell-mell to the agent's office to gaze on the Sioux Saviour. Prominent among those who strained muscle and eye in the eager throng was Cressey, of the Omaha *Bee.* Hearing of the capture of Messiah Hopkins by the Indian police while that individual was delivering 'his holy message' to the savages, Cressey rushed with great haste to Gen. Brooke's headquarters, and bursting into the room, much to the surprise of the officers there assembled, gasped out in stuttering accents:

"'Ha—, he—, ha—, have y—, y—, you got Christ in the guard-house?'

"Hopkins was a crank. Out of pity for him the General only confined him one day, and then sent an escort to conduct him to the railroad, from whence he was shipped back East to his people. As he left the agency a rough crowd gathered to see him off. Every one looked upon the man as a fanatic. Even the Sioux took no stock in his statements, although it has been said in many newspapers that the Indians regretted the departure of the Messiah. As the buggy sped away toward Rushville some wag proposed a yell for the Messiah, and willing throats of both soldiers and Indians gave vent to a mighty roar, which certainly must have been heard several miles distant.

A THIRSTY INDIAN DRINKS ACID.

"In spite of the laws against the sale of whisky or the bringing of it upon the reservation, there is not a little to be found in the tents of officers, so I am informed. The Sioux, sharp-witted as they are, keep an ever-watchful eye open for bottles and jugs. By way of illustration:

"The photographer from Omaha, Mr. Morledge,

brought a large quart flask filled with acid to develop the negatives he took.

"The fluid had a color similar to the cheap whisky sold in the West.

"One day George Beef Lights (who sang ghost dance songs for me and interpreted) came into the reporter's headquarters. Spying the flask he cried, 'Give me minnewahan.'

"'No, no,' I replied, 'it's bad, it's poison.' I was seated in a corner far off, reading, and before I could spring from my chair he had seized the flask and raised it to his lips.

"One swallow, a strangling sound, the jingling of broken glass as he dashed the bottle on the floor, and he ran out of the door yelling and coughing. We were convulsed with laughter, for it was very amusing to see the maddest Indian in Pine Ridge running around the yard, holding his stomach and shouting. The police came up to ascertain the trouble, and they laughed, too, when we told them. George never came to see me afterward, and I suppose he longs for my scalp, although really I had no part in the unfortunate affair.

"The bravest man in the employ of the Government, one whose duty as Marshal compels him to arrest desperate characters, both white and red, is George E. Bartlett. He was the first white man to visit No Water's camp on Wounded Knee Creek, and there arrest an Indian named Little, who had drawn a knife on Agent Royer. Bartlett was accompanied by several police, and by prompt pre-sentation of Winchesters secured his man without firing a shot.

"The Sioux boys and girls are especially interest-ing. Boys are the same the world over, and were you to approach the camps with your ears stopped so that you could not distinguish that a different language from your own was being spoken, you would believe you were in some Eastern village watching the gambols of the town lads. Boys play ball, shinney, run foot-races, and shoot at a mark for small prizes. Many a time have I put a nickel in a crotch of a bush to see them knock it out with their spears or shoot at it with their arrows. A few of them are good marksmen, but nearly always they miss the object shot at. A favorite trick with them is to throw the spear somewhat like a boomerang. It curves far to one side of the bush, then shoots sideways against the twigs, and by violently skaking them causes the five-cent piece to drop to the ground. It seemed to me that the double curves performed by the spear required more skill upon the part of the thrower than would a fair and square centre hit.

"The lads are full of fun. They appreciate kind-ness more than do the men. I had given them many small coins and tobacco, and they showed their gratitude by running after me in an enormous crowd whenever I approach the camp, crying, 'Muzza-ska, muzza-ska' (Money, money)!

"The missionaries and philanthropists from the

East are greatly shocked upon entering a tepee to see the women and children smoking. One portly gentleman from Philadelphia said to me :

"'Why, even the little girls cry for cigarettes. It is dreadful to think of the money raised by holy men and women East should be squandered by these degraded people for tobacco.' And the old man was right. The children actually cry for a smoke. I have seen little boys and girls barely four years of age begging for a cigarette. When it was given them already lighted they would suck away at it with remarkable bravery. The tears would roll down their cheeks and they would begin to get sick, but they would not throw away the 'weed' until it was smoked down to a short stub.

" The philanthropist would have been more deeply shocked could he have seen the treatment the barrels of clothing shipped to the Sioux receive—how the overcoats are sold for thirty cents or a dollar, the trousers and coat ditto. It is claimed that not one farmer or ranchman out of a hundred living within fifty miles of the agency ever buys clothes in town. He can get good ones for a mere trifle of the Indians after the quarterly 'missionary goods' come.

"Indian women age much more rapidly than white women. They are compelled to do much hard outside work, and consequently the furrows of age creep into their cheeks at an early period in their lives. The girl before marriage has a decidedly

easy time.   She receives callers just as do the
young ladies of civilization.   The youths vie with
each other in discoursing sweet strains upon the lover's flute near her father's lodge.   Admiring young
men bring presents, or lie in wait near her home to
speak to her words of love the moment that she appears.

'When marriage binds her to her husband there
comes about a complete change.   She associates
entirely with married women, and does not mingle
with former friends. She believes that her husband
should only assist her when she is unable to perform any task herself, and takes the same pride in
doing all the work that she possibly can that a white
woman does in keeping her home in order.   She
would no more think of permitting her husband to
do all the hard work than would the wife of to-day
expect her husband to take care of her house, or a
husband request his wife to help him at his office.

CHAPTER XXVI.

INDIANS AND SETTLERS.

The town and railroad station nearest to Pine Ridge is Rushville, Neb., which is about twenty miles away; a place of a 1,000 or more inhabitants. Mr. F. H. Carruth has given a picturesque account of it as it appeared to him in 1886 and of the semi-civilized Indians and the semi-savage white settlers.

"Rushville," he says, " was at this time a queer combination of Eastern and Western civilization. The town was about a year old, having been built when the Fremont, Elkhorn and Missouri Valley Railroad went through. The surrounding country had been partly settled with a few farmers longer, and the stockmen had been scattered throughout the region for a number of years. The land is comparatively level, the country between Gordon and Chadron being known as the Antelope Flats. Most of the town was on one street, which ran at right angles

353

to the railroad track and the law office of Judge
Trott, late of the Des Moines bar ; the liquor store
of Jim Sandoz, late of a Denver bar; the banking
house of Langham Brothers, late of Chicago; the
Niobrara Gold Mine (gambling establishment) of
Breckenridge Potter, late of St. Louis, and the First
Baptist Church, with the Rev. Mr. Cartright, late of
Brooklyn, as pastor, stood in pleasing and cheerful
proximity.   The blacksmith who shod our off mule
and got kicked over his anvil twice, and whose shop
stood next door to Mrs. Julia Grannett's millinery
store, informed me, in speaking of the gambling
house, which stood between the bank and the law-
yer's office, that you could lose your money in one
as readily as in the others ; indeed, he would prefer
to |take his chances in the gambling house, having
more confidence in the squareness of the game.   It
seemed that the able Judge Trott had been expelled
from the Des Moines bar, and that the sagacious
Langham Brothers lent money at the rate of 4 per
cent. a month; so perhaps the blacksmith was
right.

"There was, as I said, an interesting combination of
East and West in Rushville. The business men were
nearly all from the East—from 'the States,' at least,
which expression was used in its territorial sense,
notwithstanding that Nebraska had been a State for
years—but the stockmen and many of the farmers
were Western men of the most pronounced type.
Every man from outside the town—and they made

up probably three-quarters of those on the streets—
wore big, jingling Mexican spurs. Indeed, it is part
of the religion of every man connected with a Western stock ranch to never remove his spurs on any occasion whatever, with the possible exception of when
going to bed—and there are occasions in the life of
the gay and exuberant cowboy when the formality is
humorously omitted even at the time of retiring,
and the hotel landlord is confronted in the morning
with a hopeless tangle of spurs, cowboy and bed-
clothing. Besides their spurs the men also wore big
felt, or buckskin hats, with the wide leather bands
which are also peculiar to stockmen, and many of
them leather or goatskin chaparejos, or leggings.
The business men wore the ordinary attire observed
in any American city ; but it was considered among
them that some concession should be made to their
newly-made Western friends and patrons in the
matter of dress, so they hit upon the happy plan of
wearing the wide, heavy leather bands on their ordinary stiff or soft Eastern hats. To see a promising
young physician start out on his professional rounds
wearing a derby hat of the latest New York shape,
with a thick, embossed leather band two inches wide,
and fastened with a big silver buckle around it, is a
sight only occasionally afforded to mortals. I did
not see any one wearing a silk hat with leather
band, though it was gravely stated that Judge Trott
wore such an astonishing combination Sundays. So
far as we could learn, the Rev. Mr. Cartright, late

of Brooklyn, was the only man in town who still
held out against this custom.   Indeed, it was not
strictly a local idea, as we found the same thing
obtained at other towns especially at Chadron and
Hay Springs.

"Besides the business houses there were, of
course, a number of residences scattered about on
the prairie near at hand, though, like other Western
towns, a much smaller number in proportion than
will be found in an Eastern village, owing to the
fact that so many of the business men are unmar-
ried.   There was a business-like air about the
place, though it was hard to tell exactly what kind
of business was going on.   Judging from appear-
ances only any one would have said that the leading
industry was the buying and shipping of buffalo
bones.   Across the railroad track there are great
heaps of buffalo, deer, elk and antelope bones,
which had been gathered in the surrounding country
and brought to town and sold to dealers, who shipped them to fertilizer factories to be ground up.   A
half-dozen freight cars were being loaded with them.
Among the piles were many magnificent elk antlers
and fine specimens of great, broad buffalo skulls,
some of them still retaining their black horns.   The
Antelope Flats were formerly favorite feeding
grounds of the buffalo before they were extermina-
ted by butchers and other hunters.

"Near the bone piles, and evidently thankful that
it was not in them, was a pet antelope, a young one,

and as beautiful as any gazelle ever dreamed of by poet. Indeed, it gave a poetical touch to the whole town, and toned down the incongruity of the hat-bands. It was in a yard in front of a real estate office, and was as tame as possible. The town dogs seemed to pay no attention to it, reserving their scowling looks and unfriendly glances for the many Sioux Indians who 'loafed' about the streets. These Indians were from the Pine Ridge, and are the truants who are now out in the Bad Lands de-fying that sanguinary institution known as the Uni-ted States Government. Most of them were genuine wild Indians, slightiy tamed by the use of cigarettes, and with the murderous eyes and cruel mouths of full-fledged cut-throats. However, they were per-fectly harmless at that time, and no one could watch their indolent motions without being impressed with the idea that so long as they were honestly treated and well fed that they would remain harmless, their very laziness under the soothing influence of a full stomach preventing their breaking out. They lounged about all over town, and lent picturesque-ness to the scene. They went a step further than the business men in their costume, and combined elements of the savage, the cowboy, the United States soldier, and the man of fashion. Some of them had succeeded in giving up everything of the savage except the backskin moccasins, with elk-hide soles and bright porcupine quill-work on the insteps and toes. The Sioux do not seem to rise to bead-

work like many other tribes of Indians. However
dirty or torn an Indian's clothes might be, or un-
combed his hair, or unwashed his face and hands,
there was invariably one thing about his make-up
in the cleanest and best possible condition—namely,
his Winchester, fifteen-shot, forty-five calibre rifle.
Why he needed a rifle at all, since there was no
game to kill, I do not know, but he is certainly finding it very handy from his own point of view, now
that he has 'gone out.' They were all very well
provided, too, with hardy little ponies, another thing
which they find convenient since they rebelled
against the great white father. But what struck the
observer the most forcibly about a great many of
them was their smoking cigarettes. A weak and
flimsy paper. cigarette seemed as out of place in
the mouth of a heartless old savage, who perhaps
went through the Minnesota massacre of 1862, and
killed his quota of women and children, as did the
cowhide band on the silk hat of the brilliant Judge
Trott. No one to have seen them would have believed that in four years they would be again on
the warpath, and once more killing women and
children. After observing the cigarettes I looked
about expecting to see a young buck come riding in
wearing a monocle screwed in one eye. But notwithstanding that they were peaceable, we found
throughout the whole country a vague, undefined
fear of an Indian outbreak. Little was heard of it
in the towns, but among the settlers in the country

it was everywhere. It is safe to say that there was
scarcely a settler along the whole reservation, from
Niobrara to Chadron, and beyond up into the Black
Hills, who did not have at least one modern repeating rifle in his house as bright and well-kept as the
Indians'. There was an uneasy, anxious feeling
everywhere. Women and children were seldom
left alone in the houses while the men were away
very far. The feeling seemed to be much like
that which a man would have in a cage of tame lions
or tigers—there were grave doubts as to the thoroughness of the taming. And with it all, I regret
to say, there was a decided lack of confidence in
the army, whether well-founded or not I will not pretend to say. And it seems that the settler's fears
were not unreasonable after all, now that the outbreak has taken place."

Although the moment there is a rumor of war, the
white people are quick to take alarm and to cry for
the army to come and protect them, in the piping
times of peace they have, or profess to have, only
contempt for their red neighbors. At the Brule
(Sioux) Agency at South Dakota, there is a ferry
across the Missouri River; a rowboat manned by a
veteran white settler. He has, relates Mr. L. E.
Quigg, who "interviewed" him not long ago, one
set phrase in which he speaks of the redskin. He
always uses it as if it were a single word, thus:
"Themdaminjuns!" And as he guides you along under the shadow of the steep bluffs that overlook the

water everywhere, he entertains you with stories of
the noble savage.

I use ter think they wern't no virtoo 't all in themdaminjuns, an' thet th' on'y way ter make 'em good

CHANGED HIS OPINION,

was with a gun. But I've sorter changed my 'pinion.
Onct in erwhile you kin ketch rale good fellers
'mongst 'em.   I saved one of 'em from drownin' a
couple o' weeks ergo, an' he was thet grateful he
offered me my choice between ten head o' ponies
an' his wife. He said I needn't feel no constraint
'bout takin' 'em, fer the Guv'ment 'ud give him
more ponies and he could make out ter find another
wife.   They looks at ponies an' women in the same
way, On'y the woman lasts longer an' stan's more
abuse.

"Then they was another good Injun I knowed
onct. He was a p'leece up ter Crow Creek. The
agents makes all ther good Injuns p'leecemen an'
dresses 'em up in blue coats, with big brass buttons
like a regular p'leeceman. A wild Injun up the
river had murdered another an' gone off in the prairies where the agent couldn't ketch him. So he
sent this good Injun fer him an' tole him ter be sure
an' ketch him. He was gone a couple o' days an'
nights an' when he come back he had three dead Injuns layin' acrost his pony. Pinting at one of 'em,
he says to the agent: 'You tell me get Lone Eagle.'
Then he poked at one of the dead with his gun, an'
give a sorter cheerful grunt. The agent was all

RED CLOUD.

struck of a heap. 'I didn't say to kill nobody!'
says he,

GET LONE EAGLE,

"'Ugh!' says the Injun. 'You say get Lone
Eagle. I get him. Get three, no carry more.'

"'More!' says the agent, turning pale. 'What
hev you bin doin' anyhow?'

"The Injun—his name was White Hawk—give
a grunt, a lurch in his saddle, and fell dead acrost
his pony. He was all shot ter pieces, but they went
up the valley a stretch, 'bout a hundred mile er
so, an' they foun' three more Injuns layin' in a gulch.
He was tole ter ketch Lone Eagle, an' he done it.

"Thet war a downright good Injun—they's no
denyin' it, but the most 'em is onery devils. I was
pullin' a man down here onct, a Wyoming man from
ther Big Horn Mountains. He were doin' some
guv-ment work. S'he, 'You got a fine lot er Injuns
down this way.' S'I, 'Think so?' S'he, 'Yes.'
S'I, 'Where did you come acrost 'em?' S'he,
'Over yonder.' S'I, thinkin' he was one o' them Injuns' Rights folks from Philadelphy, s'I: , Air you
stuck on Injuns?' S'he, 'Not by a dern sight.' S'I,
'Well, wot makes you think they're fine?' S'he
'Why, they're the best I ever saw.' S'he, 'They're
angels 'long er the Injuns up our way.' S'he, 'We
got jist the goldarndest lot er Injuns in the Big
Horn Mount'ns they is on earth.' S'he, 'I tuck a
a contrac' las' fall from ther Guv'ment ter put up
$80,000 wuth of houses fer 'em, an' you never see

nicer little houses than the ones I put up for them‑ daminjuns. They was warm an' tight an' roofed with shingles—better houses than half the white folks in the Territory's got. Well, sir, s'he, 'wot d'you s'pos them Injuns went an' done? They tuck an' stuck their teepees 'longsider my houses, $80.000 wuth, min' ye, an' when winter sot in they tore down every single solitary house an' burnt it up fer kindlin' ! They wasn't one of 'em lef' stand‑ in' by New Years.' "

The ferryman dropped his oars, and laughed till he made the boat bob up and down like a float on a fishing line. " Them Injuns' Rights folks," he con‑

THEM INDIANS' RIGHTS FOLKS IN PHILADELPHY.

tinued, cutting off a fresh quid of tobacco and stow‑ ing it away in his cheek, " down there to Philadel‑ phy, means all right, but they don't know. They got ther noshun thet our people is alers robbin' the pore Injun, an' every time we suggests anything they sets up a howl, thinkin', 'ecause it comes from us, thet it must be bad. I jist wish they'd come out here an' stay awhile. They'd change their idees 'bout how ter manage the Injun, almighty quick. I wish they could see wot you're goin' ter see to-day. You've hit on one o' ther show-days. I'd tell you erbout it, on'y I don't wanter spile yer fun. When you come back you won't blame us fer thinkin' thet the best Injuns is the dead ones. I don't objeck ter their havin' their rights, but ez things is now, they've got a blame sight more rights 'n white people.

They's 1,200 of 'em at thet Agency. It costs $150,-
000 a year ter keep 'em in food and clothes. The
Guv'ment pays $4.75 apiece fer blankets ; an' ez
soon's they gets 'em they comes right straight over
ter Chamberlain an' sells 'em for a dollar. They
sells everything they get—ponies, clothes, hats, an'
then lies 'bout it ter the agent an' begs or steals
more."

"Are they dangerous?" I asked. That is, are
they liable to break out?"

" They're afeared. They's the wust cowards you
ever see. One night White Ghost come down ther
river ter Chamberlain an' went ter see a man wot
was shippin' cattle acrost the Reservation. The
cattle had been eatin' prairie grass along ther trail,
an' he wanted money fer it. He said ef he didn't git
ther money, he'd send his young men an' take ther
cattle.

" ' Hev you many wagons to your camp, Injun?'
says the rancher.

" 'Heap wagon, heap pony, heap gun,' says
White Ghost.

" 'You'll need 'em all, Injun,' says the rancher.
'Ef you come around botherin' my cattle, be sure
ter fetch yer wagons erlong.'

" 'How?' said White Ghost, meanin' 'wot fer?'

" 'Ter cart off the bodies of yer young men, Injun,' says the rancher.

" White Ghost tuck one o' them quick looks, an',
s'he, 'Who speaks?'"

"'Me!' says the rancher. 'I'm a big warrior, Injun. My name's Big Gun Thet Allers Kills, an' I fit in the war of ther Rebellion. Hev you heerd 'bout that war, Injun?'

"White Ghost grunted, an' the rancher says, s'he, 'Well, I was there, Injun,' s'he, 'an' I killed 926 men in one day.'

"White Ghost humped his shoulders, drored his blanket all aroun' him, and says, s'he, 'Ugh!' s'he, an' he made a break fer the door. They wasn't no harm come to them cattle!"

CHAPTER XXVII.

RED CLOUD,

A LEADER OF THE HOSTILE INDIANS—HIS TREACHEROUS NATURE—RO-
MANTIC STORY OF HIS EARLY YEARS—A MISSION TEACHER'S AC-
COUNT OF HIM—HIS DECEITFUL WORDS TO A VISITOR, AND HIS
LETTER TO A FRIEND,

One of the most famous and most hostile of the
Sioux chiefs is Red Cloud. He has for many years
been among the most influential men in the whole
nation, and his influence has invariably been bad.
He has visited the East and talked with the President at Washington. More than most of his comrades he realizes the power of the Government and
the impossibility of successfully resisting it. Yet he
has been a most persistent instigator of outbreaks
and massacres, and has played a leading part in
the troubles of 1890-91. The insurrections of 1882
and 1884 were due entirely to him.

At the same time he has managed to keep a pretty good reputation. He is crafty, versatile, and able
to assume an air of the most sanctimonious devout-
ness, even while he is plotting deviltry. His bland
and suave manners won him many friends at Wash-

ington, and he has generally been regarded as a "good" Indian, loyal and peace-loving. And whenever he has fomented an outbreak, he has taken care to keep in the background, and let some-one else catch the blame. Says a young lady who was brought up at one of the Sioux agencies: "Red Cloud, Spotted Tail, Man-Afraid of His Horses and many others have held me on their knees while the 'great talks' with my father transpired. All would with grave silence sit and smoke, the tomahawk pipe being handed from one to the other, without the utterance of a word, for perhaps an hour. Then a short harangue, a hand-shake all around, a pat on my curly head, regards to 'Capin's squaw, (my mother), and they stalked solemnly away. Old Spotted Tail had named me 'Spuss-Kerriwe' (Curly Head), and Spusskerriwe I have remained with them to this day. I have little doubt that Red Cloud would, if occasion offered, as cheerfully take a scalp from Spusskerriwe's head as of old he patted it while I sat on his knees. At least, I do not feel any curiosity to prove or disprove the proposition."

A sister of Red Cloud lives at Chattanooga, Tenn., and she tells this story of his earlier career: When but three years old he was stolen from his parents, who then resided in Wisconsin on an Indian reservation in the northern part of the State, and all track of him was lost for eighteen years, when he was found among the red men, having been brought up by them. He had forgotten his own name, but remembered that of his father and his dogs, and his identification was complete. He remained with his family a few weeks, speaking English imperfectly, but French fluently. But all his sympathies were with his adopted tribe, and he rejoined the Sioux to the grief of his parents, and brothers and sisters, and has since then been to all intents and purposes a semi-savage.

Miss Sickels, a prominent mission teacher, among the Sioux has known Red Cloud well for years, and this is her account of him :

"Across from the boarding-school of the Pine Ridge Agency, on the opposite ridge, separated by the hollow of the creek, is a two-story frame house. surrounded by some desolate-looking tepees, a few log buildings and sweat-houses. Wagons and wood-

RED CLOUD'S HOUSE.

piles complete the settlement. This is Red Cloud's camp, and the largest house is his residence—the only two-story dwelling at the agency. It was built for Red Cloud to distinguish him from the others of his band. An interview with the old man would furnish the information that he was 'the leader of his people and always wanted them to do good ways. He always wanted to work for the schools and for farms and for the Great father. He did not want his people to have any trouble. He had stopped the ghost-dance among them. They had been hungry, but he hoped everything would be all right now. He

wanted his people to do good ways.' He might
vary it a little, but this is about what he would say
to you, 'slowly and in a solemn and impressive
manner.

"For confirmation of this, see the reports in the
newspapers. They are really a correct statement
of the interviews. This is Red Cloud's formula for
interviews. It is a good idea to believe people—

INTERIOR OF RED CLOUD'S HOUSE.

when you can—but sometimes confidence is ex-
tremely hazardous, and Red Cloud's deeds and
words remind one of what the man said about his
new dictionary when he had tried to read it : 'Very
interesting, but somehow it didn't seem to hang together.' But though the deeds and words do not
seem to hang together, like the dictionary, there is
a purpose running through, which may be traced by

those initiated and familiar with the plan. The old man seems to have threaded himself in and out among all of the plots and disturbances of which I have been able to learn anything. I do not have to mention his name nor ask any leading questions. It is only necessary to take the part of listener to the casual conversations going on around me. I know from personal experience that the trouble of 1881 and 1884 was instigated solely by him in his opposition to the efforts made for progress. The threatened outbreak of 1884 had its origin in his cry of 'fraud—the teachers were getting the children into the school and making them work so as to get money out of them.' When he could not get the support of the Sioux, most of whom despise him, he tried to involve the Cheyennes. When the agent withdrew the rations and the Cheyennes decided to give their support to the school, he wrote to his Eastern sympathizers that he was 'the leader of his people and the agent was defrauding them out of their rations.'

"This, with little variation, is the real inside history of most of the trouble there has ever been at Pine Ridge Agency, and there must be some special reason why it is now, in January, 1891, the centre of hostilities. There is often a great discrepancy between the 'true inwardness' of a thing and its outward appearance.

"Having had experience and personal knowledge of Red Cloud, I watched closely to see what connection he may have had with this present affair.

"In Washington I met a soldier from Fort Wash-akie, who told me that some half breeds of the name of Genneiss had been there among the ghost-dancers this Summer, and that there was fear of an outbreak at that place. This was significant, for the reason that the Genneisses are among the most active of Red Cloud's 'missionaries.'

RED CLOUD A MISCHIEF-MAKER.

"On the train coming from Chicago I met Judge Morris, a former acquaintance, who told me that a year or two ago the Indians had come down to Chadron from Pine Ridge to celebrate the Fourth of July with an Omaha dance. In the procession, composed of Indians and settlers, that accompanied the performance, Red Cloud insisted upon riding in the carriage that preceded the Mayor and other dignitaries. He was so threatening in his manner when they hesitated that they yielded to his demands, 'fearing an outbreak.' He made a speech, saying that the land belonged to him and his people, and the time would come when they would get it back. He has a 'secretary,' and uses his assumed power among the Indians to intimidate the whites and *vice versa*.

"When I reached the agency they told me that Jack Red Cloud had been the leader in the ghost dances and in the attack that led to the appeal for troops; but that now he had 'reformed' and was an active scout, working for the Government. I discovered that by a strange coincidence the reports that he brought were not borne out by facts. Red Cloud became very pious and solicitous for the welfare of 'his people,' frequenting the office constantly. An officer told me that he said, 'Why do you discuss the plans so freely before Red Cloud?' He received the answer: 'He doesn't know what I say:' but glancing suddenly at the old rascal's face, I could see by the twinkle in his eye that he had understood.

"On the reservation the seat of the greatest trouble proved to be at Wounded Knee. Here near ly every one was a relative of Red Cloud. Teachers told me that when they taught at that camp they felt that they were in danger most of the, and time had constant annoyances; but when they taught at Little Wound's camp they felt the protection of Little Wound's influence. When I went to see Little Wound he told me that Red Cloud had been getting the people into bad ways, and when folks found it out he did not want to be blamed for it, so he said it was Little Wound who had done it. This is probably the truth, and will be readily believed by all who are acquainted with the two men.

"Two ladies from a neighboring settlement spent the day at the agency. I was busily writing in the room where they sat, discussing the times. As seemed to be inevitable in all of the accounts, the name of Red Cloud was brought in. One was saying: 'A half-breed stopped at my house yesterday afternoon. He said something about Red Cloud that I could not make out ; but I caught the words, 'people—agency—sleep—then Red Cloud'—and he grinned and drew his fingers across his throat.' Major Sword and Captain Fast Horse, the progressive leaders of the Indian police force, came to see me. During the interview they told me that 'Red Cloud always tried to work against having good ways for the people, and would do different from what the other Indians wanted him to do, and he made trouble for them.'"

At the same time this consummate red rascal would talk in the most guileless and innocent manner. To a visitor in the latter part of November, 1890, he said that the soldiers had come again to burn his house, which is a good two-story frame building, the same as Crook did fifteen years ago at the old Red Cloud Agency ; that he did not want to fight, but would if pressed. On entering the camp the first thing noticeable was the fact that there were nearly 400 war ponies in his large corral, being fed and kept ready for instant use instead of being turned out to graze. On being asked why he did not turn the ponies out, he replied, that he was afraid the soldiers would steal them ! Then he sat down and wrote as follows to a white gentleman at Omaha, who was interested in him, and had written to him about the troubles : " My friend, your letter of November 19th, is just received, and in reply would say that the soldiers are here, but I don't know what they are here for. I have spoken to my people and told them I don't want to have any trouble with the soldiers and white people living near here. About fifteen years ago General Crook burnt my house near where Fort Robinson now is, then I was willing to fight. It looks the same way now, but I don't want to have any trouble with the soldiers or white people, and will not fight unless I have to. I am too old now to make war against the whites, and my white friends here have advised me against war, and I shall take their advice. My mind is too weak to say a great deal. We have a great many schools out in the different camps, and if we go to war what will become of our schools and children?" He also wrote to a gentleman in New York, laying the blame for all the trouble entirely upon the whites. His Indians, he said, had been engaged in the ghost-dance, but it would soon have died out but for the War Department's action. One morning the Indians awoke to find the agency surrounded by soldiers. Many of the braves ran away but were followed by soldiers. The troops, Red Cloud, said, committed many depredations on the Indians at Rosebud Agency, and pillaged their villages. The braves lost their possessions and many of them the accumulations of years. "I cannot imagine what all this was done for," wrote Red Cloud, "as my people had done nothing to create any alarm among the whites. My heart is sad, but I still have a little hope for my people."

CHAPTER XXVIII.

THE LEADERS OF THE SIOUX.

LITTLE WOUND AND HIS LIEUTENANTS—YELLOW BEAR—YOUNG-MAN-AFRAID-OF-HIS HORSES—OTTI, THE SHOSHONE—HIGH BEAR—AMERICAN HORSE—JOHN GRASS, THE INDIAN JUDGE—GALL, THE GREATEST OF THE SIOUX WARRIORS AND GENERALS—SPOTTED TAIL'S ELOQUENT SPEECH.

One of the foremost chiefs in the recent troubles was Little Wound, who had for his lieutenants Broken Arm, Yellow Bear, and Yellow Hair. Little Wound is about 55 years old, a fine looking man, six feet tall, straight as an arrow, a most daring warrior, brave and straight forward himself, and appreciative of those qualities in others. He has always been on the side of peace and order and. has been a leader of the most progressive and industrious Indians. His children were the best scholars in the agency school and his followers dwelt in neat cabins and cultivated fine gardens. He often spoke to the school children and to other Indians, urging them to learn how to work and how " to make good things like what the white man has." In the threatened outbreak in 1884 he was the chief actor

376

in defending the whites and restraining the Indians from hostility.

GOOD REASONS FOR THE REBELLION OF 1890.

When Little Wound joined the disaffected Indians in 1890, the event was regarded as most significant. It was known that he would not adopt such a course except under the strongest possible provocation, and it was felt that his conduct made the situation most serious. All possible efforts were made to pacify him and win him back. Foremost among those who made such an appeal to him was Miss E. C. Sickels, the teacher whose school the chief's children had attended. Moreover when the notorious Red Cloud had some years before attempted to murder Miss Sickels and her companions, Little Wound interfered and saved her life. When Miss Sickels asked him why he had rebelled, he replied that he was very sorry and reluctant to do so, for he had been a good friend to white men all his life. But now his people were hungry. They did not get more money when the land was gone. They get 1,000,000 pounds less beef and the crops had not been good. He would like to have his men have farms and have their own houses and keep them and stay in their own homes. He was a church man (Episcopalian) and tried to do good for his people. But now they were hungry and sick. Bad men were stealing his property. He had heard about the Indian Messiah and the Ghost Dance, and wanted to see if it was true and if this new religion would help the Indians.

To another visitor Little Wound said that he had given up hope of any good in this world. He did not expect that the Indian Messiah would help his people in this life but, he said, "it will be better for us when we go to the Spirit Land." "What do you think," he was asked, "the Indian should do to better his condition?" "The only way," said Little Wound, "he can get anything is by work, but he can't get any money by working because there is no one here who has money to pay for work. If things keep on as they are now my people will all starve to death, they will all die paupers." He added that he would stop the Ghost Dances among his followers whenever General Miles or the agent said so; and he kept his word.

Yellow Bear said: "All white men think we are all bad." But he used his influence also to aid his chief, Little Wound, in restraining the Indians from hostility and in checking the Ghost Dances.

Young-Man-Afraid-of-His-Horses is one of the ablest of the Sioux chiefs, and he too has generally been friendly to the white men and progressive. His name really means not that he is afraid of his horses but that he is careful of them, afraid, that is, of their being hurt or stolen.

Otti, chief of the Shoshones, is a man of great importance among the Indians. He is wise in council, and his advice is always considered good by the Indians. He has always been slow to break peace with the white men, but once on the war-path has

CHIEF JOHN GRASS.

been one of the most dangerous of all his tribe. He is more than 70 years old, but looks and acts like a man of 50. His following, however, does not include more than 500 warriors.

High Bear, chief of the Ogallallas, comes from the Wood Mountain country in the far north. He is about 50 years and is a most dangerous enemy.

American Horse is a pretty mean Indian, greatly resembling his friend Red Cloud. He has been well described as a coward, a liar, a braggart, ambitious and deceitful both to the reds and the whites. His band is a small one, numbering only 15 lodges. But he has always tried to make the Indians believe that he was backed up by the agent and the troops, and he has tried to make the agent believe that he had the whole Indian race at his back.

JOHN GRASS AN INTELLECTUAL GIANT.

A couple of years ago the Hon. Charles Foster, chaiman of the Sioux Commission said : " At Standing Rock, we met a man whose strong sense would be conceded anywhere, and who struck me as an intellectual giant in comparison with other Indians. He is known to the white men as John Grass and to the Indians as Charging Bear, and by reason of his superior mind is the most prominent on the reservation. He could not be the leader he is, however, were he not known also to be brave. His speech in answer to the proposition we submitted to his tribe for a possession of part of their territory was by far the ablest we heard, by any chief of any following at all, addressed to us. His speech shows that he understood the treaties and acts of Congress with a regard to detail beyond the grasp of most Indians." This chief is the presiding judge of the Court of Indian offenses, being himself head chief of the Black Feet Sioux. There are few Indians now living who have done more than he for the best interests of their race.

CHIEF GALL, COMMANDER OF THE CUSTER MASSACRE,

A friend of John Grass and associate Judge of his Court, is Chief Gall, the head of the Unk-pa-pa Sioux and leader of the progressive element in that band. Years ago he was a friend and comrade of Sitting Bull, but after the Custer massacre on the Little Big Horn, there was a bitter rivalry between them. Gall was the actual commander of the Indians in the field at that battle, Sitting Bull remaining in his tent, " making medicine," and conducting the outlandish incantations that were supposed to control the fortunes of the day. After the battle Gall wanted to make peace with the whites and in this desire he was supported by most of the leading warriors. Sitting Bull on the contrary was for holding out and retreating into Canada, and in this he was supported by nearly all the medicine. men. These opposing policies split the band into two factions, and the result was that Gall, with Crow King and many other of the ablest fighting men surrendered long before Sitting Bull did. Indeed it was their secession that forced Sitting Bull into subjection.

Gall is an uncommonly brave man and is a General as well as a soldier. His ability to handle effectively a large force of Indians in the field is acknowledged by all military authorities who know him. He has always retained his native dignity and in all his negotiations, has acted with the utmost courtesy and decorum. He is a man of unquestioned honesty. His love for his people is sincere. He has never masqueraded as a patriot merely to serve selfish ends.

The sentiments of the progressive element among the Indians toward the whites and toward civilization was eloquently expressed by the famous Sioux chief, Spotted Tail, now dead, in his address to a Government Commission in 1877. He said:

" My friends, your people have both intellect and heart; you use these to consider in what way you can do the best to live. My people, who are here before you, are precisely the same. I see that my friends before me are men of age and dignity, and men of that kind have good judgment, and consider well what they do. I infer from that, that you are here to consider what shall be good for my people for a long time to come. I think each of you has selected somewhere a good piece of land for himself with the intention to live on it, that he may there raise his children. My people are not different. We also live upon the earth and upon things that come to them from above. We have the same thoughts and desires in that respect that the white

people have.   This is the country where they were
born, where they have acquired all their property,
their children and their horses.   You have come
here to buy this country of us; and it would be
well if you would come with the goods you propose
to give us, and to put them out of your hand so we
can see the good price you propose to pay for it.
Then our hearts would be glad.

My friends when you go back to the Great Father,
I want you to tell him to send us goods; send us
yokes and oxen, and give us wagons so we can earn
money by hauling goods from the railroads.   This
seems to be a very hard day; half of our country
is at war, and we have come upon very difficult
times.   This war did not spring up here in our land.
It was brought upon us by the children of the Great
Father, who came to take our land from us without
price, and who do a great many evil things, the Great
Father and his children are to blame for this trouble.
We have here a storehouse to hold our provisions,
but the Great Father sends us very little provisions
to put into our storehouse, and when our people become displeased with our provisions and have gone
north to hunt, the children of the Great Father are
fighting them.   It has been our wish to live here
peaceably, but the Great Father has filled it with
soldiers who think only of our death.   Some of our
people who have gone from here in order that they
may have a change, and others who have gone north
to hunt, have been attacked by the soldiers from

other directions; and now, when they are willing to come back, the soldiers stand between them and keep them from coming home. It seems to me there is a better way than this. When people come to trouble it is better for both parties to come together without arms, talk it over, and find some peaceful way to settle."

CHAPTER XXIX.

THE BEGINNING OF WAR.

DAKOTA SETTLERS PANIC-STRICKEN—GENERAL MILES ON THE SITUA-
TION—PINE RIDGE REGARDED AS THE FATAL POINT—ROSEBUD
INDIANS BREAK LOOSE—TROOPS HURRIED TO THE SCENE—A COAL
MINE FOR A FORT—A NIGHT'S ALARM—A MUCH-SCARED SAD-
DLER—GOVERNOR MELLETTE'S LETTER.

About the middle of November, 1890, it became
evident to everybody that there was serious trouble
ahead. The Indians had massed themselves together in a menacing attitude, and threatened violence unless their wrongs were redressed. The authorities did not deny the existence of the wrongs,
but demanded the entire submission of the Indians
as an indispensable preliminary to any discussion
of the matter. As for the settlers in the Dakotas
and elsewhere near the reservations, they became
abjectly panic-stricken. They huddled together in
mass-meetings and clamored wildly for protection,
for arms, for troops, for cannon, for the whole military strength of the nation. They looked for a repetition of the horrors of the first Sioux war, and
were alarmed beyond description. At Mandan,
North Dakota, the panic reached its height. It was

386

rumored that the Indians were about to sack and
burn the town and massacre the inhabitants. Settlers from all about moved in to the city for shelter,
and the people of the city held mass-meetings, and
asked for arms and ammunition. Resolutions were
adopted calling on the President and Secretary of
War to protect them. All sorts of stories were
afloat, and all found ready credence. One evening,
it was said, two Indians at Mandan went into a hard-
ware store and called for ammunition. The store-
keeper asked what they wanted it for, and they said
to shoot white men, and they drew imaginary scalp-
ing-knives around their heads. A settler named
Ardrom came from ten miles out of town and stated
that six Indians camped near his place that morning. He told them to be careful of fire. They
told him to mind his own business, and ominously
tapped their guns, showed their ammunition, and
drew their fingers about the tops of their heads. At
Bismarck, too, a reign of terror prevailed, and people gravely talked of the probability of that city being destroyed by the Sioux.

MILITARY PRECAUTIONS.

Gen. Ruger, at St. Paul, and Gen. Miles, at Chicago, were watchful, but did not share in the panic
of the people. Orders were issued for the troops
at Fort Yates and Fort Lincoln to keep in readiness
for marching at short notice. The seven companies
at Cheyenne, Wyoming, received similar orders, and
so did those at Fort Robinson, Nebraska. Gen.

Miles regarded Pine Ridge as the most threatened point. On November 18th four companies of infantry were started from Omaha for Pine Ridge, and troops were also ordered thither from Fort McKinney, Fort Robinson, and Fort Niobrara. Gen. Miles now spoke out plainly and admitted that the Indians had got beyond control of the agents. "Discontent," he said, "has been growing among them for six months. The causes are numerous. First was the total failure of their crops this year. A good many of them put in crops and worked industriously, and were greatly discouraged when they failed, as they did utterly in some districts. Then the Government cut down their rations, and the Appropriation Bill was passed so late that what supplies they received came unusually late. A good many of them have been on the verge of starvation. They have seen the whites suffering, too, and in many cases abandoning their farms."

The alarm at Mandan began, after a few days, to subside. Army officers laughed it out of existence. One of them said that the place was no more in danger than was St. Paul. "The Indians located nearest to Mandan are about thirty-five miles away on the Cannon Ball River. They are thrifty, industrious, peaceable people who have taken up claims built huts and houses, own cattle, ponies, and wagons, and are in good circumstances. They are Christianized Indians, having no faith in aborigina superstitions and disliking this new Messiah craze

for they say that it interferes with the progress of
the people. I found that there was nothing having
the appearance of war or indicative of war in this
Messianic belief. The Indians say that the whites
are to be destroyed, but by the Christ alone and
without aid from the red men." At Yankton, also,
people kept their confidence. At Pierre there was
no panic. At Jamestown some anxiety was felt.

But troops continued to press on to Pine Ridge,
sure that there the trouble would be most serious.
On November 19th there were rumors of fighting,
which were not, however, confirmed. Rushville was
thronged with refugees from Pine Ridge, both whites
and Indians. Gen. Brooke left Omaha for the
Pine Ridge agency. Gen. Miles hoped to be
able to cope with the hostile Indians. "The dis-

LOCATION AND NUMBER OF HOSTILES.

affected camps, scattered over several hundred miles
of territory," he said, "aggregate in round numbers
6,000 warriors. The troops scattered over this
extensive territory number about 6,000, and not
more than 1,500 of this number are effective
mounted troops."

From Pine Ridge came this message on Novem-
ber 20th: "The dancing Indians have the agency
and the surrounding country in a state of terror.
The ghost dances under the lead of Little Wound,
Six Feathers, and other chiefs are still going on at
Wounded Knee Creek, White Clay, and Medicine
Root. There are 600 of the painted redskins

dancing this afternoon at White Clay, ten miles out
from the agency, and they have their guns strapped
to their backs as they dance.

"This morning a large band of Indians left Rosebud Agency and headed this way. It is within the
bounds of possibility that the dancing Indians may
consolidate their forces at Wounded Knee, and in
that case a fight may be expected at any moment.
Medicine Root, the furthest point from the agency
where the dancing is going on, is thirty miles away,
Wounded Knee is fifteen, and Porcupine twenty-
five.

"Gen. Brooke, who is in command of the troops
which arrived this morning, held a long consultation
during the forenoon with Indian Agent Royer and
Special Indian Agent Cooper. It is probable that
with the force at hand no attempt will be made to
stop the dancing at present. Both the Indian
agents said at the conclusion of the interview that
the situation was certainly grave. They confirmed
the reports of armed Indians dancing at different
points, and said that parties of them were probably
moving about the reservation. Several days will be
passed by the troops and agents in making a study
of all the phases of the excitement, but until troops
are here in greater force the reds will not be mo-
lested.

"The Indians at all the four points mentioned are
dancing and telling stories of having seen and talked
with the Messiah.

"The wives and children of all the traders and other whites about the agency have left for the safer points along the railroad, and the men here are prepared for the worst.

"Three companies of the Ninth Cavalry (colored) from Fort Robinson and five companies of infantry from Omaha marched in this morning and camped. Special Indian Agent Cooper, who has been among the Cheyennes pacifying them, came in yesterday and is working in co-operation with Agent Royer. The troops are under command of Gen. Brooke, who arrived with them this morning. Several more companies are expected to-night or to-morrow from Fort Niobrara, Fort Meade, and Fort McKinney. With their help it is thought that the Indians can be held in check and controlled. They have been beyond all restraint for some time since. The ghost dance craze has driven No Water, Little Wound, and Six Feathers so far that they have openly defied the agent and the Indian police.

A PANIC AND ALMOST A MASSACRE.

"When the Indians came in last week (Wednesday) to draw their rations of beef the agency people were thoroughly alarmed. The authority of the Indian police was entirely ignored. Little Wound used so many threats and grew so troublesome that Thunder Bear and one or two of the police took him in charge and started with him for the guardhouse. An uprising of the ghost-dancing Indians was narrowly avoided. Knives were drawn and the disaffected reds began to call to each other to set fire to the building, as the whites were in their power. Little Wound was surrounded and rescued by his friends.

"Within the last two weeks the agent and a posse of police were compelled to leave the vicinity of the ghost dance at the point of a lot of Winchester rifles in the hands of No Water and Little Wound's men. What effect the arrival of the soldiers will have on the Indians cannot be told. When the news that they were coming reached the agency some one informed the boys and girls in the Indian school, and almost created a stampede. The Indian children are afraid of troops, and it was only with the greatest difficulty that many of them could be prevented from leaving the building and bolting to the various camps of their friends and relatives."

Rumors went out that the Two Kettle Sioux were joining the hostiles, and Capt. Norville hurried to their settlement on Bad River to see about it. They positively denied to him that they were disloyal. Crow Eagle and Hump Rib, the two head men of the band, told the Captain that emissaries had visited them from the Cherry Creek Indians, and one evening, while they were having a pleasant little dance, one of Big Foot's men came and addressed them and told them about the new Christ, and how he was going to lead the Indians to happiness and destroy the whites. He said they knew this was going to happen, and urged them to come

over to the Cheyenne River and join with them in
their ghost dances, but they told him they would
not not go, and neither had they been there. They
told the Captain they wished he would have it said
in the Pierre papers that they were not going to
join the new Messiah craze. Further, they stated
that within the past few days several of the hostiles
had appeared among them, making threats that if
they did not join them enough force would be sent
against them to at once massacre the Two Kettle
tribe without warning. These Indians stood in
great fear of the hostiles, and said they were going
into hiding immediately, until the Great Father sent
his soldiers to protect them. The Captain also
learned that White Buffalo, a son of Sitting Bull,
who was with the Two Kettle band, had recently
had his star taken from him because he would not
make the arrest of an Indian Messiah agent, who
was an old bosom friend of his. He sent word to
his father, stating that he was under arrest because
he was a son of Sitting Bull.

A COAL MINE AS A FORT.

A curious feature at this stage of the troubles
was reported from Mandan. The people of that
place were so fearful of attack that they fitted up a
big coal mine as a place of retreat. They stocked
it with provisions and ammunition, and for many
days were ready to flee into its impregnable recesses at the first onset of the dreaded Sioux

Late in the evening of November 23d, the Pine

Ridge Agency had a taste of an Indian scare. While a party of gentlemen were talking with Agent Royer, in front of his house, they were startled by a weird, unearthly howl from away across the creek, where Jack Red Cloud's men were encamped. It was a loud, piercing cry that sounded like the last long howl of a drunken cowboy. Then it was taken up and answered from two or three points along the hills to the north. That was enough. The Indian police asleep in the office were routed out in breathless haste. Hatless and bootless they darted out and hurried off into the hollow of the creek in the direction of the yelling. Every white man in the agency who was awake heard the yells with a shiver. Others who were not awake were routed from their beds and, loading themselves with pistols and shot-guns, hurried toward the agency buildings.

The yelling was echoed back and forth through the Indian camp for five or ten minutes, then stopped as suddenly as it began. In a few minutes the police came in with a Sioux in white man's clothes, but whether he had been doing the howling could not be determined. The scare plainly showed the intense strain upon the people there. It was only a little scare, but it plainly showed that the slightest possible row or shooting scrape of any kind might lead to a fight.

SAW THE MESSIAH.

At Standing Rock Agency, Mr. Stewart, the

agency saddler, while out buggy riding visited the Indian camp, four miles from town, and saw the Indians perform the Messiah dance. The Indians were all nearly naked and painted hideously. They gathered around Stewart, who was badly frightened at their threats. One Indian pointed toward the blazing sun, shaking Stewart with the other hand and saying: "See! See! There he is now. The Indian Messiah is coming now. See! See!" Stewart was compelled to look at the sun, and when he acknowledged he saw the Messiah the Indians seemed greatly pleased. Stewart was then released, and returned to the agency as fast as his horses would bring him.

Two Indian scouts were sent from Fort Yates to Sitting Bull's camp to see the state of affairs in that direction. Being known to Bull as military scouts, they were at once suspected as spies and were treated harshly by Bull and others. Bull asked them their business out there. They said they were after two deserters from the post, which, of course, Bull knew to be untrue. Bull told them he understood there were 2,000 soldiers coming to take him and his property. "But," said he, "I have runners coming and going every day, and know everything that is going on there, and as soon as these soldiers come I will take my family and ponies and those that will follow me and leave here, and they will not get me.'

Continuing, he said to the scouts:

"You see we have abandoned the white men's houses and are living in our native tepees, and will not return to the houses nor to the agency."

The supposition was that if Bull heard of any serious trouble at the lower agency, or if the military attempted to take him, he would at once break camp on the Grand River and join the hostiles at the lower agencies, thereby declaring war against the Government. Bull's son-in-law, when questioned as to whether or not Bull was coming in, said: "No; he is never coming until the military overpower him and make him."

The view taken of the situation at this time by Governor Mellette, of South Dakota, may be seen from the following letter which he sent on November 26th to Gen. Miles:

"Scotty Phillips, who has a thousand head of cattle and lives at the mouth of the Grand Stone Butte Creek, eighty miles up Bad River, with an Indian family, and Waldron, the cattleman, seven miles this side of Phillips, left their places at 2 P. M. yesterday to bring me intelligence. Phillips is a very cool, courageous man, was a good scout through the Sioux trouble of 1875–76, and Cheyenne troubles of 1879. He is a reliable man of nerve, good judgment, and good character. He reports that he was never afraid of Indians before, and thinks there will be an uprising very soon, and bases his belief as follows: Eight days ago five lodges, containing twelve bucks, armed with Winchesters and laden

YOUNG-MAN-AFRAID-OF-HIS-HORSES.

with ammunition, camped at his house going from Rosebud to a large camp which is formed on White River, at the mouth of Pass Creek. He talked with them an hour. They were surly and defiant in manner; one said he had seen the time when he used to beat out the brains of children and drink women's blood, and that the time was coming when they would do it again. He said Phillips was raising horses for Indians to ride; that the country was just as good now as in buffalo time, as there were plenty of cattle in it. Phillips knew these Indians well, Yellow Thigh being their leader.

"White Field, a settler at Mouth Pass Creek on White River, had his house broken open by the Indians and all his horses and goods stolen about ten days ago. Phillips in the last few days has had twenty cattle killed by the Indians and Waldron seven that they know of. Three half-breeds from White River stopped at Phillips' house night before last and said they expected to find the settlements destroyed when they got home. The threats are against the half-breeds and all Indians who won't join the ghost dance. Phillips says everybody who has been among the Indians any length of time, without exception, says that there is going to be an uprising, and that very quick. The Pass Creek dance has been running for a month. Phillips and Waldron say it is Short Bull's headquarters, and they think it is a point fixed for concentration for all the bands. They think there are now 1,000 lodges and 1,500 warriors there.   Indians claim they won't give up Short Bull and will fight when the soldiers try to arrest them.   They say as soon as the fight begins a hailstorm will kill the white soldiers. The Indians say they have shirts that are bullet-proof.

"I know Phillips well, and would take his judgment on the situation in preference to anybody I know.   If you deem this information of any importance I can send a messenger to further investigate. I urgently request, however, that you establish a post at Chamberlain and at Forest City.   Both points are reached by rail.   I have requested the Secretary of War, and again make the application through you, for 1,000 guns and ammunition to be shipped to me at Huron."

CHAPTER XXX.

FROM BAD TO WORSE.

An Ominous Thanksgiving—Scenes at an Issuing of Beef—"Buffalo Bill"—Plenty Bear's Report—Medicine That Was Not Bullet Proof—An Era of Uncertainty and Lies—Two Deeds Determined Upon.

HUNTING DOWN GAME.

Thanksgiving Day at Pine Ridge was celebrated by an issue of beef to about 2,600 of the Indians assembled there. It was little more than the aboriginal idea of hunting down game and slaughtering it, with the single exception that the game came out of a corral and was furnished by the Government. Ninety-three scrawny steers had been gathered at the beef corral about two miles out in an open prairie to the east of the agency building. About the little office and gate at 9 o'clock there assembled a motley crowd of interested Indians and half-breeds, and a smaller crowd of white men who came to see the sights. About one in every three Indians carried a rifle of some kind.

At the call of a dilapidated redskin, who holds the exalted position of royal haranguer for the Pine

Ridge Agency, they fell into lines stretching away from the gate of the cattle-pen. The Indians were arranged in bands of thirty, represented by the name of the head man on the books of the agency clerks. One clerk called this head man's name, the haranguer shouted it out to the crowd, and a weazened steer was allowed to pass the gate. All the men who belonged to that particular band put spurs, whip, and lariat to their ponies and started them out upon the open prairie. They were all lean enough to run well, and for an hour the whole plain was covered with frightened steers and yelling Indians. As soon as the steers ran out of the pen they demonstrated that they were as fleet as the Indian ponies. In almost every instance it was a long chase. Attempts to lasso the cattle generally failed, and a regular fusilade followed. Several Indians have been killed heretofore by this firing, yet the only rule is that no shooting must be done within half a mile of the corral. Once outside that limit the steers were shot down as soon as the ponies placed their riders in a position to get in a shot.

The danger to the Indians and the picturesqueness of the scene were enhanced by the squaws and wagoners. When the first steer dropped a portion of these people who had collected back of the horsemen near the pen started for the carcass. Another party bolted out upon the prairie at the fall of every succeding animal. They were soon in the midst of the mêlée, and the maddened steers and excited horses ran about among the little knots of hungry women and children who had gathered to the bloody feast, too anxious for the tidbits to await the close of the hunt. When the last steer was down the first and many others were upon their way toward the Indians' stomachs.

AN INDIAN FEAST.

Men and women fell upon the jerking and quivering bodies of the overheated animals, and before the hide was half off the eating had begun. There was no cooking. As quick as the knife exposed the liver and the choice portions of the entrails, which are dear to the Sioux epicure, they were cut out, and the butchers and their waiting children began the feast. A drive across the prairie was enough to send a qualm through the stomach of the toughest white man who saw the feast for the first time. The eating of the "fifth quarter," as the Indians call the viscera, and the use of the hide of the animal to prevent the meat from getting into the prairie sand, were too disgusting to permit of a calm observation. Each one of these scrawny animals was portioned off for the heads of families who made up the band of thirty Indians to whom one steer was allotted to last them for two weeks. Even when it it is considered that little more than the bare horns, hide, and hoofs escape the Indian's stomach, the supply was scant, indeed. The show was, for a few moments, wild and exciting, and then it changed to a most disgusting spectacle.

The only reason given for not slaughtering the steers decently and serving the meat from the block is that the Indians want the hides. One of them is worth at the traders' store about $2 or $2.50. All the rest of the animal that the Indian eats could be given to him decently and in order. Serving the meat from the block was tried once. There was no appropriation to pay for butchering. The hides were used for that purpose, and then a howl went up. Instead of paying the butcher, the Department of Indian Affairs ruled that the hides belonged to the red man, and the old system was resumed.

At the same time four cannons were planted in a commanding position, and 1,200 soldiers were encamped close by the agency. The agent declared that 4,000 hostile Indians from the Rosebud Agency were approaching.

BUFFALO BILL.

On November 27th Col. Cody, "Buffalo Bill," arrived at Bismarck from New York, accompanied by his old partner, Frank Powell, known as "White Beaver," and R. H. Haslan, known as "Pony Bob," who once rode 108 miles in eight hours and ten minutes. Special conveyances were engaged to take the party to Standing Rock Agency. Buffalo Bill had a commission from Gen. Miles to go direct to Sitting Bull's camp on Grand River to get at the bottom of the Messiah craze, with almost unlimited authority to act. This was Buffalo Bill's first visit to that section since the Custer massacre.

And now matters hastened toward a crisis. The Rosebud Indians, under Chief Two Strike, united with Short Bull's band, also from Rosebud, and made all preparations for war. They made "medicine" to render themselves bullet-proof, and put on their war-paint. Chief Little Wound went to the agency and reported that his endeavors to pacify and restrain his followers had been unavailing. Plenty Bear, an old-time friendly Indian who lived at Wounded Knee, twenty-five miles northeast, came in with an alarming report to Agent Royer. He stated there were 364 lodges, being over 2,000 Indians, at Wounded Knee, and they had resumed the ghost dance with many war-like accompaniments. He said they were formed in the regular war dance proper, and were swearing vengeance upon the whites for conspiring to stop the dances. They had taken an oath to resist interference if it cost the last drop of their hearts' blood. Plenty Bear witnessed the dance in person.

PREPARATIONS FOR WAR.

The agency people were informed that Short Bull, one of the leading ghost dancers of the Rosebud Agency, had been in the camp about the agency attempting to induce the Pine Ridge Indians to join the Rosebud forces on Porcupine and Medicine Root Creeks. Early one morning about fifty of the Indian police began a search of the camp. It was not a fruitless errand. While Short Bull was not found, the policemen discovered that Good Thunder

and one or two other ghost dancers had left the camp
some time at night with Short Bull.

At a war dance at Pine Ridge the bullet-proof
"medicine" was used, and Chief Porcupine was selected as the man upon whom its efficacy should be
tried. He was placed in the centre of a ring and
the Indians opened on him. At the first discharge
he was shot through the thigh. The Indians at first
declared he was not injured, and would not permit
the onlookers to give him any assistance. He was
put in a tepee, and finally they declared he would
be all right in a little while.

The uncertainty that prevailed was thus described
by the correspondent of the *Chicago Tribune*, writing from the Pine Ridge Agency on November
30th:

"Gen. Brooke and his 1,200 soldiers are watching the agency and the few friendly Indians.
Three or four thousand Rosebud Indians are running things on the northern end of the reservation,
and nothing is being done. It is likely that something would be done if Gen. Brooke was not compelled to await the orders of the Indian fighters at
Washington. He could at least round up the wandering Rosebuds and stop their depredations upon
the property of the Indians who are here.

"White liars, red liars, and all the intermediate
tinges are busily at work. Stories of the most
alarming character are told about once an hour and
contradicted in less time. First, the rumor comes

that the Rosebuds are painting themselves, dancing, and preparing for a fight. Then the other side has a story ready. The Indians are only alarmed at the presence of the troops. They do not credit any messages sent them by the Indian police, and would be ready and willing to come into the agency at once if some person in whom they have confidence would go out and tell them so. For the last four days Special Agent Cooper and Mr. Royer have declared that they had sent them instructions to come in. They have not done so, and the agents say they have had no communication with either Two Strike or Crow Dog, the leaders of the band. Royer and Cooper had a long talk this morning with Red Cloud, Big Road, and one or two of the minor chiefs there. They were instructed to send for the Rosebud Indians, and it remains to be seen whether that move will have any effect.

THE ROSEBUDS.

"The reports made of the movements of the Rosebuds are of the most conflicting character. It appears certain, however, that the whole outfit moved about ten miles further away from the agency, going north along Wounded Knee Creek to its junction with White River. Rocky Bear, the chief of Buffalo Bill's band of show Indians, returned last night from a trip to the Rosebud camp. He said that he could see nothing warlike in their movements. They were badly frightened about the soldiers and suspicious of all movements about Pine Ridge Agency. So far as he could learn with a talk with Two Strike and Crow Dog, they could be readily persuaded to come here if they could be convinced that Agent Royer wanted them here and wanted to talk to them. He did not see any of the work of the thieves during his trip, as he only went to his own house on Wounded Knee Creek. Rocky Bear explained that he did not care to go near any other house for fear that if they had been broken open he would be accused of the robbery. So far as his own property was concerned, it was safe and intact.

"The opposite of this report comes from a couple of Indians who were examined by Cooper late last night. One of them said that he came over from Rosebud because he had married a Sioux, and his wife was determined to come to this agency. According to his story, the Rosebuds were getting ready for a fight. Their horses were painted and their camp was constantly picketed and guarded by their young warriors, who had been selected for that duty. The squaws and young bucks were talking of war, and medicine to render the braves bullet-proof was being prepared. These two agreed with Rocky Bear in only one particular, which was that a council of the Rosebuds was to be held either last night or to-night, at which their course of conduct was to be decided upon.

"Another rumor that startled a good many people was that a large force of Sioux had left the Cheyenne River Agency and moved south and east, as if to join the Rosebud or the Pine Ridge malcontents.

"Late last evening the crowd about Agent Royer's office was thrown into a fever of nervous excitement by the appearance of an Indian leading a white sorebacked pony. He had streaks of red upon his flanks and quarters, and an attempt had been made to wash them out. Half-breeds and Indian policemen declared that this pony had been painted for the war-path, and that he came from the Rosebud camp, but who brought him and under what circumstances could not be learned. This is a fair sample of the information that reaches the agency from the camp of the hostiles. Should the Rosebuds refuse to come in and the troops attempt to call them to an account a stampede or fight might be expected. As it is they are wandering about the northern part of the reservation at their own sweet will, and as long as the soldiers and Indians are as far apart as they are now the warfare will be confined to an exchange of lies"

TWO DECISIVE PROJECTS.

About this time talk began seriously to settle upon two projects: To arrest Sitting Bull, and to disarm the Indians. These acts were, indeed, soon decided upon and executed; but with tragic and disastrous results.

CHAPTER XXXI.

DELAY AND DISASTER,

WAITING FOR SOMETHING TO TURN UP—INCREASED RATIONS COME TOO
LATE—DEPREDATIONS BY THE HOSTILES—A FRUITLESS POW-WOW AT
PINE RIDGE—THE INDIANS FIGHTING AMONG THEMSELVES—TROOPS
HURRYING ON TO THE BAD LANDS.

Before the two decisive moves were made, however, there was a fortnight more of delay, "waiting for something to turn up." The authorities were naturally reluctant to begin a struggle which was certain to be serious. At the same time they neglected to take any of those steps for the amelioration of the condition of the Indians, which justice and humanity required, and which alone could have brought about a peaceful solution of the difficulty. They simply waited, hoping that very severe weather would set in and stop the ghost-dancing, and starve and freeze the Indians into unconditional submission.

UGLY PREPARATIONS.

The statesmanship of this policy was not appreciated by the Indians' who kept on with their war-like preparations. On December 1st, Judge Burns, of Deadwood, came in to the Pine Ridge Agency, having passed through the hostile camp. There was, he said, no doubt that the red workers for war were preparing thoroughly for a great struggle, and that they had no thought of giving up their purpose. A member of the camp proclaimed his approach when he was a long way off, so that when he neared the camp he found it bristling with preparation for an attack. The hostile band was made up almost exclusively of young men, who had disregarded the advice of their old chiefs, taken the reins into their own hands, and vowed to fight until death. The ghost dance, Judge Burns said further, was being done all night long, and was varied during the day with the old-time war dance. He corroborated fully the previous reports as to the abundance of food and ammunition which they had, and said, they were making up a big supply of a new pattern of tomahawk, more ugly than the old style.

INCREASE OF RATIONS.

Little Wound made another desperate effort for peace, and narrowly escaped being killed by his own tribesmen for his pains.

The Secretary of the Interior now ordered an increase of rations, in the hope that such action would pacify the Indians, but it was too late. When the Indians were informed of it, they thought they were being tricked again, and they only hurried their preparations to flee to the Bad Lands, and there sell their lives as dearly as possible. General Miles, in the meantime, sent troops forward as speedily as possible, until he had 2,000 mounted men and a large force of infantry within reach; enough, he thought, to deal with the 4,000 Indians who were on the war path. The hostile Indians were massing their forces between Pine Ridge and the Bad Lands, and General Miles was trying to encircle them with a cordon of troops. On December 5th a report stated: "The situation has not materially changed. The hostile Rosebud Indians sleep upon their arms, prepared constantly for an attack. They have three lines of signal couriers between the agency and their camp, and any movements of the troops would be known in a few moments. They have taken all they wish of the Government beef herd and burned the buildings and corrals. They are living high and are happy. They have moved to the edge of the Bad Lands. Military preparations proceed rapidly. Unless the Indians come in within a very few days the troops will be equipped and in position, when an advance may be ordered."

DAILY OUTRAGES,

At the same time, depredations and outrages were of daily occurrence. On December 5th, William McGaa and John O'Rourke, farmers, came in from the White Earth River country with a tale of woe. These men were half-breeds, with full-blooded Indian wives, as are nearly all the settlers in the valley. Both had come to the agency as requested when the troops arrived, because they had learned obedience, leaving their farms to the protection of the Great Father and the tender mercies of the fanatical ghost dancer. Both brave, stalwart men, they stood up in the crowded, dingy little room that serves as an office, with choked voice and hardly repressed tears, and told the sad account of their distress and ruin. William McGaa lived on White River, at the mouth of Porcupine Creek, forty miles from the agency. He found his home a wreck. Twelve work horses had been stolen, the heavy work harness cut into pieces, the wagons broken to pieces, and every useful article in house and barn demolished. Windows had been broken; pictures, tables, chairs, cupboards and bedsteads chopped into fragments; trunks broken open, and his wife's and children's clothes torn into shreds; the sewing machine lay in a hundred pieces mingled with those of the crockery. All the accumulated annuity goods of clothing, blankets, cloth of various kinds, as well as extra provisions, had been stolen. Mr. McGaa lost also one stallion which cost him $500, and 225 head of cattle. John O'Rourke's ranch was at the mouth of Wounded Knee Creek, and the scene at his home was but a repetition of that at McGaa's, even to the breaking of the clock, and the theft of the well rope. Here they were not content with mere destruction, but added insult to injury by arranging his choicest set of dishes in the centre of the floor and leaving them defiled beyond description. Between the houses of these two men were the homes of many friends. All was wreck and ruin. Dick Stirks lost a work horse and a lot of range horses and cattle, as well as ranch and home.   William Valangry was homeless, losing horses and cattle.   John Steele had a handsome house, well furnished ; it was gone, and so were forty head of cattle known to be slaughtered, and over 100 head of horses.   Yellow Bird lost his shelter and over fifty horses, and a large herd of cattle.   Charley Cooney was ruined, without counting seven horses and twenty cows stolen. Mrs. Cooney, a widow, lost everything.   At her home the marauders left evidence that they were not suffering for even the luxuries of life, for coffee and sugar were sprinkled all over the floors and around the yard.   John Davison, one of the boss farmers in the employ of the Government, was left destitute, losing everything.   Henry Kerns and Mrs. Fisher were left homeless, penniless and suffering.   Baptiste Courier, better known as Big Bat, an old-timer even among the Indians, lost seventy-five horses and thirty-eight cows. The Government ranch, the head-quarters of John Dwyer, the chief herder for the agency, was burned and everything destroyed. The leaders of the war party said that they would sweep the country.

A CONFERENCE WITH GENERAL BROOKE.

Through the efforts of Father Jule, the Roman Catholic priest at Pine Ridge, a conference was held on December 6th between General Brooke and a number of the chiefs.   The Indians came in to the camp bearing a flag of truce and armed with Winchester and Springfield rifles.   The entrance of the

From Photographs taken on the spot by the *Philadelphia Press* Artist.

WHITE BEAVER AND BUFFALO BILL.

novel procession produced much excitement at the agency. First came the chiefs, who were Turning Bear, Big Turkey, High Pine, Big Bad Horse, and Bull Dog, who was one of the leaders of the Custer massacre. Next came Two Strike, the head chief, seated in a buggy with Father Jule. Surrounding these was a body guard of four young warriors. All the Indians were decorated with war-paint and feathers, while many wore ghost-dance leggings and the ghost-dance shirt dangling at their saddles. Bunches of eagle feathers were tied in the manes and tails of most of the ponies, while the backs of the docile little animals were streaked with paint,

The warlike cavalry proceeded at once to General Brooke's spacious headquarters in the agency residence. At a given signal all leaped to the ground, hitched their ponies to the trees, and guided by Father Jule they entered the General's apartments, where the council was held, lasting two hours.

At the beginning of the pow-wow General Brooke explained, that the Great Father, through him, had asked them to come in and have a talk regarding the situation. A great deal of misunderstanding and trouble had arisen by the reports taken to and fro between the camps by irresponsible parties, and it was, therefore, considered very necessary that they have a talk face to face. Through him he said the Father wanted to tell them if they would come in and live near the agency, where he, General Brooke, could see them often, and so not be compelled to depend upon hearsay, that he would give them plenty to eat and would employ many of their young men as scouts, etc. He said he heard they were hostile Indians, but he did not believe it. The soldiers did not come there to fight, but to protect the settlers and keep the peace. He hoped they (the Indians) were all in favor of peace, as the Great Father did not want war. As to the feeling over the change in the boundary line between the Pine Ridge and Rosebud Agency, he said that and many other things would be settled after they had shown a disposition to come in, as asked by the Great Father.

CONTRACTED BROWS AND LOW GRUNTS.

Wounded Knee was suggested as a place that would prove satisfactory to the Great Father to have them live. The representatives of the hostiles listened with contracted brows, sidelong glances at one another, and low grunts.

When the General had concluded his remarks, Turning Bear came forward and spoke in reply. He is a fine specimen of the blanket-wrapped Indian. Turning Bear gave expression to the following ideas: It would be a bad thing for them to come nearer the agency because there was no water or grass for their horses here. He couldn't understand how the young men could be employed as scouts if there was no enemy to be watched. They might come in, but as the old men and old women had no horses, and as their people had nothing generally to pull their wagons, it would take them a long time to

come. If they did come they should want the Great
Father to send horses and wagons out to the Bad
Lands camp and bring in the great quantities or
beef, etc., they had there and take it anywhere to a
new camp that might be agreed on.

In conclusion, the speakers hoped that they would
be given something to eat before they started back.

To this the General replied that he intended before the council opened that before its close he
would tell them that they should be given feed or
words to that effect. As for horses and wagons being sent after the beef (after they had been stealing
and butchering in so high-handed a manner), the
General said that and many other things would be
considered after they had acceded to the Great
Father's request to move in the agency. Any reference whatever to the wholesale devastation, depredations, thieving, burning of buildings, etc., was
studiously avoided on both sides. After the pow-
wow was over the Indians were conducted to the
Quartermaster's department and there given a big
fat feed. Then the squaws living at the agency
came out in gala day feathers and gave a grand
squaw dance.

Soon after this fruitless pow-wow, the hostile In-

FIGHTING AMONG THEMSELVES.

dians began fighting among themselves. The con-
flict was for the leadership between Two Strike and
Short Bull, each wishing to control the united bands.
Two Strike was supported by Turning Bear, Big

Turkey, High Pipe, Big Bad Horse, and Bull Dog
and their bands. The other party, with Short Bull
as leader, included Chiefs Crow Dog, Kicking Bear,
High Hawk, Eagle Pine, and a host of Standing
Rock and Cheyenne Agency Indians. The fight
was bitterly contested for several hours, and several
Indians were killed. The valley in the edge of the
Bad Lands was crowded with mounted Indians, clad
in full war rig, feathers and rifles flashing in the air,
as the two parties went dashing, wheeling, circling
over the small plain.

As a result of this disturbance Two Strike and
his followers started in toward Pine Ridge again,
while Short Bull, Kicking Bear, and a smaller following, went north, further into the Bad Lands.
Then General Brooke sent out 300 friendly Indians
to join Two Strike at the river and go with him back
to the Bad Lands and try and bring Short Bull and
his crowd in peaceably, if possible ; by force, if necessary. The warriors were selected entirely from
the friendliest, none of the police or scouts being
permitted to go. If this party was successful it was
to bring in Short Bull, Kicking Bear, and their
chiefs, providing there were no scapegoats for punishment for the sins of the whole crowd, and reliev-
ing Two Strike and others from blame. At the same
time Lieutenant Casey with his Cheyenne scouts and
Captain Adams' troop of the First Cavalry, set out to
head Short Bull and his party, and the Sixth, Seventh
and Eighth Cavalry hurried on to the Bad Lands.

CHAPTER XXXII.

CATASTROPHE.

Matters reached a crisis at last, on December 15th, not, however, at Pine Ridge, but forty miles North of Fort Yates. It was reported that Sitting Bull and his band were about to make their way to the Bad Lands to join the hostiles there. Accordingly a detachment of troops and Indian police were sent to arrest the turbulent chief. A fight occurred, and Sitting Bull was killed. Of this tragedy and the events immediately surrounding it, we have already given a full account in a preceding chapter. It may well be recorded here, however, that there seemed to be ample reason for thinking that Sitting Bull was going to the Bad Lands and that his arrival there would have meant war. For on the very evening before he was killed, the Bad Lands were

A GREAT LIGHT SUDDENLY BLAZE UP

ablaze with signal fires. People at Pine Ridge saw, that night a great light suddenly blaze up in the

421

northwest in the direction of the Bad Lands. The light faded to a sullen glow and then rapidly spread along the sky for a distance of a couple of miles. Men posted in Indian signals in the camp said that this meant that the Indians in the Bad Lands had determined to fight. The Indians in the camp of the friendlies on being asked what the signal meant declined at first to talk, but being pressed finally said it meant that their brothers in the Bad Lands would be on the war path within one sun, and that all Indians who did not join them would be dogs and enemies forever. The friendlies, however, disclaimed any intention of obeying the signal.

The death of Sitting Bull created tremendous excitement all through the Indian country. Instead of causing relief, it aroused the keenest apprehension. It was feared that many settlers would fall victims to the vengeance of the Sioux, and thousands of refugees flocked to Bismarck and Mandau for safety.

General Miles now set out from St. Paul for Deadwood, by way of Standing Rock. He telegraphed back that Chief Two Strike had come into General Brooke's camp, at Pine Ridge and surrendered, but that part of his band still remained out. There had come in with him 184 lodges, containing about 800 Indians. General Miles established his headquarters for the time at Rapid City, with 150 soldiers. General Carr was at the junction of Rapid and Cheyenne rivers, with 400 soldiers, ready to move on to Pine Ridge as soon as trouble began.

Seven companies of the 17th Infantry were sent from Fort Russell to Pine Ridge.

"My information" said General Miles, "was reliable and positive of Sitting Bull's emissaries and runners going to different tribes and inciting them to hostility. The order for his arrest was not given too soon, as he was about leaving with 100 fighting men. The effect has been disheartening to many others. I have

TO DESTROY OR CAPTURE.

directed the troops to destroy or capture the few who escaped after his death, from Standing Rock. General Brooke has more than 1,000 lodges, or over 5,000 fighting Indians, under his control at Pine Ridge, but there are still 250 lodges, or over 1,000 fighting Indians in the Bad Lands that are defiant and hostile."

A courier came to General Carr's camp, on December 18th, to report that a party of fifteen men were besieged fifty miles from there on Spring Creek at Daly's ranch. The Indians had made three attempts to fire the ranch. One was nearly successful. One of the occupants, M. H. Day, Aide-de-camp to the Governor of the State. The courier had to make a break through the Indians, firing both pistols right and left. One of their bullets penetrated his overcoat. He rode by a circuitous route to our camp. General Carr sent Major Tupper with 100 men to the rescue. Near Smithville a large number of Indians were seen in a small creek, in the brakes. A number of shots were exchanged.

While some of the Goverment wagons were crossing Spring Street Creek, they and escort were attacked by about forty Indians and over 100 shots were exchanged. One soldier was wounded, and another had a bullet through his hat. A troop of Captain Well's cavalry came to their rescue and the Indians ran away. General Carr sent a troop of cavalry up into the Bad Lands to watch any movement of the hostiles. A signal service was established between the troop and camp. The troop reported about seventy teepees in the Indian stronghold, wholly inaccessible. The only known outlet for these Indians was a trail which goes up Cottonwood across the road from Rapid Creek to Wounded Knee. This pass was closed next day by the Sixth Infantry.

The military authorities at Pine Ridge, on December 18th, counted the returned Indians and issued rations to them. There were 1,024. A grand coun-

HIS HEART WAS BROKEN.

cil was held. Red Cloud told them that his heart was broken. They had caused a deal of trouble, and their stock was there eating grass (a very serious thing, there being so much stock there), and they were eating his rations, but he was willing to give the grass and rations, and he grunted. He would count it all nothing if the trouble could be settled. If those who were out would not come in and the soldiers were forced to kill them, he should feel sorry, for they were his relatives, but he must say that it was just.

The next day brought this news from the camp on Cheyenne river: "From twenty to thirty ranchers rode or drove into camp to-day all heavily armed and all agree that the Indians are augmenting their forces and growing bolder hourly. It was ascertained early this morning that the deserted ranch and outlying buildings of a man named Wilson were burned last night, having first been looted. M. H. Day, aide-de-camp to Governor Mellette, rode in with four other men from his ranch to-day. He reports that besides the seventy tepees, which contain about 350 hostiles, between Battle and Spring Creeks, he saw another large band further down the Cheyenne River, which will number at the very least 300.

"Three heliograph stations had been established —one in camp, one on the top of the high bluffs, and one which had followed up as nearly as practicable Captain Stanton's command. About 2 P. M., a soldier was seen coming down the bluff, putting his horse to a full gallop, and immediately the heliograph lines began working, The rider crossed the river and reported to General Carr that Captain Stanton was in an engagement with the Indians. General Carr gave orders for Lieutenant Scott and Troop D to go to his assistance. Within a few minutes the

CHARGING UP THE BLUFF.

troop was charging up the bluff to the scene of action. When the soldier dismounted his hard-ridden horse dropped dead. Other troops were immedi-

ately put in marching order. After some hours
Captain Stanton and the troops returned. He said
that after noon he had noticed a large party of Indians with a herd of ponies coming from the east
and heading for the Bad Lands. He immediately
gave chase and after running several miles gradually drew up to the Indians, who began firing, but
their bullets went wide of the mark. Shots were exchanged for some time, when the Indians made for
a creek called Wounded Knee. They went down
this creek and were lost to view in the Bad Lands.
Captain Stanton followed them for some time, but
fearing an ambush, withdrew his troops and returned to camp."

A ranchman named Tom Hetlund, who lived
thirty-five miles up Bad River, went to Pierre on December 20th, with a strange story. "He said the
peaceable, christianized, half civilized Two Kettle
Sioux had been seized with a sudden frenzy, and
were imitating the wildest orgies of the ghost dances indulged in by the hostiles. His account was
as follows: "Night before last some Indians were
returning from a little social gathering when a sight

CHILLED THEM TO THE BONE.

met their eyes that chilled them to the bone. One
of their number directed attention to the top of a
bluff and there stood a figure in white perfectly mo-
tionless. Suddenly one of them cried out in Sioux:
'It's Sitting Bull!' Then did the marrow in the
bones of these Indians grow cold, and their teeth

chattered like beans in a barrel. The phantom suddenly commenced waving an arm as if motioning them to follow, and with the speed of a bird glided from hill top to hill top, finally disappearing in the direction of the Bad Lands. Only one interpretation could be given this ghostly visitation. Sitting Bull was thus identified as really the simon-pure, long-danced for Messiah, and he was beckoning them to join his followers and avenge his spirit. A ghost dance is the consequence, and the spirit has moved down the river, and it has affected them as far down as Willow Creek."

Acting under General Brooke's authority, 500 friendly Indians left Pine Ridge, on December 20th to attempt to bring in the hostiles. The Indians at Fort Yates were quiet, and 39 of Sitting Bull's band who had left the Agency a few days before, sent word that they would return. General Carr sent out a cavalry force to intercept the band that was reported as moving towards the Bad Lands. Big Foot and Hump surrendered and returned to the agency, Every day the cordon of troops around the Indians was drawn tighter.

Big Foot brought in with him 150 of Sitting Bull's warriors, and this greatly weakened the force which the hostiles expected to gather in the Bad Lands. Had Big Foot and Hump gone into the Bad Lands, other northern tribes would have joined them and swelled the force to at least 1,000 fighting men. Had this been done, according to General

Miles, the Indians could have massacred as many settlers as the Sioux did in 1862.

Stands First, a clever Indian scout, spent a day in the hostile camp. When he attempted to present the peaceful mission on which he had been sent, the Indians pointed their guns at him and drowned his voice with their war cries. One of their leaders

LISTEN TO NO MORE PEACE TALK.

told him that they would listen to no more peace talk and would never again allow an advocate of peace to leave their camp alive. He said that the white soldiers were cowards and afraid to fight and called Stands First a women and a slave of the white men.

A genuine sensation was enjoyed at Pine Ridge on December 22d. The police arrested in Red Cloud's camp a fellow who pretended to be the In-

THE INDIAN MESSIAH.

dian Messiah. When they pulled the blanket off him, however, they found him to be a white man, an intelligent but harmless crank named Hopkins, who had come there from Iowa. He claimed that he was there in the interest of peace and had come there because the Indians had misinterpreted his message. He wanted to go on to the Bad Lands and preach to the Indians there, but the agent sent him instead to Chadron escorted by some policemen. Some of the Indians were indignant over his arrest while others laughed and said that he was a crazy fool. None of the chiefs believed in him, and Red Cloud spat in his face and said: "You go home. You are no son of God."

At about the same time A. I. Chapman, an Indian scout, returned from Nevada, whither he had been sent to interview the so-called Messiah at Walker's Lake. He reported his mission as follows: "The Messiah, Quoitize Ow, as he calls himself, is a full blooded Piute Indian and has always been peacefully disposed. He spoke freely of his call to

EXPERIENCE WITH THE ALMIGHTY,

preach. His first experience with the Almighty was one afternoon while hunting. Hearing a noise he started to learn the cause when he was suddenly thrown to the ground. He was then taken to Heaven and there saw all the whites and Indians that have ever lived in the world. He was afterward brought back to earth and returned to his senses on the same spot where he was stricken down. While he was in Heaven, God told him he had been looking for a man whom he could trust to reform the world, and he had picked out Quoitize Ow. So Quoitize Ow set out to perform his mission. He taught the Indians that they should work and avoid fighting except in self defense. Last summer the Indians told him that unless it rained soon the crops would fail. He told them to go home and it would be all right, and in three days there was a heavy fall of rain." Chapman thought Quoitize Ow was only indirectly to blame for the Indian uprising, his doctrine having imbued the Indians with a more independent spirit to resist their wrongs.

Two cow boys reported to General Miles that they had seen Two Strike and Kicking Bear leave the cabin of the latter's brother-in-law, about ten miles from Rapid City, and go toward the Bad Lands. A troop of cavalry was immediately started after them, but after chasing them 13 miles lost track of them in the Bad Lands. Another troop went out in pursuit of another party of run away Indians and exchanged some shots with them, but only succeeded in capturing two squaws and one pappoose.

There were no further hostilities of importance until the day before Christmas. On that day about 80 hostile Indians made two attempts to break into a camp of Cheyenne scouts at the mouth of Battle Creek. The first attack was quickly repulsed with a loss of one scout killed and two wounded and two Indians killed and several wounded. The second attack was made after dark and was led by Kicking Bear himself. Hot firing was kept up for an hour or more and a number of the attacking Indians were killed and wounded.

The next day the Indians who had come in with Hump and Big Foot broke out again and made for the Bad Lands, and General Carr and a force of cavalry men started in pursuit. Serious depredations were renewed at many points. On hearing this news General Miles remarked that he was tired of fooling with the Indians, and thought that the best thing to be done was to attack them at once.

More peaceful news came soon, however. On December 28th it was announced that the 7th Cavalry, under Captain Whitesides, had captured Big Foot and his band on Porcupine Creek without a conflict, and all the other Indians in the Bad Lands

DECIDED TO COME IN.

had decided to come in and surrender. This news was confirmed and great was the rejoicing thereat, for it was believed that the Indian war had thus been brought to an end.

It was on Sunday morning that Big Foot surrendered ; a bright warm day. An Indian scout who had been sent forward came hurrying in waving his hat with the good news that Big Foot was only eight miles away. "Boots and saddles" was sounded and the cavalry men hurried forward. Descending the slope to the Porcupine Valley they found Big Foot's band drawn up in line of battle. There were more than 150 fighting men, heavily armed. Had a shot been fired there would have been a desperate battle. But Big Foot advanced from his side alone, and Captain Whitesides went forward alone to meet him. Big Foot began a long talk, telling how tired he was of running around and how much he wanted to make peace with the white men. The Captain however, told him that there was only one

SURRENDER AT ONCE.

thing to be done, to surrender at once. "All right," said Big Foot, "I surrender." And in a moment the whole band of fighting men and 250 women and children beside had given themselves up. They were all marched over to the old camp of the 7th Cavalry on Wounded Knee. There the troops formed a cordon around them and sent for reinforcements. Among the prisoners were all of the Sitting Bull party who fled after that chief's death.

By permission of the *Illustrated American*.

INTERIOR OF TENT OF LIEUT. BROWN AT PINE RIDGE AGENCY.

CHAPTER XXXIII.

RED WAR.

Colonel Forsythe Takes Command at Wounded Knee—The Indians Suspicious and Uneasy—Preparations to Disarm Them—A Desperate Outbreak — The Indians Outnumbered and Slaughtered Without Mercy—Incidents of the Battle—Death of Captain Wallace—List of the Killed and Wounded Elaine Goodale's Report.

Sitting Bull was dead, and thus the first of two decisive measures was accomplished. Now came the second, the disarming of Big Foot's band. Although these Indians had now surrendered in entirely good faith, they were most suspicious and uneasy, The tragic fate of Sitting Bull had alarmed them, and they only half trusted their white captors. There were those among them who belived that they were all to be put to death, and when the surrender of their weapons was talked of this belief was much intensified. They naturally supposed that their arms were to be taken from them only to render them defenseless, and therefore, easier victims. It was in this state of mind that they went into camp on the bank of Wounded Knee Creek, a

435

place destined to become famous as the scene of one
of the most bloody Indian battles of recent years.

Colonel Forsythe arrived at the camp on Wounded Knee Creek early on the morning of December
29th, with orders from General Brooke to disarm
Big Foot's band. Colonel Forsythe assumed command of the regulars, which comprised two battalions of 500 men, with Hotchkiss guns. It was
feared that the Indians would offer resistance and

EVERY PRECAUTION WAS TAKEN.

every precaution was taken to prevent an escape
and to render the movement successful. Colonel
Forsythe threw his force around the Indian camp
and mounted the Hotckiss guns so as to command
the camp, and at eight o'clock issued the order to
disarm the redskins.

The preparations were quickly made. The command was given to the Indians to come forward from
the tents. This was done, the squaws and children
remaining behind the tepees. The braves advanced
a short distance from the camp to the place designated, and were placed in a half circle, the warriors
squatting on the ground in front of the tent, where
Big Foot, their chief, lay sick with pneumonia. By
twenties they were ordered to give up their arms.
The first twenty went to their tents and came back
with only two guns. This irritated Major Whiteside, who was superintending this part of the work.
After a hasty consultation with Colonel Forsythe
he gave the order for the cavalrymen, who were all

dismounted and formed in almost a square, about twenty-five paces back, to close in. They did so, and took a stand within twenty feet of the Indians. When this had been done a detachment of cavalry

TO SEARCH FOR ARMS.

went through the tepees to search for arms. They found about fifty rifles. But in the meantime the Indian warriors, who were firmly and naturally convinced that they were about to be put to death, raised their plaintive death chant. Then in the twinkling of an eye they changed it to their war-song, and before the startled soldiers fully realized what was happening, the Indians drew their rifles from beneath their blankets and opened fire. Those Indians who had no guns rushed on the soldiers with tomahawk in one hand and scalping-knife in the other. The troops outnumbered the Indians, three or four to one, and the case from the first was hopeless. It was simply the last desperate death struggle of brave men who believed they were all to be massacred and who meant to sell their lives as dearly as possible.

The fight lasted for over an hour. During this time Captain Wallace and seven troopers were killed and fifteen wounded, including Garlington, of Arctic fame. The slaughter among the savages was terrible, despite the fact that the soldiers had to run

'REMEMBER CUSTER.''

them down in their ambuscades. When the fight had fully begun the troopers cheered one another

with the cry, "Remember Custer." The regiment
fought as only men with a revengeful grievance can
fight.   There was no disorder after the first shock
of surprise had passed away. On foot and mounted
the troopers deployed in all directions, driving the
savages from cover and sending them in disorder to
the more impregnable buttes to the north.

Nearly 100 Indians fell before the sheet of flame
that swept down from the batteries and guns of the
United States troops.   The manner in which Big
Foot's band turned upon their captors, stood before
the terribly raking fire and shot down so many soldiers, rivals anything that has accompanied the Indian wars of America.   Though encumbered with their
squaws and pappooses, they almost snatched victory
from defeat, and displayed a degree of reckless daring and bravery that has rarely been equalled.

The instant the attack began the soldiers, maddened at the sight of their falling comrades, hardly
awaited the command, and in a moment the whole

A SHEET OF FIRE,

camp was a sheet of fire, above which the smoke
rolled, obscuring the central scene from view.
Through this horrible curtain single Indians could
be seen at times flying before the fire, but after the
first discharge from the carbines of the troopers
there were few of them left.   They fell on all sides
like grain before the scythe.

Indians and soldiers lay together and, wounded,
fought on the ground.   Off toward the bluffs the

few remaining warriors fled, turning occasionally to
fire, but now evidently caring more for escape than
battle.   Only the wounded Indians seemed possess-

THE COURAGE OF DEVILS.

ed of the courage of devils.   From the ground
where they had fallen they continued to fire until
their ammunition was gone or until killed by the
soldiers.   Both sides forgot everything excepting
only the loading and discharging of guns.

It was only in the early part of the affray that
hand to hand fighting was seen.   The carbines were
clubbed, sabres gleamed and war clubs circled in
the air coming down like thunderbolts.   But this
was only for a short time.   The Indians could not
stand that storm from the soldiers.   It was only a
stroke of life before death.   The remnant fled and
the battle became a hunt.

It was now that the artillery was called into requi-
sition.   Before the fighting was so close that the
guns could not be trained without danger of death
to the soldiers.   Now with the Indians flying where
they might it was easier to reach them.   The Gatling and Hotchkiss guns were trained, and then began a heavy firing, which lasted half an hour, with
frequent heavy volleys of musketry and cannon.   It

A WAR OF EXTERMINATION.

was a war of extermination now.   It was difficult to
restrain the troops. Tactics were almost abandoned.
About the only tactics was to kill while it could be
done, wherever an Indian could be seen.   Down in-

to the creek and up over the bare hills they were
followed by artillery and musketry fire, and the engagement went on until not a live Indian was in sight.

More than ninety Indians were killed by the
deadly fire from the Hotchkiss guns and the unerring
aim of the soldiers. But when the smoke cleared
away it was found that the firing of the redskins had
been only a degree less effective than that of the
well-trained troopers. Twenty-five brave soldiers
were scattered on the field and thirty-five others
were suffering from serious wounds

Chief Big Foot was lying in his tepee, dying of
pneumonia, when the battle began. He slowly
drew himself up, but had hardly reached an erect

TWENTY BULLETS STRUCK HIM.

position when at least twenty bullets struck him,
and he pitched forward, never to rise again. His
squaw rose to her feet with a Winchester in her
hand, when a bullet struck her in the heart and she
sprang convulsively in the air, rolling down the hill
like a ball.

Colonel James Forsythe, in command of the
troops, showed only the greatest personal courage
and most soldierly qualities. Unarmed, in the very
thickest of the fight, with bullets buzzing around
him and men falling at his side, he gave his orders
as quietly and coolly as if sitting in a parlor. His

HIS COOLNESS, KIND-HEARTEDNESS AND JUSTICE.

coolness, kind-heartedness and justice were never
better illustrated than his action when he became

satisfied that his men were safe from further injury. While his men were boiling with rage and fired with the almost uncontrollable fever of battle, burning to revenge comrades slaughtered in cold blood, he gave the order to cease firing, with the words: " We did not come here to butcher them."

Major Whiteside was equally cool and in full possession of his faculties as if on parade, and added fresh laurels to his long brilliant record.

Lieutenant Rice, who was leading his company over a series of knolls south of the creek, had two horses shot from under him and Lieutenant Robinson, who was in his rear, also narrowly escaped death from a bullet which cut the horn of the saddle. When the troopers got fairly at work they

POURED A DEADLY FIRE.

poured a deadly fire into the savages, who were hurrying with their guns to the crags and cliffs and buttes which surround the camp. Many of the hostiles leaped upon their ponies before the battle had fairly opened and fled toward the Bad Lands.

The Indians formed no order of battle. Each man fought for himself, and the soldiers were at a disadvantage from the start. Captain Hayden and his artillerymen worked desperately to get their guns to perform effective service, but they were so slow at their work that most of the casualties had occur-

SHELLS BEGAN TO BURST.

red before the shells began to burst over the ambuscades of the hostiles. Captain Hayden had one

Hotchkiss gun, which was used to some effect before the howitzers began to work. The Indians have an everlasting hatred for cannon, and the men who work them, and it was noticeable that in this battle the heaviest fire from the enemy was directed toward the artillerymen, among whom there were several casualties.

The death of Captain Wallace caused universal regret. He had gone to a tepee to direct the search for arms when the firing began. At first it was sup-

KILLED AT THE OPENING VOLLEY.

posed that he had been killed at the opening volley from the Indians. When his body was recovered he was found lying at the entrance of a tepee with his empty revolver in his hand. Every chamber had been discharged. His head had been crushed in, front and back, by stone battle-axes. There was no braver man in the whole army than he. He was in Reno's command at the time of the Custer massacre. When Reno was driven to cover Wallace's Adjutant fell from his horse mortally wounded. Wallace threw himself from his horse under a terrific fire from the savages, seized the wounded man, vaulted into his saddle, and bore the officer toward the rear. The officer knew that he was dying, and told Wallace to drop him and save himself. Wallace carried the officer over a mile, forded two streams, and was nearing a place of safety when the savages got so close that he was forced to abandon the officer in the bush, dismounting for that purpose and remounting after he had hidden him away. He was under a hot fire all the time and showed unlimited pluck.

Captain Wallace was born in South Carolina, on June 29th, 1849. He was appointed a cadet at the Military Academy from South Carolina in 1868, and was graduated in June. 1872. He was at once assigned to the 7th cavalry, with the rank of second lieutenant. He became a first lieutenant on June 25th, 1876, and from that date until June 6th, 1877, he was adjutant of the regiment. He became a captain on September 23d, 1885, and for a long time was in command of Troop L, of his regiment.

Lieutenant Garlington, who was wounded in the arm in this battle, was born in South Carolina and was appointed a cadet in the United States Military Academy from Georgia in July, 1872, and was graduated June 15th, 1876. He became Second Lieutenant of the Seventh Cavalry June 15th, 1876, and First Lieutenant June 25th of the same year. He accompanied the expedition for the relief of Lieutenant Greely to the Arctic regions in 1883. When his ship, the Proteus, was lost in Smith's Sound, Garlington retreated with the crew to Upper Nairk, nearly 500 miles away. Garlington was the Adjutant of the Seventh Cavalry at the time of the Custer massacre, or soon after, and he was the officer who signed the order placing the only living representative of civilization which escaped alive from the scene of that awful slaughter, on the pension roll.

It was a horse, which, scarred and maimed, came back riderless to the regiment, and was always cared for as a pensioner of the Government.

The following is a complete official register of the killed and wounded in the battle of Wounded Knee, with statement of places in which the mortal injuries were received:

KILLED.

SEVENTH CAVALRY, COMPANY A.

Kranberry, A., arm and side.
Dyer, A. C., sergeant, chest.
Frey, Henry, head.
Johnson, George, head.
Regan, Michael, head.
Logan, James, head.

COMPANY B.

Coffey. D. C., sergeant, head.
Forest, Henry A., head.
Costillo, John, head.
Cook, Ralph H., heart.
Milzo, William S., head.
Newell, Charles H., abdomen.

COMPANY C.

Devreede, John, chest.

COMPANY D.

Reinecky, Frank E., head.

COMPANY E.

Nettles, Robert H., head.
Keedner, J., head.

COMPANY I.

Bone, Albert G., chest.

Koon, Gustave, head.

Kelley, James E., head.

Cummings, James, abdomen.

Zehnder, Bernhard, chest.

COMPANY K.

Wallace, George D., captain, head.

Hodges, W. J., sergeant, abdomen.

Adams, William, back.

McCue, John M., back.

Murphy, Joseph, head.

McClints, William F., head.

NON-COMMISSIONED STAFF.

Corwin, R. W., sergeant-major, Seventh Cavalry, hospital corps.

Polock, Oscar, groin.

WOUNDED.

Ernest A. Garlington, first lieutenant, company A, Seventh cavalry.

Thomas Harran, private, company B, Second infantry.

Robert Brunner, private, company B, Second infantry.

John Coffey, private, light battery, First artillery.

Harry L. Clifton, corporal, company K, Seventh cavalry.

James Ward, sergeant, company B, Seventh cavalry.

William Toohey, sergeant, company B, Seventh cavalry.

John McKenzie, private, company B, Seventh cavalry.

Harry H. Thomas, private, company I, Seventh cavalry.

Christopher Martin, private, company A, 7th cavalry.

John F. Frittle, first sergeant, company E, Seventh cavalry.

Daniel McMahon, private, company A, Seventh cavalry.

Adam Neter, private, company A, Seventh cavalry.

Harry Stone, private, company B. Seventh cavalry.

Fred Woder, private, company K, Seventh cavalry.

Hugh McGinnis, private, company K. Seventh cavalry.

William Davis, private, company K, Seventh cavalry.

Edward A. Sullivan, private, company K, Seventh cavalry.

Samuel F. Smith, private, company K, Seventh cavalry.

Henry Howard, private, company I, Seventh cavalry.

Charles Campbell, quartermaster sergeant.

Gottlieb Hipp, private, company I, Seventh cavalry.

Frank Lewis, private, company B, Seventh cavalry.

H. L. Hawthorn, first lieutenant, Second artillery.

Alvin H. Hazelwood, private, company H, Seventh cavalry.

George York, private, company D, Seventh cavalry.

James Christenson, private, company K, Seventh cavalry.

Harry Lincoln, private, company A, Seventh cavalry.

William H. Green, private, company G, Seventh cavalry.

George Lloyd, sergeant, company I, Seventh cavalry.

Herman Kranberg, private, company A, Seventh cavalry.

George Elliott, private, company K, Seventh cavalry.

Ervine Schrievner, private, company C, Seventh cavalry.

General Miles sent the following official report of the conflict to the Secretary of War, dated at Hermosa, S. D., December 30th: "Colonel Forsythe says sixty-two dead Indian men were counted on the plain where the attempt was made to disarm Big Foot's band, and where the fight begun on other parts of the ground there were eighteen more. These do not include those killed in ravines where dead warriors were seen, but not counted. Six were

brought in badly wounded, and six others were with
a party of twenty-three men and women, which
Captain Jackson had to abandon when attacked by
150 Brule Indians from the agency. This accounts

for ninety-two men killed and leaves few alive and
unhurt: The women and children broke for the hills
when the fight began, and comparatively few of them
were hurt and few brought in; thirty-nine are here,
of which number twenty-one are wounded. Had it
not been for the attack by the Brules an accurate
account would have been made, but the ravines
were not searched afterward. I think this shows
very little apprehension from Big Foot's band in the
future. A party of forty is reported as held by the
scouts at the head of Mexican Creek, These consist of all sizes and the cavalry from Rosebud will
bring them in if it is true. "These Indians under
Big Foot were among the most desperate. There
were thirty-eight of the remainder of Sitting Bull's
following that joined Big Foot on the Cheyenne
River and thirty that broke away from Hump's following when he took his band and Sitting Bull's Indians at Fort Bennett, making in all nearly 160 warriors. Before leaving their camps on the Fort Chey-
ennne River they cut up their harness, mutilated

their wagons and started south for the Bad Lands,
evidently intending not to return, but to go to war.
Troops were placed between them and the Bad

Lands and they never succeeded in joining the hostiles there. All their movements were intercepted
and their severe loss at the hands of the 7th Cavalry may be a wholesome lesson to the other
Sioux."

Mr. Royer, the agent at Pine Ridge, made on December 31st his report of the battle to the Commissioner of Indian affairs, as follows:

" From the best information I can obtain, Big
Foot and his band surrendered to Major Whiteside,
and while they were disarming them, an Indian
known as their 'medicine man' rose from his seat
and began to cry out, ' Kill the soldiers, their bullets will not have any effect upon our ghost shirts,'
at the same time stooping to the ground, picking up
handfuls of dirt, throwing it up in the air, and, after
a short performance of perhaps two minutes, he
fired his gun in the direction of the military, which

STARTED THE WAR.

started the war that resulted in the killing of Captain Wallace and twenty-five soldiers, wounding thirty-five soldiers, some fatally, and the killing of a
large number of Indians known as the Big Foot
band, or the hostile band of Sitting Bull Indians,
who escaped from the police and military at Standing Rock Agency, immediately after the killing of
Sitting Bull.

" I am unable at this time to give the exact number of Indians killed, but will in a few days obtain
some knowledge of the matter, and report fully to

you the substance of my information. The Rev. Charles S. Cook, Episcopal minister at this agency, is kindly allowing his church to be used to shelter the wounded Indians. He has thirty-eight of the number in his church, and is doing a missionary's part to see that they are properly cared for. This battle occurred at a point about twenty miles northeast from the agency, known as the Wounded Knee store, recently occupied by Prescott and Robertson, on the morning of the 29th, 1890.

"I am informed that the millitary had every preparation made to feed and care for the Indians, and their intention was to take them to Gordon, Neb. (the nearest railroad point), but the attack, which ended practically as I have stated, upset all plans.

"Lieutenant Standing Soldier, who was for a long time lieutenant on the police force at this agency, but now employed by the United States as a scout, on the night of the 30th inst. arrived at the agency from Porcupine Creek with sixty-three Indians who belonged to the Big Foot band, consisting of eighteen men and the balance women and children. The men were disarmed after their arrival at the agency by the scouts and agency police, and placed under millitary guard. I am told that this little band are some that became lost from Big Foot during the excitement following the killing of Sitting Bull at Standing Rock Agency, and were at the time of their capture hunting for the Big Foot band. They were not informed of the fight until after they were safely

BUFFALO BILL.

under guard, and then only in a mild way, that they might not become excited over the loss of their leader"

A ghastly account of the battle-ground has been given by Dr. Charles A. Eastman, of Boston, a full blooded Sioux, who visited it after the conflict. He wrote on January 3 :

" On Thursday morning I visited the field of battle, where all those Indians were killed, on the Wounded Knee, last Monday. I went there to get the wounded, some who were left out. The soldiers brought with them about twenty-five, and I found eleven who were still living. Among them were two babies, about three months old, and an old women who is totally blind, who was left for dead. Four of them were found out in a field in the storm, which was very severe. They were half buried in the

TERRIBLE AND HORRIBLE SIGHT

snow. It was a terrible and horrible sight to see women and children lying in groups, dead. I suppose they were of one family. Some of the young girls wrapped their heads with shawls and buried their faces in their hands. I suppose they did that so that they would not see the soldiers come up to shoot them. At one place there were two little children, one about one year old, the other about three, lying on their faces, dead, and about 30 yards from them a women lay on her face, dead. These were away from the camp about an eighth of a mile.

" In front of the tents, which were in a semi-circle, lay dead most of the men. This was right by one of

the soldiers' tents. Those who were still living told
me that that was where the Indians were ordered to
hold a council with the soldiers. The accounts of
the battle by the Indians were simple, and confirmed
one another, that the soldiers ordered them to go
into camp, for they were moving them, and told
them that they would give them provisions. Having

TO GIVE UP THEIR ARMS,

done this they (the Indians) were asked to give up
their arms, which was complied with by most of
them, in fact all the old men, but many of the
younger men did not comply, because they either
had no arms or concealed them in their blankets.
Then a order was given to search their persons and
their tents as well, and when a search was made of
a wretch of an Indian, who was known as Good-for-
Nothing, he fired the first shot, and killed one of the
soldiers. They fired upon the Indians instantane-
ously. Shells were thrown among the women and
children, so that they mutilated them most horribly.
I tried to go to the field the next day, with some
Indians, but I was not allowed to. I think it was a
wise thing not to go so early. Even Thursday I
thought I would be shot. Some of the Indians
(friendly) found their relations lying dead. They
waited and began to put out their guns. My friend,
Louis De Coteau, was with me, but left me when
they acted in this manner. Before he left me the
hostiles appeared. We did not take in all the

wounded. Those we could not carry away we left in a log house and gave them food."

A little Indian baby girl about three months old, one of the survivors of the battle of Wounded Knee, who lay for three days beside the dead body of its mother, was adopted by Mrs. Allison Nailor, a wealthy lady of Washington. Major John Burke, manager of Buffalo Bill's Wild West Combination, stood as god-father to the child, and had it christened Maggie C. Nailor, the first name and initial being those of the child's new found benefactress.

Miss Elaine Goodale, the poet, who had devoted some years to educational work among the Indians, made this report to the Commissioner of Indian affairs, concerning the battle at Wounded Knee:

"I was not an eye-witness of the fight and my information has been obtained chiefly from Indian prisoners who engaged in it and half-breeds who were present, and from parties who visited the battlefield several days after the encounter.

"The testimony of the survivors of Big Foot's band is unanimous on one important point, namely, that the Indians did not deliberately plan a resis-

NOT A WAR PARTY

tance. The party was not a war party, according to their statements (which I believe to be true), but a party intending to visit the agency at the invitation of Red Cloud.

"The Indians say that many of the men were unarmed. When they met the troops they anticipated no trouble. There was constant friendly intercourse between the soldiers and the Indians, even women shaking hands with the officers and men. The demand for their arms was a surprise to the Indians, but the great majority of them chose to submit quietly. The tepees had already been searched and a large number of guns, knives and hatchets confiscated when the searching of the persons of the men was begun. The women say that they too were searched and their knives (which they always carry for domestic purposes) taken from them. A number of the men had surrendered their rifles and cartridge-belts when one young man (who is described by the Indians as a good-for-nothing young fellow) fired a single shot. This called forth a volley from the troops and the firing and confusion became general.

I do not credit the statement which has been made by some that the women carried arms and participated actively in the fight. The weight of testimony is overwhelmingly against this supposition. There may have been one or two isolated cases of this kind, but there is no doubt that the great majority of the women and children, as well as many unarmed men and youths, had no thought of anything but flight, They were pursued up the ravines, and shot

SHOT DOWN INDISCRIMINATELY.

down indiscriminately by the soldiers.

It is reported that one of the officers called out, "Don't shoot the squaws," but the men were doubtless too much excited to obey. The killing of the women and children was in part unavoidable, owing to the confusion, but I think there is no doubt that it was in many cases deliberate and intentional. The 7th Cavalry, Custer's **old** command, had an old grudge to repay.

The party of scouts who buried the dead, report sixty-four bodies of men and boys, forty-four of women and eighteen of young children. Some were carried off by the hostiles. A number of prisoners, chiefly women, have since died of their wounds, and more will soon follow. The party who visited the battlefield on January 1st, to rescue any wounded who might have been abandoned, and brought in seven, report that nearly all the bodies of the men were lying close about Big Foot's Sibley tent while the women and children were scattered along a distance of two miles from the scene of the encounter.

CHAPTER XXXIV.

FATHER CRAFT AND HIS WORK.

A Devoted Priest—Descendant of a Seneca Chief and Successor of Spotted Tail as Chief of the Brules—His Interview with Red Cloud—Arraignment of the Government.

Among those who were seriously wounded in the fight was the Rev. Francis J. M. Craft, a Roman Catholic clergyman. He was born in 1854, in New York City, where his father, Dr. Francis Craft, was a leading physician. Father Craft received his early education in the public schools, and then studied medicine at the College of Physicians and Surgeons. He was graduated with honors, but poor health prevented him from practicing. Then he turned his mind toward theology, and abandoning the Protestant Episcopal Church, in which he had been reared, he became a Catholic. He entered the Theological Seminary at Troy, and was ordained there in 1878.

Father Craft is directly descended from one of the greatest Seneca Indian chiefs, and recently the Seneca Indians of New York State

MADE HIM A CHIEF,

and the historical badge of the tribe, made of silver,

458

and supposed to be three hundred years old, was presented to Father Craft. His natural inclination was to help the Indians, and he chose missionary work among the Western tribes as his field of labor.

For eleven years the priest labored among the Sioux at Pine Ridge, Standing Rock, and Rosebud Agencies. He has been instrumental in establishing schools for the Indian children and a house for the Sisters of Charity, of whom many are native Indian women. Father Craft also lent all his energies toward a peaceful settlement of all difficulties, and tried in every way to prevent the Indians from becoming contaminated by their association with bad white people.

He was made chief of the Brule band of Sioux by the dying decree of Chief Spotted Tail, who, according to the Indian custom, had the right to transfer the chieftainship to any one he might name. Spotted Tail's words were: "Let the first black robe that comes among you be my successor."

Father Craft was the first to come, and he arrived in time for Spotted Tail to sign his name to the paper making Father Craft chief. This Spotted Tail did

IN HIS OWN BLOOD,

pricking a vein in his arm for the purpose. Father Craft then obtained a drop of his own blood in the same manner and signed his name. This made the compact sacred and sealed the Father as Spotted Tail's successor after the Indian custom. Father

Craft afterward, in the presence of a large number of the tribe, consecrated it to the Sacred Heart.

In the summer of 1890, Father Craft's horse fell upon him and so disabled him that he was granted a leave of absence. He came to New York and spent his time mostly in the examination, with Gen. O'Beirne, of the Indians returning from the shows in Europe. At the request of friends he proceeded to Washington to consult with Gen. Schofield, Secretary Proctor, and Gen. Miles on the occasion of Gen. Miles' visit to the capital. He intended to return to New York, but instead of doing so he set out hastily for the scene of the Indian disturbances.

From Rosebud he wrote to the War Department that

EVERYTHING WAS QUIET.

He then proceeded quietly to Pine Ridge, where he took part in the discussion of affairs. He it was who advised that Indians be sent out to the Bad Lands after the braves who were still out.

In his work among the Indians, Father Craft had many bitter opponents, and his life was often threatened. But he was a formidable opponent. He was one of the best shots with rifle or revolver in all the country, and on several occasions when men wanted to fight him he satisfied them amply by drawing his revolver and with unerring aim

PLANTING BULLET AFTER BULLET

in chips that were floating far out in the river. Just

before the battle at Wounded Knee Father Craft had the following interesting interview with old Red Cloud:

He asked the chief:

"What, in your opinion, is the cause of the trouble among the Indians?"

"Everybody seems to think that the belief in the coming of the Messiah has caused all the trouble. This is a mistake. I will tell you the cause.

"When we first made treaties with the Government, this was our position: Our old life and our old customs were about to end; the game upon which we lived was disappearing; the whites were closing around us, and nothing remained for us but to adopt their ways and have the same rights with them if we wished to save ourselves. The Government promised us all the means necessary to make our living out of our land, and to instruct us how to do it, and abundant food to support us until we could take care of ourselves. We looked forward with hope to the time when we could be

AS INDEPENDENT AS THE WHITES,

and have a voice in the Government.

"The officers of the army could have helped us better than any others, but we were not left to them. An Indian Department was made, with a large number of agents and other officials drawing large salaries, and these men were supposed to teach us the ways of the whites. Then came the beginning of trouble. These men took care of themselves but not of us. It was made very hard for us to deal with the Government except through them. It seems to me that they thought they could make more by keeping us back than by helping us forward. We did not get the means to work our land. The few things given were given in such a way as to do us little or no good. Our rations began to be reduced. Some said that we were lazy and wanted to live on rations, and not to work. That is false. How does any man of sense suppose that so great a number of people could get to work at once, unless they were at once supplied with means to work, and instructors enough to teach them how to use them?

"Remember that even our little ponies were taken away under the promise that they would be replaced by oxen and large horses, and that it was long before we saw any, and then we got very few. We tried, even with the means we had, but on one pretext or another we were shifted from place to place or were told that such a transfer was coming. Great efforts were made

TO BREAK UP OUR CUSTOMS,

but nothing was done to introduce the customs of the whites. Everything was done to break the power of the real chiefs, who really wished their people to improve, and little men, so-called chiefs, were made to act as disturbers and agitators. Spotted Tail wanted the ways of the whites, and a cowardly assassin was found to remove him. This was charged upon the Indians, because an Indian did it, but who set on the Indian ?

"I was abused and slandered, to weaken my in-fluence for good and make me seem like one who did not want to advance. This was done by the men paid by the Government to teach us the ways of the whites. I have visited many other tribes, and find that the same things were done among them. All was done to discourage and nothing to encourage. I saw the men paid by the Government to help us all very busy making money for them-selves, but doing nothing for us.

"Now, don't you suppose we saw all this? Of course we did, but what could we do? We were prisoners, not in the hands of the army, but

IN THE HANDS OF ROBBERS.

Where was the army? Set by the Government to watch us, but having no voice in setting things right, so that they would not need to watch us. They could not speak for us, though we wished it very much. Those who held us pretended to be very anxious about our welfare, and said our con-dition was a great mystery. We tried to speak and clear up this mystery, but were laughed at and treated as children. So things went on from year to year. Other treaties were made, and it was all the same. Rations were further reduced, and we were starving, sufficient food not given us, and no means to get food from the land were provided. Rations were still further reduced. A family got for two weeks what was not enough for one week.

"What did we eat when that was gone? The people were desperate from starvation—they had no hope. They did not think of fighting. What good would it do? They might die like men, but what would the women and children do? Some say they saw

THE SON OF GOD.

All did not see Him. I did not see Him. If He had come He would do some great thing as He did before. We doubted it, because we saw neither Him nor His works. Then Gen. Crook came. His words sounded well; but how could we know that a new treaty would be kept any better than the old one? For that reason we did not care to sign. He promised to see that his promises would be kept. He, at least, had never lied to us. His words gave the people hope. They signed. They hoped. He died. Their hope died with him. Despair came again. The people were counted, and wrongly counted. Our rations were again reduced. The white men seized on the land we sold them through Gen. Crook, but our pay was as distant as ever. The man who counted us told all over that we were feasting and wasting food. Where did he see this?

"How can we eat or waste what we have not? We felt that we were

MOCKED IN OUR MISERY.

We had no newspapers, and no one to speak for

us. We had no redress. Our rations were again reduced. You who eat three times each day, and see your children well and happy around you, can't understand what starving Indians feel. We were faint with hunger and maddened by despair. We held our dying children, and felt their little bodies tremble as their souls went out and left only a dead weight in our hands. They were not very heavy, but we ourselves were very faint, and the dead weighed us down. There was no hope on earth, and God seemed to have forgotten us. Some one had again been talking of the Son of God, and said He had come. The people did not know; they did not care. They snatched at the hope. They screamed like crazy men to Him for mercy. They caught at the promises they heard He had made.

"The white men were frightened, and called for soldiers. We had begged for life, and the white men thought we wanted theirs. We heard that soldiers were coming. We did not fear. We hoped that we could tell them our troubles and get help. A white man said the soldiers

MEANT TO KILL US.

We did not believe it, but some were frightened and ran away to the Bad Lands. The soldiers came. They said: 'Don't be afraid; we come to make peace, and not war.' It was true. They brought us food, and did not threaten us. If the Messiah has really come, it must be in this way. The people prayed for life, and the army brought it.

The Black Robe, Father Jule, went to the Bad
Lands and brought in some Indians to talk to Gen.
Brooke. The General was very kind to them, and
quieted their fears, and was a real friend. He sent
out Indians to call in the other Indians from the
Bad Lands. I sent all my horses and all my young
men to help Gen. Brooke

SAVE THE INDIANS.

Am I not right when I say that he will know how to
settle this trouble ?   He has settled it.

"The Indian Department called for soldiers to shoot
down the Indians whom it had starved into despair.
Gen. Brooke said, ' No, what have they done? They
are dying. They must live.' He brought us food.
He gave us hope. I trust to him now to see that
we will be well treated. I hope that the despair
that he has driven away will never return again. If
the army had been with us from the first there never
would have been any trouble. The army will, I
hope, keep us safe and help us to become as independent as the whites."

"What do you think of the killing of Sitting
Bull ?"

" Sitting Bull was nothing but what the white men
made him.   He was

A CONCEITED MAN

who never did anything great, but wanted to get
into notice, and white men who had something to
make by it, encouraged him and used him. When
they had made him as great as they could they killed

him to get a name by it. The fight at his arrest
would have been made for any one arrested in the
same way. If he was a little man, he was a man,
and should not have been murdered uselessly.
What is worse, many good men were killed also.
The soldiers came in time to prevent more murders,
but too late to save all. If the army had wanted to
arrest him they knew how to do it, and never would
have done it in that way. You see how they are
doing here. The agent does not interfere with the
army, and the army saves lives and does not do
anything foolish. No Indian wants to fight; they
want to eat, and work, and live; and as the
soldiers are peace-makers there will be no trouble
here.

"The Indian Department has almost destroyed us.
Save us from it. Let the army take charge of us.
We know it can help us. Let it manage our affairs
in its own way. If this can be done I will think
that all this late trouble has been only a storm that
broke the clouds. Let the sun shine on us again.
There is one man whom we named

'BIG-LONG-TRAVELER'

(Gen. O'Beirne), who some years ago helped us when
we were in trouble and were about to starve. He
was the first and the only one who made the whites
take away the little cattle they brought to cheat us,
and made them bring cattle of full weight. Ask
him to tell people what we suffer and what we need.
He made people treat us well once while he was

with us. I wrote to him to come here again when we were in trouble, and make our case known. He understands it. Get him to help keep the army in charge of us."

Father Craft also wrote a letter to the *New York Freeman's Journal*, in which he said that in the beginning the Indians hoped for much aid from the Government to enable them to become like white men. They were, however, in every way abused, mocked, and discouraged. Instead of being wards, they have felt they were the victims of unscrupulous politicians, who benefited by their misery.

Father Craft continued: "I know what I say, for I have

SHARED THEIR SUFFERINGS

for many years. In their despair Gen. Crook brought them hope. Their confidence in him led them to hope that he would be able to realize their hopes. His death was their death-blow, and they felt it.

"Indians are not fools, but men of keen intelligence. Reductions in rations increased these fears. Even Indian agents protested against such cruelty. Mr. Lee, who took the census, made grave mistakes; counted less than the real numbers, and made false reports of prosperity that did not exist. It is not to be wondered that they believed in a Messiah, whom they at first doubted, and listened to every deceiver who promised hope.

"Interested whites took advantage of this state

of affairs and howled for troops. The army indig-
nantly protested against their false statements, but
had to go to the scene of the supposed danger.

"Interested whites persuaded them that their entire destruction was aimed at, and the Indians ran
away in fear and despair. Father Jule calmed them,
and I brought them back to the agency, and the

KINDNESS OF GEN. BROOKE

convinced them of their safety. The General's plan
to send Indians after those still out was good, and
would have succeeded if the General were left alone.

"Just as the tree can be traced from its smallest
branch to its root, so can the Indian troubles be
traced to starvation and misery of the Indians."

CHAPTER XXXV.

AFTER THE BATTLE.

A Profound Sensation Caused—Varying Comments and Prophecies—Alarm at Pine Ridge—List of the Troops in Service—Murder of Lieut. Casey—Agent Royer Removed—Red Cloud's Flight—The Case of Col. Forsythe.

A profound sensation was caused throughout the whole country by the news of the Battle of Wounded Knee, and the most extreme comments were made on both sides. Some denounced it as a wicked massacre of red men. Others hailed it as a piece of righteous punishment inflicted upon incorrigible savages. Its effects were also variously estimated. It was by many thought to be the beginning of a long and bloody war of extermination, while others believed it would end all the troubles and insure immediate and lasting peace. As is usual, the truth lay in neither of these extremes. It was generally felt, however, that the military authorities now had the upper hand, and that henceforth the Indians would be kept on the defensive.

Credit is to be given to the Indians who were

enlisted as scouts and police by the Government. They were

TRUE AS STEEL

and did their duty nobly. Conspicuous among them were No Neck, Yankton Charlie, Rocking Bear, Long Wolf, and Black Heart. The chief of the scouts, Frank Gruard, and Little Bat also did most valuable work.

After the battle Col. Forsythe went into camp on Porcupine Creek near the scene of the fight. His position was not a safe one, and reinforcements were hurried forward to his relief. No further attack was made upon his command, however. Big Foot's band had been practically annihilated, and all other hostile Indians in that part of the country were over-awed by their fate.

At Pine Ridge Agency the news of the battle created great excitement and alarm. Pandemonium broke loose among the 5,000 Indians there, and a large number of them broke away and fled toward the Bad Lands, while many others joined the troops and

PREPARED FOR DEFENSE

against the hostiles. Soon sounds of war were heard about the agency. A friendly Indian village near by was burned by the hostiles. The settlers from all around came flocking in. All the women and children were huddled together in one house and guarded by the infantry, and all night long every one at the agency remained awake in instant expectation of attack. An outbuilding at the Catholic Mission School was burned by mischievous Indians, and it was rumored that the whole school had been destroyed, but the rumor happily proved unfounded.

The New Year did not open peacefully. New Year's Day saw 3,000 Indians, 600 of whom were fighting men, encamped in the Bad Lands about fifteen miles from the Pine Ridge Agency. They were in a spot greatly resembling the famous lava beds of California where the Modocs under Captain Jack made their last stand. It was

A STRONG SITUATION,

but the troops surrounded it on all sides and Gen. Miles felt sure that he would make them surrender without a struggle. There were now on the scene of action the First, Second, Third, Seventh, Eighth, Twelfth, Seventeenth, Twenty-first, and Twenty-second Regiments of Infantry, and the First, Second, Fifth, Sixth, Seventh, Eighth, and Ninth of Cavalry, Battery A of the First Artillery and Battery F of the Fourth Artillery.

Red Cloud now sent in a letter, claiming that he was a prisoner and begging the soldiers to come and save him from the other Indians who were determined to drag him into the war. A number of his followers voluntarily came in and surrendered themselves, and promised that they would be followed by the whole band.

Matters remained in about this condition for sev-

eral days. Foraging parties were sent out to capture all the cattle and ponies that could be found,
and to secure hay from the outlying ranches which
had been deserted by the settlers. Hay and provisions were very scarce, the weather was severe,
and the 8,000 troops were by no means in a comfortable position. On January 25th an attempt was
made by the Indians to move to the northward, and
preparations were made for action, but no serious
trouble ensued.

Two days later

ANOTHER DEPLORABLE TRAGEDY

occurred. Lieut. Casey, a fine officer of the 22d
Infantry, went out from Gen. Brooke's camp to visit
the hostile Indians and, if possible, induce the chiefs
to come in and have a conference. He passed a
small band of Ogallalas, who were butchering cattle and who appeared to be friendly. Two of them,
however, set out to follow him. A little further on
he met Peter Richards, a son-in-law of Red Cloud,
who had been sent by the latter to warn him not to
come nearer to the hostile camp, as it would be
dangerous for him to do so. Lieut. Casey said that
he would at least go on a little further, to the top
of a small hill, whence he could get a view of the
hostile camp. Richards tried to dissuade him from
even this. While the two were talking there was a
shot, and Casey fell from his horse dead,

SHOT THROUGH THE BRAIN.

The shot was fired by one of the two Ogallalas who

had been following Casey. Richards would have shot the murderer, but was himself unarmed. When news of the murder was brought to the camp, Gen. Brooke sent out a detachment to recover Casey's body, which was found stripped but not mutilated. Lieut. Casey was about forty years old, and had been in command of a troop of Cheyenne scouts for about a year. He was earnestly devoted to the best interests of the Indians, and his death was greatly lamented by both Indians and his army comrades.

A decided change in the situation was effected on January 8th. At this date the Secretary of the Interior dismissed Mr. Royer from the agency at Pine Ridge, and placed Capt. Pierce, of the 1st Infantry, temporarily in command. At the same time, the Pine Ridge, Rosebud, Standing Rock, Cheyenne River, and Tongue River reservations were placed temporarily

UNDER MILITARY CONTROL,

with Gen. Miles in supreme command. Mr. Royer was removed because, in the opinion of the Indian Office, he was not equal to the emergency. In ordinary times he had performed his duties well, but in time of war he was lacking in nerve.

The general situation was summed up by the Indian Office at this date as follows: There were in all about 20,000 Sioux Indians on the northern reservations. Of these, 16,500 were living in peace. This left about 3,500 men, women, and children more or less hostile, and to deal with them Gen. Miles had 8,000 well-equipped soldiers.

After the murder of Lieut. Casey, Red Cloud became panic-stricken and fled to the agency for protection from his fellow-Indians. His escape from them, according to his own story, was a narrow one. His son Jack had to

SMUGGLE HIM OUT OF CAMP,

and then his daughter took him by the hand and led him through the snow and on foot across eighteen miles of wretched country to the agency. He was nearly blind, and without his daughter would certainly have lost his way and perished in the blizzard that was then raging. Twice during the flight they were fired upon by Indians, and had to lie down and burrow in the snow to escape the bullets. Young Red Cloud also came into the agency, bringing with him one of Lieut. Casey's revolvers which had been stolen by his murderer.

Col. Forsythe was much criticised for his management of the battle at Wounded Knee, and was relieved from the command and an inquiry was ordered. It was said that the troops were so placed that in the firing many of the men were killed by their own comrades. The testimony of the officers and men, however, was unanimously in his favor, and he was

HONORABLY ACQUITTED

by the investigating committee. Gen. Schofield

thus explained the reason for Col. Forsythe's sus‧ pension:

"It had been suggested, by a person whom I can‧ not mention, that it would be well to look into the matter of the fight on Wounded Knee Creek the other day, inasmuch as the reports state that sev‧ eral Indian women and children were killed. Ac‧ cordingly, Gen. Miles, at a suggestion from here, relieved Col. Forsythe of his command, pending an investigation of the circumstances of that fight, which investigation is probably now being conducted by Gen. Miles."

One officer remarked: "It is preposterous to say that it is necessary in an Indian skirmish to stop firing long enough to find out just what sort of an Indian you are shooting at. The women and the men look very much alike in their blanket costume, and the former are quite

AS FIERCE FIGHTERS AS THE MEN.

A Sioux squaw is as bad an enemy as a buck at times. The little boys, too, can shoot quite well as their fathers."

An officer of the 7th Cavalry said: "The story that the men shot down women and children is a lie. The fact is, nothing was left undone to save them. I heard many men cry out, 'Don't shoot! that's a woman!' The people who killed women and chil‧ dren were the Indians themselves."

CHAPTER XXXVI.

DOUBT AND FEAR.

Losing Faith in Indian Promises—Strange Scenes in Church—A Wagon Train Attacked—A Midnight Pow-wow—Two Daredevil Brules—The Fortifications—An Unexpected Advance—Much Talk but Little Action.

So the campaign at Pine Ridge dragged its way along in doubt and uncertainty. Every morning brought reports that the Indians were coming in to give themselves up, but every evening saw the promise unfulfilled. They were coming. But in such matters time is an element which does not concern the Indian. So many times, indeed, did he promise to come in without keeping the promise that no man could tell when the final entry would be made. A correspondent one day had an interview with Father Jule. He is the Jesuit missionary who induced the Indians to promise to come in just before the battle of Wounded Knee. They were on the point of keeping the promise when the news of the engagement sent them flying back in fear. Said that gentleman :

479

"I have so often heard that the Indians are com-

BELIEVE THEM NO MORE.

ing in only to be mistaken, that I shall believe them no more until I see them.

Father Jule was almost the only man at the agency who paid much attention to religious duties. Besides his church and school there were two churches—The Presbyterian, the pastor of which was the Rev. Mr. Sterling, and the Church of the Holy Cross, Episcopal, the rector being the Rev. C. S. Cook. In the Government school, religious services were held generally by the Catholics. In the first mentioned there was no service on January 11, wrote a correspondent; the windows were barred and to the west was stationed a line of breast-works, and adjacent were several tents of infantry soldiers; in the Episcopal church fifteen wounded

AT THE POINT OF DEATH.

women and children lay, some at the point of death and all in pain, the result of the fight on Wounded Knee. The pews had been torn from their places and on either side of what had been the main aisle were beds of loose hay on which lay the unfortunates. The sanctuary was given up to the groaning little ones, while in the choir three hostiles moaned in misery. On the lectern were rolls of bandages, pieces of lint and cloth which had served to stanch the flow of blood from the wounded victims. This lectern was presented to the church by Calvary church of New York, and at it had officiated the

Rev. A. L. Southard, the Rev. F. L. Hawks, the Rev. Cleveland Coxe and the Rev. E. A. Washburn. Neither of these worthy men, nor those who succeeded them doubtless ever imagined that this would be one of the uses to which the desk should be put in this distant country. The little church was of Gothic design and was beautifully hung with evergreens, reminiscent of the Christmastide—the period of peace and of good-will, which was made memorable there by the blood spilled. In the school Father Jule said mass and delivered a short sermon. One-half of the worshippers were Indians, among whom was Red Cloud. The old chief knelt and rose up, made his genuflexions and crossed himself like the others present. Throughout he held an English prayer-book, which, however, he was unable to read. He devoted his attention to the pictures of the several parts of the mass, many of which he could scarcely distinguish because of his failing sight.

The party sent to Wounded Knee to bury the dead Indians found and buried eighty-four bucks and sixty-three squaws and children. . It was also found that five had been buried by the Indians. In addition to this total of 152, others, who had been carried away by hostile scouts, etc., were heard of, sufficient to swell the number of dead Indians, as a result of the battle of Wounded Knee, to fully 200.

Another conflict occurred near Wounded Knee on January 5. As a number of wagons with supplies were known to be coming thither on the road from

Rapid City, it was thought best to send out a detachment to protect them. So thirty men were picked, and immediately started down the road. They had not gone over ten miles when they discovered the wagons, thirteen in number, drawn up

ATTACKED BY A BAND.

in the form of a square, and being attacked by a band of about fifty Indians. The detachment put their horses to a full gallop, whereupon the Indians withdrew to an adjoining hill. The detachment now joined the teamsters, who numbered only nineteen. Sacks of grain, bundles and boxes were thrown up in front of the besieged men as breastworks. The Indians noticing this immediately returned and began an attack, circling around the wagons, but keeping at a distance of 800 yards. As a result the shots from their Winchesters were not effective, often falling short of the mark. The carbines of the soldiers were used with much more effect, a number of Indians being seen to fall from their horses.

Meantime the band was augmented until it numbered some 100 warriors in all, besides some who had been posted off in the adjoining hills, One soldier at the beginning of the fight, while arranging the breastworks, was shot in the shoulder, but not seriously wounded. A soldier was detailed to re-

BESIEGED BY THE INDIANS.

turn to camp and report that the detachment was besieged by the Indians. He selected a fast horse and made a break at an opportune moment, the attention of the Indians being attracted to movements made on the other side. As soon as the object of the ruse was seen about twenty Indians gave chase to Private Collins, and fired shot after shot at him, but as he had a fast horse he soon distanced them.

They then returned with the others to the attack. Three more Indians were seen to fall from their horses, and were picked up and carried away by their companions. Four cavalry horses were shot and killed, as were a large number of Indian ponies.

While the large body of Indians was being engaged by the majority of the soldiers and citizens, a few Indians scattered about, dismounted, and, setting as close as possible, began firing into the

TRYING TO STAMPEDE THEM.

horses, trying to stampede them. Had not some of the soldiers been holding and guarding the horses the Indians would undoubtedly have succeeded in obtaining their object. By this time things were getting pretty hot for the besieged party, and bullets were flying as thick as hailstones, and it was hard to distinguish the Indians through the smoke. The citizens had been fighting them for six hours, and the soldiers about three hours. A little before 2 p. m. a commotion was seen among the Indians, and they gradually retreated, when it was seen that troops were coming in full charge to the rescue. Every one gave three resounding cheers as the troops rode up, and the Indians scattered in all directions, Troop F, giving chase. They were pursued until near nightfall, when the chase was abandoned, the wagon train and every one returning to camp, bringing the dead Indians and some ponies with them.

There was a big pow-wow in the hostile camp on

A BIG POW-WOW.

January 9th. It was a starlight night, and the red-skins stood or squatted in a great circle around the council fire. Many of the Ogalallas, led by Little Wound and Big Road, made speeches urging sur-render, but the young dare-devils were still obstinate. After wrangling and fighting they finally agreed to move on the agency next day and to go into camp on the White Clay Creek, five miles from Pine Ridge, and near the Catholic Mission. This was the story told by Young-Man-Afraid-of-his-Horses. Next morning two young Brules dashed up to the agency buildings. They had just come from the hostile camp. One fellow had a streak of blue paint across his nose. Both were in white shirts. They leaped nimbly off their ponies and bolted through the crowd to General Miles's headquarters, dragging their rifles behind them. The leggings of the leader had the zodiac worked upon them in beads. Indian po-licemen fell upon them and disarmed them. They then said they wanted to see General Miles. They

MEANT NO HARM.

were escorted to headquarters, where they were profuse in assurances that the Brules meant no harm. General Miles told them to go back to their camp and tell their people to surrender without further trouble. Then they dashed away, laughing at the Indian police. These daring fellows were not 20 years old, and doubtless came to the agency on some mysterious mission. Their boldness simply showed the craziness of the young dare-devil Brules,

General Miles telegraphed on January 12th that the Indians were within two miles of the Pine Ridge Agency. They were of course surrounded by troops, and the closer in they came, the stronger the encircling cordon was. During that day a number of men and squaws from the hostile camp arrived on horseback and in wagons, in all stages of dilapidation. The arrivals, however, were not as numerous as had been expected, the main body of Indians still remaining near the mission. As the refugees or visitors reached the outposts they were deprived of their arms by the guards. The wily

ONLY A FEW WEAPONS.

hostiles, however, displayed only a few weapons, and these were later returned to them when the owners went back to the hostile camp. It is not at all improbable that many of the warriors had arms concealed about their persons.

The announcement that a large number of the hostiles had at length arrived within gun-shot of the pickets spread with rapidity through the camp of the Indians. Immediately hundreds of squaws and children gathered in the vicinity of headquarters, whence a view of the bluffs, beyond which the hostiles were stationed, could be obtained. They waited patiently for their brothers, lovers and husbands to appear, but as evening drew on and their devotion was not rewarded they gradually retired to their tepees.

Colonel Henry, who was expected with his four troops of the 9th Cavalry to reach the agency in company with Colonel Wheaton and his command, was ordered to White Clay to ·follow General Brooke, whose headquarters were established with Colonel Sanford's command. The latter was within a few miles of the Indians, and would press them more closely unless in the meantime they have gone into camp within the agency. Colonel Sanford's command comprised of one troop each of the 1st, 2d and 9th Cavalry, the Cheyenne Scouts, formerly commanded by the late Lieutenant Casey and now in charge of Lieutenant Getty, and Companies A, C, G and H of the 2d Infantry. Colonel Wheaton was about eight miles west of the agency with Companies B, D, E and F of the 2d.

There was of course no certainty as to what the Indians would do. General Miles himself was in doubt as to what to expect of them. They might. he said, get to within gunshot of the agency and

WITHIN GUNSHOT OF THE AGENCY.

then break away to the camp which they had just abandoned. Fear of all kinds of punishment seemed to have taken possession of them, and it was

WHITE THUNDER.

generally understood that one injudicious act on the
part of the soldiers or the mad act of some implacable hostile would precipitate a fight, the consequences of which could scarcely be imagined. Lieutenant Taylor, of the 9th Cavalry, went to the Indians
with a couple of his scouts with the intention of
leading them at the proper time to the places designated for their camp at the agency. Where they
were resting the ground was rolling, and offered advantages to the cavalry which were denied to them at
Wounded Knee. They were virtually surrounded by

SURROUNDED BY TROOPS.

troops and in a disadvantageous position, and revolt
would most surely have resulted disastrously to them.
Major Whiteside, in command of the 7th Cavalry,
had his men ready to move at a moment's notice,
and could reach any point of the agency within five
minutes. The same was true of Captain Capron
with his battery and Gatling guns, as also of the
1st Infantry under Colonel Shaftner. The latter
had about 300 men, about 260 of whom were
mounted, ponies for this purpose having been
procured.

The fortifications commanding the hostile camp
were about three-fourths of a mile north of the
agency. They occupied several prominent bluffs
and commanded the valley, which was nearly two
miles wide and about as many miles in length. They
were guarded by a Hotchkiss gun, which had a
range of four miles. This belonged to Captain

Capron.   There were also Companies B and H, of
the 1st Infantry.   Both batteries and Infantry were
under the command of Captain Dougherty.   At the
nothern extremity of the valley, beyond White Clay
Creek, and at the base of a semi-circular, pine-covered
bluff, the hostiles had their tents. Their village
comprised about 300 tepees, with about 800 Indians,
who seemed to be well supplied with ponies.   The
view was picturesque and the site was one from
which the Indians might easily retire were they not
closely followed by General Brooke and his command.

Shortly before noon of January 12, Frank Gourard,
who had been to the hostile camp, arrived and announced that the Indians were not coming in.   Up
to midday the chiefs who were expected to hold a
big talk with General Miles, had not made their appearance, and it began to look as if Gourard's report
was correct, but shortly after noon it was discovered

MADE A RAPID ADVANCE.

that the hostiles had made a rapid advance.   Major
Baker, the paymaster, had visited the fortifications
to pay off the company, and all of the men were in
the camp a hundred yards away except one, who
was left as a guard near the guns.   Suddenly two
Indians were seen on the crest of a hill but a short
distance beyond the other pickets ; then others appeared on the hills to the northwest ; then more
than a dozen were seen on the various elevations,
and then a body of more than 100 warriors rose to

the crest of the hill behind which the hostiles were. The number was steadily increased to 400 by accessions of bands ranging in numbers from five to twenty-five. Captain Dougherty was immediately notified. He dispatched a courier to headquarters to inform General Miles of the movement. Then hurrying to the fortifications he had the gun prepared for action. The range-finder adjusted his sights, and the cave in which the ammunition was stored was opened. A line of skirmishers were sent out beyond the fortifications on the crests of the hills. The activity at headquarters was stirring. Orders

BE IN READINESS.

were sent to the cavalry to saddle and be in readiness to move southwest of the camp. General Miles, accompanied by Buffalo Bill and his staff, rode to the fortifications and made a circuit of the camp. Extra ammunition was issued and when everything was in readiness the troops waited a movement. After two hours General Miles received word that the Indians did not mean to make any advance, but they would like to talk with him. The General sent them word to go quietly into camp and he would receive ten of their chief men. Then the warriors disappeared from the hilltop and an hour later they were camped with the end of their column on the plain.

The friendly Indians held a council and decided that they wanted none of the hostiles in their camp. They dug rifle pits and said that if even a solitary warrior came among them and caused trouble they would arrest him, and if he resisted they would kill him. Still, this did not give a feeling of security. If a fight took place no one would know a friendly from a hostile, and the fight would become simply a battle between all the Indians and the whites.

The next day found General Miles still patiently

PATIENTLY WAITING FOR THE INDIANS.

waiting for the Indians to come in. The hostile Indians still remained in the camp, about two miles from the agency. They did not attempt to come nearer with the exception of those who desired to visit some of the friendlies, and who were compelled to take a circuitous route around the agency to reach them. These were generally met about half a mile beyond the breastworks by pickets, by whom they were compelled to surrender their arms until after their return from the visit. Young-Man-Afraid-of-his-Horses came in from the camp to arrange for a meeting of the hostile chiefs with General Miles.

Arrangements were made, and on January 14, Little Wound, Little Hawk, Crow Dog and Old Calico came in from the hostiles to talk with General Miles, under the escort of Young-Man-Afraid-of-Horses. This council made satisfactory progress. Colonel Corbin, Assistant Adjutant-General, announced that the chiefs had assented to the surrender of their arms, and that the latter would probably be brought in that night or the next day.

A reported uneasiness among the young men in

IN FIGHTING TRIM ALL NIGHT.

the hostile camp had kept the troops in fighting trim all night, but the outbreak did not occur. A Rosebud Indian explained to General Brooke that the reason he did not return to the agency after the fight on Wounded Knee was because, when he attempted to do so, the Indian police fired on him, driving him back to the hostiles. He said he could not tell whether the latter would remain out or not, because there were a number of young men among them who could not be controlled.

CHAPTER XXXVII.

IN AT LAST.

The Hostiles Come to Pine Ridge—A Motley Procession—Their Weapons Left Behind, Hidden Away—What the Chiefs Said—General Miles's Generous Conduct—Troops Returning Home—A Delegation of Indians on Their Way to Washington—Letter from "Buffalo Bill."

To everything there must be an end, except to eternity. The deliberate slowness of an Indian is not quite eternal. So at last it ended, and the hostiles came in to the Pine Ridge Agency. This was on January 15. At noon they were strung along the west bank of White Clay Creek for a distance of two miles. They were mounted, walking, riding on wagons, and, in fact, were advancing in every manner known to them. They were driving and leading immense herds of ponies Some of them entered the friendlies' camp, others pitched their tepees on the west bank of the White Clay. These were the Ogalallas. The Brules, however, were camping in the bottom around Red Cloud's house and half a mile from the agency buildings. Frank Gourard, the scout, estimated the number of lodges at 742,

494

though he could not estimate the number of Indians, The latter could not, however, be fewer than 3,500. The Indian camp two miles from the agency had been broken up. General Brooke had been ordered to march in with his command from below the mission.

The advance guard of the hostiles had scarcely reached the agency when Big Road sent word that

COLLECTED THE ARMS

he had collected the arms of his followers and wanted to surrender them to the agency. When the weapons came in they were found to consist of simply two short guns, a heavy rifle and a broken carbine, two Sharp's rifles and one Winchester—nine guns in all. This surrender was an evidence that the Indians did not propose to give up all their guns, that they had hidden their best weapons in the hills. On this basis the entire hostile band would be expected to give up about 100 guns, when it was known that every man was the owner of a weapon. American Horse, Standing Bear, White Horse and Spotted Horse asked protection from the hostiles camped among them.

This movement of the hostiles was the result of a visit paid to General Miles the day before by Two Strike, Kicking Bear, Lance High, Hawk and Eagle Pipe. They had a big talk with General Miles. The same subjects were considered as in the morning

LEAVE THEIR CAMP.

session with Little Wound, Big Road, Crow Dog and Turning Bear. It was agreed that the hostiles would leave their camp and pitch their tepees on the west side of the White Clay Creek, immediately opposite and less than half a mile from the agency. It was also decided the Indians would surrender their arms to their respective chiefs and that the arms would be taken. The latter would receipt for them, placing the name of each man upon his gun. The weapons would then be sold and the proceeds returned to the Indians. It was also decided that the chiefs would attempt to control their young men, and failing in this they would themselves arrest those who refused to act as good Indians and turn them over to the agent. General Miles was pleased with the friendly disposition manifested by the chiefs, and proposed to allow them several days in which to

EVIDENCE OF HIS GOOD WILL,

redeem their promise. As an evidence of good will the General sent to the hostiles several thousand pounds of flour and several hundred pounds of coffee and sugar. The General also considered with them several of the important contracts which the Indians said had been violated, and guaranteed that in future these contracts would be complied with to the letter. The chiefs were equally pleased with the kindly treatment they had received at the hands of General Miles. The General demanded the surrender of the slayer of Lieutenant Casey and the chiefs promised to accede to the demand.

Short Bull, of the leading hostiles, was missed from both detachments of chiefs. His absence was explained by those who came on the ground that so many wild young men desired to accompany him to the agency that he deemed it a measure of policy to remain home.

INTERVIEW WITH EAGLE PIPE.

A correspondent had an interview with Eagle Pipe, in which a number of facts were ascertained regarding the big talk with the General. Among them was the novel one that the Indians demanded the abolition of the Rosebud Agency and the establishment of one more general agency at Pine Ridge. The reason they advanced for this radical move was the fact that the Indians were continually moving from one agency to the other, contrasting the methods of each, and longing for the comforts of Pine Ridge as compared with the many disadvantages which they claimed to have experienced at Rosebud. This proposition Eagle Pipe, who, by the way, was one of the most influential of Rosebud or Brule chiefs, said General Miles had promised to consider. He also said that they would attempt to control all their young men, and would talk to them on the subject when he should return home. He

INDULGING IN THE GHOST DANCE.

said also that they had been recently indulging in the ghost dance, but that there were only a few of them, and they generally discontinued it when he advised them to do so.

In anticipation of the camping of the hostiles on the west side of the agency, General Miles ordered the strengthening of the breastworks around the Ogalalla school, all of which command the proposed camping-grounds, General Colby and Buffalo Bill, of the Nebraska National Guard, had a talk with General Miles regarding the return to their homes of the militia camped along the frontier towns. They were assured that the men need no longer be retained. General Colby telegraphed his commands that they might return.

General Miles telegraphed to General Schofield at Washington as follows:

"In order to restore entire confidence among these Indians I have found it necessary to send a

A DELEGATION TO WASHINGTON.

delegation to Washington to receive assurance of the highest authority of the good intention of the Government toward them. This will answer a double purpose, namely, satisfy them, bridge over the transition period between war and peace, dispel distrust and hostility, and restore confidence. It will also be a guarantee of peace while they are absent. I ask that my action may receive the approval of the Department by telegraph. Everything is progressing satisfactorily, and I can see no reason why perfect peace may not be established."

As soon as the Indians got into the agency and

CALLED A COUNCIL.

fairly settled, the Ogalailas called a council, which was held at "Loafer's Camp," in the vicinity of the friendlies. Six hundred Brules were present. The former had prepared a feast of hot coffee and boiled dog. The braves squatted in a circle, in the centre of which steamed the viands. The only white man present was Lieutenant Taylor, 9th Cavalry, commanding the famous Ogalalla scouts. Among the Ogalallas present were Chiefs Standing Soldier, American Horse, Standing Bear, Fast Thunder, Spotted Horse, White Bird and Bad Wound. Among the Brules were Chiefs Short Bull, Hole in His Pants, Kicking Bear, High Pipe, Iron Bull and Two Strikes. American Horse reviewed the circumstances which had led up to the present difficulty and had impelled General Miles to issue the order disbanding the Indians. The order, he said, ought to be complied with, and they should return

RETURN TO THEIR HOMES.

to their homes and bring their young men to respect their white friends, dissuade them from violence and compel their children to return to school. Short Bull said that he had been in trouble with the whites before, but that he had signed a treaty which always prompted him to be a good friend of the white man. A great many of the Rosebud Indians wanted to come to Pine Ridge agency because they knew they would be treated better there. Rosebud was in a hole. They were starved there sometimes. They wanted to leave it and live with their brothers in one place. People carried lies about the Indians when they were separated. They wanted to live in

one family, then everything would be all right.
High Pine and Two Strikes also spoke.

They were followed by Standing Soldier, a fine
young man of the Taylor scouts. He said that some
had come to the agency to make trouble and had
killed friendly Indians ; that had caused the soldiers
to be sent against them and made General Miles
command them to lay down their arms. He hoped

BRING PEACE AGAIN.

all of them would comply with the order, because it
would bring peace again. A short time ago, he said,
he had brought to White Hat (Lieutenant Taylor)
a good many of Sitting Bull's men. They were now
in camp. The scouts, when they were brought in,
were told they had given up their arms and reminded
where they were to remain and had been well
treated and their ponies had been fed with grain and
hay. If Big Foot and his band had come in they
would have been treated in the same manner. The
trouble which killed him and his people was brought
on him by his own people. If they were here now
they would tell them something.

Dr. McGillicuddy then gave them a talk in which
he pointed out the errors which they had made in
the past—the leaders they had followed and the result which had followed. He gave them good
advice and encouraged them to obey regulations in
the future.

Lieutenant Taylor was asked to speak, and said
that he knew many Ogalallas and was satisfied that

they were friendly. He did not know the Brules so well, but felt that there were many brave men among them that would listen to reason The trouble they had experienced had been occasioned by a variety of circumstances In the greater part of the Indian troubles he observed the Indians had always good excuse for bringing it on. They thought they had some excuse in bringing it on. He thought they had some excuse in this

TROUBLE WAS NOW OVER.

instance ; the trouble was now over and if they wish to remain in peace all they had to do was to comply with the order of General Miles, Those who had good sense and judgment should set an example to and control the young men, of whom he knew many lived in their tribes. They had turned in very few guns and knew they had many more. It was now the middle of winter. The Great Spirit had given them extraordinarily good weather, differing from all other winters. If a blizzard should now come up their children and women would die and the soldiers would suffer. He hoped they would immediately comply with General Miles' order that the soldiers could soon go home and would be comfortable. If they complied with General Miles' order some of them would be allowed to go to Washington to see the great father and state their grievances. He closed by stating that their rights would be recognized by the present officers who had been placed over them. The council closed in the best possible

humor, and it was noticed that some of the Brules
had heard arguments and facts against their rebellious course to which they attached considerable
importance.

An interesting estimate of the situation at this
date was made by that experienced Indian manager,
Col. W. F. Cody, "Buffalo Bill," in *The Philadelphia Press.* He said: "The situation to-day, so far

BEST MARKED TRIUMPHS.

as the military strategy goes, is one of the best
marked triumphs known in the history of an Indian
campaign. It speaks for itself, for the usual incidents to Indian warfare, such as raids on settlers
and wide devastation, have been wholly prevented.
Only one white man has been killed outside the
military circle. The presiding genius and his able
aides have acted with all the cautious prowess of the
hunter in surrounding and placing in the trap his dangerous game, at the same time recognizing the value
of uninjuring the game for future occasions. I speak,
of course, of the campaign as originally planned to
overcome and pacify the dissaffected portion of the
Ogalallas, Wassachas, and Brules, the Big Foot
affair being an unlooked-for accident. The situation

A DESPERATE BAND CORRALED.

to-day, with a desperate band corraled and the possibility of any individual fanatic running amuck, is
most critical, but the wise measure of holding them
in a military wall, allowing them to quiet down and
listen to the assurances of such men as Young-Man-

Afraid-of-His-Horses, Rocky Bear, No Neck, and other progressive Indians, relieves the situation so that, unless some accident happens to the military end of the active warfare, it seems a complete, final and brilliant success, as creditable to General Miles' military reputation as it is to the humane and just side of his character.

Neither should praise be withheld from General Brooke, Carr, Wheaton, Henry, Forsythe, and the other officers and men of the gallant little army who stood much privation, and in every instance I have

SYMPATHY FOR THEIR UNHAPPY FOE.

heard them speak they never expressed great sympathy for their unhappy foe, and regrets for his impoverished and desperate condition. They, and the thoughtful people here, are now thinking about the future. In fact, the Government and nation are confronted by a problem of great importance as regards remedying the existing results. The larger portion of the Ogalalla Sioux have acted nobly in this affair, especially up to the time of the stampede. The Wassachas and Brules have laid waste the reservation of the Ogalallas, killed their cattle, shot their horses, pillaged their houses, burnt their ranches; in fact, poor as the Ogalallas were before the Brules have left them nothing but the bare ground, a white sheet instead of a blanket, with Winter at hand, and the little accumulations of thirteen years swept away. This much, as well as race and tribal dissensions and

personal enmity, have they incurred for stand
ing by the Government. These people need as
much sympathy and immediate assistance as any
section of country when great calamities arouse the
sympathy of the philanthropist and the Government.
This is now the part of the situation that to me
seems the most remarkable. What are we going
to do about it? Intelligent and quick legislation
can now do more than the bullet,

WHITE EAGLE.

CHAPTER XXXVIII.

WHO SHALL BE THE VICTIM?

DISCUSSION OF THE INDIAN QUESTION BY THE REV. W. H. HARE, MIS-
SIONARY BISHOP—HOW THE TROUBLE WAS BROUGHT ABOUT, AND
WHO SHOULD BE HELD RESPONSIBLE FOR IT—REFLECTIONS INSPIRED
BY THE CONFLICT AT WOUNDED KNEE.

Amid all the flood of comment and discussion
that was let loose in the press and on the platform
at this time, nothing was better worthy of notice
than some remarks of the Rev. W. H. Hare, the
Protestant Episcopal Missionary Bishop, of Niobrara. He had spent many years among the Indians, and well understood their nature, their wrongs,
and their needs. These were his comments upon
the situation, immediately after the battle of Wounded Knee:

"A disaster often produces a disposition in the
public mind to lay blame on some particular person,
or set of persons, on the assumption that some particular person, or set of persons, must have been
guilty of an intentional wrong. And it is probable
that the present Indian trouble, especially the tragic
affair on Wounded Knee Creek, will call this ten-

dency into action, and that some official person, civil or military, or some one set of persons—the Indians, the settlers, the Indian Bureau, or the military—

WILL BE MADE A SCAPE-GOAT.

With some, the cause of all the trouble will be the untamable ferocity of the Indians; with others, thieving or blunders in the Indian Department; with others, the heartless brutality of the soldiers— and so on. Or worse, perhaps, some one representative of a class, some one person, an agent, the Commissioner of Indian Affairs, an officer of the army, will be singled out, and on him an incensed public will pour the vials of its wrath. This process of retribution reaches its end with neatness and dispatch, and this fact commends it to some. The assumption on which it is based, that some person or set of persons has been guilty of an intentional wrong, is like a clasp-knife; it occupies little room (in the mind), it is portable and quickly made ready for use, and, when used, inflicts a wound. This is just what many want.

"But the important question is, Is this assumption, in the particular case under consideration, true, and is it just to make any one person, or class of persons, a scape-goat on which to lay the sins or mistakes of many, or the natural result of an

IRREPRESSIBLE CONFLICT?'

"A careful study of the whole situation for some years past will lead, I think, to the following conclusions. Three modes of dealing with the Indians

have had their day. The first said, 'Fight them.'
The second, 'Feed them.' The third, 'Lead them
on to self-support.'

"This last has been the controlling principle for
several years past, and in carrying it out the design
has been to bring the Indians in from a roving life
and confine them to reservations; then to settle
them on individual and separate farms ; to sell their
surplus land for their benefit, and to stimulate them
to labor and self-help by reducing the prodigal issue
of rations which marked the relinquishment of the
chase, to an amount which would be sufficient, if
supplemented by their own essays in stock raising
and farming and other labor, to keep them from
suffering. This plan of operation is a wise one, and
I believe has been so esteemed, not only by judicious friends of the Indians in the East, but by the
most practical missionaries living on the reservations.
Such was the *plan* of action. Now let us watch it
in *operation* among the Sioux of South Dakota.

"For several years it worked, on the whole, very
well. The Indians were gathered on reservations,
and

THE BORDER WAS QUIET.

Many of the Indians broke off from the camps where
they had huddled, and took farms, and not infre-
quently a whole band under the lead of a well-dis-
posed chief, and prompted by the promise of a church
or school, would settle on an eligible tract along a
creek, and go to farming and raising stock. The

rewards of their efforts were not inconsiderable, and in some settlements the domestic cattle would average, perhaps, three or four to each man, and in the fall their stores of corn, potatoes, pumpkins, and even wheat and oats, were delightful to see. Missionary and educational effort was kindly received, and kept pace with all this advance, and generally went ahead of it. The counsels of the missionary and the promise of a chapel or a school-house frequently, if not generally, preceded the determination to give up the dance and go off and begin a farming settlement. In a few years eight to a dozen camp-schools were built on each of the chief subdivisions of the great Sioux reserve. Lone women lived in them, or a man and his family, and taught unmolested and secure. The Episcopal Church alone counted seven or eight thousand of the people among the habitual attendants on its religious services. Its communicant members numbered over 1,700 in the year 1890; the people made collections for charitable objects, such as home and foreign missions, and the women showed warm interest in forming and conducting regular branches of the Woman's Auxiliary, with native president, secretary, and treasurer.

"The time seemed now to have come to take a further step and divide the great Sioux reservation up into

SEPARATE RESERVES FOR EACH IMPORTANT TRIBE,

and to open the surplus land to settlement. The

needs of the white population, with their business and railroads and the welfare of the Indians, seemed alike to demand this. Commissioners were, therefore, sent out to treat with the people for the accomplishment of this end, and an agreement which, after much debate had won general approval, was committed to them for presentation to the Indians. The objections of the Indians to the bill, however, were many, and they were ardently pressed. Some preferred their old life, the more earnestly because schools and churches were sapping and undermining it. Some wished delay. All complained that many of the engagements solemnly made with them in former years, when they had surrendered valued rights, had been broken, and here they were right. They suspected that present promises of pay for their lands would prove only old ones in a new shape (when milch cows were promised, cows having been promised in previous agreements, the Indians exclaimed, 'There's that same old cow'), and demanded that no further surrender should be expected until former promises had been fulfilled. They were assured that

A NEW ERA HAD DAWNED,

and that all past promises would be kept. So we all thought. The benefits of the proposed agreement were set before them, and verbal promises, over and above the stipulations of the bill, were made that special requests of the Indians would be met. The Indians have no competent representative body. The commissioners had to treat at each agency with a crowd, a crowd composed of full-bloods, half-breeds, and squaw-men, a crowd among whom all sorts of sinister influences and brute force were at work. Commissioners with such a business in hand have the devil to fight, and can fight him, so it often seems, only with fire, and many friends of the Indians think that in this case the commission, convinced that the acceptance of the bill was essential, carried persuasion to the verge of intimidation. I do not blame them if they sometimes did. The wit and patience of an angel would fail often in such a task.

"But the requisite number, three-fourths of the Indians, signed the bill, and expectation of rich and prompt rewards ran high. The Indians understand little of the complex forms and delays of our Government. Six months passed, and nothing came. Three months more, and nothing came.* But in the midst of the winter's pinching cold the Indians learned that the transaction had been declared complete, and half of their land proclaimed as thrown open to the whites. Surveys were not promptly made; perhaps they could not be, and no one knew what land was theirs and what was not. The very earth seemed

---

* A bill was drawn up in the Senate under Gen. Crook's eye, and passed, providing for the fulfillment of the promises of the Commission, but it was pigeon-holed in the House.

SLIDING FROM BENEATH THEIR FEET.

Other misfortunes seemed to be crowding on them. On some reserves their rations were being reduced, and lasted, even when carefully husbanded, but one-half the period for which they were issued.* In the summer of 1889, all the people on the Pine Ridge Reserve, men, women, and children, were called in from their farms to the agency to treat with the Commissioners, and were kept there a whole month, and, on returning to their homes, found that their cattle had broken into their fields and trampled down or eaten up all their crops. This was true, in a degree, elsewhere. In 1890, the crops, which promised splendidly early in July, failed entirely later, because of a severe drought. The people were often hungry, and, the physicians in many cases said, died when taken sick not so much from disease as for want of food.†

"No doubt the people could have saved themselves from suffering if industry, economy, and thrift had abounded, but these are just the virtues which a people merging from barbarism lack. The measles prevailed in 1889, and were exceedingly

---

* The amount of beef *bought* for the Indians is not a fair criterion of the amount he *receives*. A steer will lose 200 pounds or more of its flesh during the course of the winter.

† This is doubtless true of all the poor, the poor in our cities and the poor settlers in the West.

The testimony regarding the existence of hunger is exceedingly conflicting, but at Pine Ridge Agency, at least, it seemed to me conclusive that it was general and extreme.

fatal. Next year the grippe swept over the people
with appalling results. Whooping-cough followed
among the children. Sullenness and

GLOOM BEGAN TO GATHER,

especially among the heathen and wilder Indians.
A witness of high character told me that a marked
discontent, amounting almost to despair, prevailed
in many quarters. The people said their children
were all dying from diseases brought by the
whites, their race was perishing from the face of the
earth, and they might as well be killed at once.
Old chiefs and medicine men were losing their
power. Withal, new ways were prevailing more
and more which did not suit the older people. The
old ways which they loved were passing away. In
a word, all things were against them, and, to add to
the calamity, many Indians, especially the wilder element, had nothing to do but to brood over their
misfortunes. While in this unhappy state, the story
of a Messiah coming, with its ghost dance and
strange hallucinations, spread among the heathen
part of the people. The Christian Indians, on the
whole, maintained their stand with praiseworthy patience and fortitude; but the dancers were in a
state of exaltation approaching frenzy. Restraint
only increased their madness. The dancers were
found to be well armed. Insubordination broke
out on several reserves. The authority of the
agent and of the native police was overthrown.
The civilized Indians were intimidated.

ALARM SPREAD EVERYWHERE.

No one knew what was coming. The military were summoned to the agencies. Their appearance did not dampen zeal, but fanned the flames. Why should they fear who wore the bullet-proof sacred shirt? When one of the women, wounded in the fight, was approached as she lay in the church and told by Miss Goodale she must let them remove her ghost dance shirt in order the better to get at her wound, she replied, 'Yes, take it off. They told me a bullet would not go through. Now I don't want it any more.' Hence, when Col. Forsythe's cavalry overtook Big Foot's band (off their own reserve, and apparently bent on mischief) and endeavored to take from them their arms, after their surrender, the commanding officer's forbearance and coolness availed nothing. The prayers of the medicine man and his assurances that the bullets would not penetrate their ghost dance shirts prevailed, and although two pieces of artillery were trained upon them, and the soldiers who surrounded them outnumbered the Indian warriors three or four times, they fell suddenly upon the troops with savage fury, and continued fighting often even when wounded and dying. The soldiers retaliated with terrible results. Indian men, women, and boys engaged in the fight, and Indian men, women, and boys paid the penalty. What is to follow no one knows.

SUCH IS THE SAD STORY.

"But I do not think the reasonable conclusion is

that some one person, **or set of** persons, should be made a scape-goat or become the victim of an incensed people's wrath.

"Some say, The Commissioner of Indian Affairs gives too much attention to schools and should devote more to empty stomachs. Well, a while ago the complaint was that the Indian Department seemed to think that all the Indians needed was beef and flour, sugar and coffee.

"Some say, Missionaries should preach less and teach housewifery and the arts of healthy living more. So be it, and let funds be supplied.

"Some say, The military are peremptory and severe. Perhaps they are (in a fight, but not otherwise); but to be a fair judge one should first take a taste of campaigning in the Indian country.

"Some say, The Indians are madmen and savages. Let those who say so remember how they themselves feel when, from continued slights, or affronts, or disappointments, they are sore all over.

"No. We need no victim. We need no scape-goat.

"But these things we do want. A profound conviction in the mind not only of a few, but of the PEOPLE, that

THE INDIAN PROBLEM IS WORTH ATTENDING TO.

Next, that officials placed in charge of the difficult Indian problem should be protected from the importunity of hungry politicians, and that the employees in the Indian country, agents, teachers, farmers, carpel ters, should not be changed with every shuffling of the political cards. The abuse here has been shameful. Next, that Congress, especially the House of Representatives, shall consider itself bound in honor to make provision for the fulfillment of promises made to the Indians by Commissioners duly appointed and sent to the Indians by another branch of the Government. The evils which have arisen from a violation of this comity have been most serious. Next, that testimony regarding Indian affairs should not be swallowed until careful inquiry has been made as to the disinterestedness of the witness. An honest man out here

BURNS WITH INDIGNATION

when he reads in the papers that So-and-So, represented as being fully informed on the whole question, affirms that Indians have no grievances and ought to receive no quarter, when he knows that the lots which the witness owns in a town near the Indian country would no longer be a drug in the market if Indians could be gotten out of the way. Next, let it be remembered that this crisis has lifted evils in the Indian country up into the light, and left the good things in the shade. But the goods things are real and have shown their vigor under trial. There is no reason for losing faith or courage. Let all kind and honest men unite with the higher officials of the Government, all of whom, I believe, mean well, in a spirit of forbearance toward each other, of willingness to learn, and of mutual helpfulness, to accomplish the results which they all desire.

"I believe an inspired Apostle, after studying the Indian question in South Dakota to-day, would write as one did in a time of distrust and perplexity of old, 'Be ye steadfast, unmovable, always abounding in the work of the Lord, forasmuch as ye know that your labor is not in vain in the Lord.'"

CHAPTER XXXIX.

THE INDIAN IN CONGRESS.

STARVED INTO HOSTILITIES—CRIME TOWARD THE INDIANS—DIFFICULTY
WITH THE INDIAN SERVICE—WENT TO HIS GRAVE THROUGH GRIEF—
THE BANE AND CURSE OF THE INDIANS—THEY HAVE NOTHING TO
EAT—GO UPON THE WAR-PATH—LACK OF PROPER PROVISIONS—AC-
CEPT ANY PROPOSITION—THE SIOUX ARE STARVING—SOLVING THE IN-
DIAN QUESTION—MOST PIOUS HYPOCRITE—PROPOSE AN INVESTIGA-
TION—GREATEST INDIAN THAT HAS LIVED.

Early in the history of the more serious part of
the campaign, the Indian troubles attracted the attention of Congress. For two days, December 3d
and 4th, the United States Senate discussed the
condition of the Sioux and the best means of re-
storing peace. The subject came up on the introduction of a joint resolution by the Committee on
Military Affairs, authorizing the Secretary of War
to issue arms and ammunition to the people of
North and South Dakota for purposes of self-
defense.

Mr. Voorhees, in opening the debate, said that if
the proposition were one to issue a hundred thousand rations of food to the starving Indians, it would
be more consistent with Christian civilization. Maj.-
Gen. Miles, he said, had stated in public interviews
that the Indians were driven to revolt or rebellion,

519

or into savagery, by starvation; and it was, in his judgment, an inexpiable crime on the part of the Government to stand silently by and do nothing except furnish arms to the whites. Gen. Miles had stated to the public, as he had previously stated to him, that the Indians were being

STARVED INTO HOSTILITIES,

and that they preferred to die fighting rather than be starved to death. Mr. Voorhees regards the policy pursued in the administration of Indian affairs as a crime revolting to man and to God. The Indians had no newspapers to make known their sufferings and privations. They had been suffering for years in silence. There was blood-guiltiness somewhere in connection with it. He had intended to introduce a resolution asking for an investigation on the subject, but he had an entire respect for the ‟Committee on Indian Affairs, and he had no right to assume to instruct that committee. But somewhere there was blood-guiltiness that would have to be answered for. The hostilities into which the Indians in the Northwest were being starved would result not merely in the destruction of the lives of many Indians, but of the lives of thousands of American citizens and hundreds of American soldiers. That condition of things had been brought about by a niggardly, parsimonious, or dishonest policy—he knew not which. While he was willing that the joint resolution should pass, and that the people of the Northwestern States should be armed, he could not refrain from emphasizing the occasion by those few words. When he had asked Gen. Miles whether something could not be done to prevent hostilities, the General's answer was that he feared it was too late. Whether it was too late or not, he was glad that his skirts were clear of any of the blood that would be shed, growing out of a policy of starvation, iniquity, and

CRIME TOWARD THE INDIANS.

The policy had been pursued to take the lands of the Indians and not pay enough for them to keep the Indians from starving to death when dispossessed of their homes.

Mr. Hawley said he did not know that he had any objection to the remarks of the Senator from Indiana, except that they were, perhaps, a little florid and exaggerated. He, too, had been thinking (as he presumed most American citizens had been) that 100,000 rations of food would be worth more than 100,000 ball cartridges, and he had been hoping that the time would arrive when an appropriation would be made for that purpose. An allegation had been made that the Sioux Commission had made certain promises to the Indians which had been entirely disregarded by Congress, and that there had been constant irritation ever since. It had been also said in the public press that the allowance of rations had been fixed at a certain figure long ago, and had been gradually diminished on the theory that the Indians were going over to civilization or were dying out, whereas neither was the case.

Mr. Dawes, chairman of the Committee on Indian Affairs, satirically expressed his delight that the Senator from Indiana had discovered the real cause of the present troubles among the Indians, because those who had lived among them and who had had much to do with them (Gen. Miles and others) were much perplexed as to what was the cause and what was the remedy. There was a great diversity of opinion on the subject. A good deal of what the Senator from Indiana had stated was undoubtedly true. There was a large body of those Indians starving, or at least short of food, and that condition aggravated the feeling prevalent among them. But he doubted that that was the origin of the evil, or that a supply of food would be the cure for it. The Indians who were starving were Indians who had been led by a religious craze to abandon their homes and follow the standard of their chiefs on the war-path, leaving all their sources of supply and the means of support which they had hitherto enjoyed. The

DIFFICULTY WITH THE INDIAN SERVICE

all along in the past had been a constant change of policy. Heretofore for years it had been impressed upon Congress that the best way to treat the Indian was to starve him into self-support. "Root, hog, or die," had been the phrase sometimes put over the door of those who administered the affairs of

STANDING BEAR.

the Indians, and the policy had been to cut down, year by year, the rations required by treaties, and to give notice to the Indians that next year they were to have only so much, and that the difference must be supplied by the labor of their own hands. He thought it well to hold out every inducement to the Indians to turn from dependence on Government rations and to supply their own support; and that it was well to resort to all the devices within the limits of justice and reason to induce them to do it.

As to the suggestion in the public press that the Government had failed to keep the promises made to the Indians by the Sioux Commission, and that Gen. Crook (the head of that Commission) was so wounded by the lack of good faith on the part of the Government that he

WENT TO HIS GRAVE THROUGH GRIEF,

the truth was that the Commission had made two sorts of stipulations with the Indians. One of them had been written out in plain language and enacted into law by Congress, and that stipulation the Commission had taken out to the Indians, asking them to accept it. The Commission had no power to alter it in one iota. The Indians had had cause of complaint on account of the non-fulfillment of other agreements, and the Commission had told them that it had no authority as to these matters, but that it would use its influence with the Government in the case. The Commission had reported to the Interior Department and to the President, just as it had told the Indians it would do. The Commission had then gone to the Indian Department with forty representative Indians. The Indian Committees of both Houses had been invited to the conference. The agreement was read over in the presence of the Indians and of the Commission, and all had assented to it. It had then been embodied in a bill that was drawn up by Gen. Crook and his associates, and was submitted to Congress by the President. The bill thus framed to the complete satisfaction of the Indians had passed the Senate without the dotting of an "i" or the crossing of a "t," but where it was now he did not know. He knew, however, that the skirts of the Executive and of the Senate were clean of any attempt to depart one iota from the assurances given to the Indians by the Commission. Mr. Dawes said that he realized the danger and the necessity of some present relief to bring around composure among the Indians and to extricate them from the lead of such bad Indians as Sitting Bull and Red Cloud, who were

THE BANE AND CURSE OF THE INDIANS.

Mr. Voorhees said he did not know whose fault it was that the Indians were not fed. It might be the fault of Congress, or it might be the fault of dishonest men. The Indians were armed with Winchester rifles, and were in a state of starvation and desperation. They could enter the field with 6,000 fighting men, and with the advantage of their knowledge of the country they could fight 6,000 of the best American troops on terms of equality. He asked the Senator from Massachusetts whether those Indians had enough to eat; whether Gen. Miles was right or wrong; and whether the Indians were being starved into belligerancy.

Mr. Dawes said he had heard to-day, for the first time, that the Indians were on the war-path because they were starving. They had been on the war-path for three or four weeks. They had been holding meetings, and had been giving themselves up to the delusion that the time had come to go back to barbarism and away from civilization, and they were starving in consequence of that. He was not disposed to deny that there had been distress among the Indians, as there had been among the white people in that region.

Mr. Voorhees—Does not Gen. Miles say that these Indians have been hungry for two years?

Mr. Dawes—He may have said it to the Senator from Indiana.

Mr. Voorhees—He says it in his published interview.

Mr. Dawes—The great difficulty in dealing with those 6 000 Indians who are congregating under leaders and are on the war-path is that

THEY HAVE NOTHING TO EAT.

They are away from their tepees. They belong to that class of Indians who never did a day's work in their lives.

Mr. Pierce said that he had sometimes wondered that the white people in that region did not themselves go on the war-path because they were hungry. The Indian seemed to get hungry, as well as noble, the further people got away from him. He lived within a few miles of the great Sioux Reservation. He had been there for the last two months, and this was the first time he had heard it asserted that the Indian was on the war-path because he was hungry. He saw Indians every day in the town where he lived, and they were sleeker and better fed, apparently, than the Senator from Indiana.

Mr. Voorhees—Does the Senator suppose that Gen. Miles does not know what he is talking about, or that he does not know better about Indian affairs than a citizen of Dakota?

Mr. Pierce—I am nearer to the Indians than Gen. Miles is. I have no doubt that in some of the agencies there are Indians who complain of insufficient food. But I do question whether Gen. Miles made the statement attributed to him in the newspapers. The trouble with the Indians is that they are fed and clothed and allowed to live on the bounty of the Government, and that, therefore, as the old adage says, "the devil finds mischief still for idle hands to do." I apprehend that you might take the same number of white people and put them on a reservation, and feed and clothe and take care of them, and that in less than six months they also would

GO UPON THE WAR-PATH.

Mr. Dawes having handed to Mr. Pierce a copy of the New York *Tribune* containing an account of the interview with Gen. Miles, Mr. Pierce read the words "insufficient food-supply and religious delusion—not a disposition on the part of the savages to go to war." He had no doubt that the religious craze was at the bottom of the whole business, and that the Indians themselves did not attribute their disposition to any lack of food.

Mr Voorhees took the copy of the *Tribune* from which Mr. Pierce had read, and quoted from other parts of the interview statements to the effect that the Indians were starved into fighting, and would prefer to die fighting rather than to starve peacefully. He asked Mr. Pierce why he had not read that. Mr. Voorhees paid a high compliment to the soldierly and other good qualities of Gen. Miles, and said that he would take his statement far sooner than that of a Senator who lived near the Sioux Reservation, and who, with his people, wanted to get the Indian lands as soon as possible. The one was a reliable officer; the other was the fox lying around the pen where the geese were, waiting to get some of them.

It is interesting to observe, at this point, that on the very day when this debate occurred, Col. Heyl, Inspector General of the Division of the Missouri, said: "The principal cause of the Indian troubles is

LACK OF PROPER PROVISIONS

in the way of rations—principally meat rations. The latter was reduced 1,000,000 pounds for the Pine Ridge Reservation alone, and the authorities there have a practice of issuing a steer at the weight at which it was received. For instance, the agency might get a steer in the fall that would weigh 1,000 pounds. In the spring it would not weigh more than 800 pounds, but it would be issued as 1,000 pounds all the same. Of course, the Indians would lose the difference. This is one great source of dissatisfaction.

"The Indians generally, I think, are inclined to

ACCEPT ANY PROPOSITION

made to them by the military authorities of a peaceful nature, but when I left there there was a big snow-storm and blizzard coming, which I think will cool the ardor of the young bucks. While I was there Gen. Brooke enlisted ninety Sioux braves as Indian police, and armed them with Springfield rifles. They were made a guard for the Indian camp. The best evidence that these Indians were all acting in good faith was that they all cut their hair off short. When an Indian cuts off his scalp-lock and has his hair cut short you may feel sure that he has effectually departed from war-like customs. I do not anticipate a winter campaign in the Indian country in that sense of the word, but troops will be kept there as against any possibility that might happen this winter, or any attempt to go on the war-path in the spring. The Indians are not properly fed, and there will be the probability of trouble until they are."

The next day the debate in the Senate was resumed. Mr. Voorhees said that he did not want to delay the passage of the joint resolution; but after what had transpired yesterday, he thought it due not only to himself but to Gen. Miles, as well as to the country to submit some matter which had since come to his hands. That was an interview with ex-Governor Foster, of Ohio, published in *The Cincinnati Enquirer.* All the Senators were acquainted with Mr. Foster, who had recently served on an important Indian Commission, and his views ought to have and doubtless would have great weight. Mr. Foster said in that interview: "In my opinion, the difficulties might be easily avoided. The whole matter has been brought about by a combination of bad policy and of the incompetency of some officials.

THE SIOUX ARE STARVING.

Give the Sioux plenty to eat and there will be no further trouble."

Mr. Teller asked whether he understood Mr. Voorhees to say that these Indians did not have enough to eat.

Mr. Voorhees—You understood me to say that Governor Foster said so.

Mr. Teller—And the Senator accepts that as correct?

Mr. Voorhees—I think that Governor Foster tells the truth. The great stubborn fact confronts the country that in some way or other these Indians are starved into fighting.

Mr. Dawes, commenting on the interview with ex-Governor Foster, said that there was nothing in it which failed to corroborate his statement yesterday as to the cause of the Indian troubles. It rather supported what he had said. It was true that there were five or six thousand Indians there in a starving condition, and the peril to the peace and to the lives of white people was just as great whether it arose from one cause or another, and it had to be met and guarded against by a supply of food. In that peril it was, perhaps, unwise to take up time in inquiry into the cause. There was a habit, Mr. Dawes said, of

SOLVING THE INDIAN QUESTION

every once in a fortnight by a column of a newspaper, or by an interview with somebody, made up principally of charges of injustice and fraud on the part of the Government. It seemed to him that people were misled in that regard. For the last ten or fifteen years the Indians had been, in the main, treated fairly and squarely. He knew and appreciated ex-Governor Foster, but that gentleman was not quite so well acquainted with the condition of things among the Sioux Indians as were men who lived among them and had charge of them. Mr. Foster had made a mistake in saying that the lands had been taken from the Sioux first and their consent obtained afterward. No such thing had been done, and the story of the whole case showed that it was not so. Mr. Dawes went on to say that the public mind had been perverted by an army of newspaper men out in the Indian country. ,

Mr. Blair asked Mr. Dawes whether any application for food had been made to the Government by the Indians.

Mr. Dawes—Not by these hostile Indians. But the Government thinks that as a matter of precaution against an outbreak, it would be better to feed them, just as sometimes in time of war an enemy has to be fed.

Mr. Blair—If they were hungry and wanted to be fed, would they not naturally apply for food instead of making war?

Mr. Dawes—I believe that Sitting Bull and Red Cloud have availed themselves of the present conditions to draw on these Indians, making use of the prevalent delusion as a means. This Sitting Bull is the

MOST PIOUS HYPOCRITE

in this country, and that is saying a good deal.

Mr. Reagan assumed that, if there was any danger of an outbreak, some communication would have been made to Congress from the Executive Department, and he said that he was not prepared to assume that the Executive was derelict in his duty.

Mr. Hawley said that the Secretary of War had sent a communication asking for authority to distribute arms to the Governors of the States where Indian hostilities were feared.

Mr. Allison spoke of a question by Mr. Reagan as a pertinent one. Why, he asked, had there been no communication from the Executive Department respecting the question? He took it that the reason was that there was no occasion for such communication. He took no stock whatever in the suggestion that the uprising was caused by the starvation of the Sioux. Senators who believed that there had been any dereliction on the part of agents should

PROPOSE AN INVESTIGATION

and have the matter probed to the bottom. He did not believe it,

Mr. Voorhees interpreted Mr. Allison's remarks as a contradiction of Mr. Foster's statements, and said that Mr. Foster was the peer, in intelligence and honor, of any man in public life.

Mr. Paddock remarked that Mr. Foster had not been in the Sioux country within the last two years.

Mr. Voorhees replied by saying that, if the Sioux had been starved two years ago, it was all the worse for Mr. Paddock's side of the question. He accepted Governor Foster's statement in preference to that of Mr. Allison, who was necessarily ignorant of the question.

Mr. Allison—When it comes I shall be ready for it.

Mr. Voorhees—Yes.

Mr. Allison—What I meant to say was this: That if the statements are true that these Indians have been starving, then those who believe so should invite an inquiry. I have not been on the reservation, and know nothing respecting the truth or falsity of the statement.

Mr. Voorhees—But you declare with great earnestness that you do not believe a word that Governor Foster has said on this subject. The Committee on Indian Affairs can summon him by telegraph and can examine and cross-examine him. That is the way to get at the facts of the case. Governor Foster says in this interview: "Sitting Bull is only a feeble old man hardly respected in his tribe," and yet the Senator from Massachusetts seems to lay the whole blame on him.

Mr. Dawes—Gen. Miles told me, the last thing before he took the cars, that Sitting Bull was the

GREATEST INDIAN THAT HAS LIVED

in this country.

Mr. Voorhees—Why not send for Gen. Miles and have him before the Committee on Indian Affairs?

Mr. Dawes—Gen. Miles has no personal knowledge on the subject of the uprising of the Sioux. He had been on the Pacific Coast for the last two or three years, and has come to his new assignment very lately. Governor Foster got all his information on the subject of the Sioux a year and a half ago.

Mr. Voorhees read some further extracts from the Foster interview, and then, referring to Mr. Dawes' criticism of the newspapers, said: "I thank God for newspaper men, especially in dark places, and to every newspaper man who has thrown a single ray of light on this miserable business I return my heart-felt and profound thanks. Newspaper men may get things wrong sometimes, but in the main, in the great volume of what they do, they contribute to the light and knowledge of the world and to the cause of justice. That is what I have to say to the Senator from Massachusetts in reference to his criticism of newspaper men.

After remarks by Messrs. Stewart, Vest, and Morgan, the joint resolution was amended so as to apply to the States of North and South Dakota, Wyoming, and Nebraska, and was passed.

CHAPTER XL.

THE INDIAN BUREAU.

SHALL IT BE UNDER CIVIL OR MILITARY CONTROL?—RECORD OF THE
ARMY—GENERAL GRANT'S EXPERIMENT—IMPROVEMENT IN ADMINIS-
TRATION—CENSUS OF THE INDIANS—MANY INDIANS CIVILIZED AND
PROSPEROUS.

Another topic that was much discussed was whether the Indian Bureau should remain in the Interior Department or be transferred to the War Department. The transfer was strongly urged by the "army circle" at Washington. Years before, the Indians had been under the control of the War Department, and the army never had forgiven the transfer of it to the Interior, and had never lost a chance to urge that it be given back to them.

On this occasion they argued that if the Indians were placed

UNDER MILITARY CONTROL

wars would be prevented, and scandals arising from dishonest administration would be known no more. In this, however, they did not argue wisely. As a matter of historical fact, the entire Indian frontier, from the Seminole country, in Florida, to the great

Western rivers and lakes, was frequently disturbed
by Indian hostilities, usually the result of the en-
croachment of white settlers, but sometimes of
causes for which officers of the War Department
were more or less directly responsible, during the
entire period of military control after the last war
with Great Britain; and more than once in that
period was the good fame of the military branch of
the Government tarnished by bad conduct on the
part of some of its officers and agents. No intelligent man will contend that the power and the
morals of the army and its agents are stronger or
better now than they were in the "good old days"
to which reference has been made. There were
good and valid reasons for the transfer of Indian
affairs from the War Department, in which the control had so long resided, to the civil branch of the
Government—reasons which are as cogent now as
they were when the transfer was made.

THE INDIAN TREATY SYSTEM

became firmly established as a Government policy
during the period of military control. It was entered upon, it is true, when the Indian tribes of the
South and what was then the great but sparsely
settled West were relatively a thousand times more
powerful than they now are; when hostile foreign
influences dominated most of the tribes from Ohio
westward, when Pontiac and Tecumseh loomed like
giants on the western horizon, and long before the
battle of Tippecanoe had been fought. Nobody

criticised the policy then, and the Interior Department ought not to be held responsible for its existence now. Indeed, the civil administration deserved credit for a change of policy in 1854, which resulted in a large number of treaties in which, for the first time, provisions were incorporated for the allotment . of lands in severalty and for the employment of other means and agencies designed to civilize and influence Indians to engage in peaceful pursuits. It is true that these provisions were greatly neglected through a series of years, during four of which the energies of the nation were devoted to its preservation. It is not more deplorable that some

INDIAN AGENTS AND SUPERINTENDENTS BECAME DE-
MORALIZED

in the war period than that scores of army quartermasters, paymasters, commissioners, and officers of still higher rank were accused and found guilty of dishonesty and fraud, or that some army officers in the first few years after the war were detected in violations of the trusts, both military and civil, which were committed to them. It may be remembered that when Gen. Grant became President of the United States, in 1869, he determined to purify the Administration of Indian affairs. To that end he appointed as Commissioner of Indian Affairs an accomplished officer who had been a member of his personal staff during the war, who was the titular chief of the Six Nations, and a man in whom he reposed the most perfect confidence. At the same

time he detailed for duty as Indian agents a number
of officers of the regular army.   It may be remembered also that after two years' trial, the experiment
was abandoned.   President Grant, apparently, was

NOT SATISFIED WITH THE RESULTS.

Before that time the Indian frontier had been virtually destroyed and white settlers had poured into
and over the immense region of which during the
entire period of War Department control of Indian
affairs the savage tribes had been left in unmolested
occupation, with the exception of a few small and
scattered trading posts; the difficulties of Indian
administration had increased tenfold, and the number of Indians with whom the agents of the Government had to deal directly had greatly increased also.

Since 1871 there has been a steady if not rapid
improvement in the management of Indian affairs,
and the Indians themselves have been responsive,
in a visible degree, to the efforts in behalf of their
civilization.   According to the returns of the eleventh
census, more than 35,000 Indians in the United
States to-day are taxed citizens, counted in the
general population.   This does not include nearly
65,000 members of the

FIVE CIVILIZED TRIBES

in Indian Territory, more than 8,000 Pueblo Indians
in New Mexico, nearly 3,000 Cherokees in North
Carolina, and more than 5,000 Iroquois in the
State of New York.   In addition to these, there are

GROUP OF INDIAN CHIEFS WHO VISITED PRESIDENT HARRISON.

at least 45,000 Indians on the reservations who obtain a livelihood by farming, herding horses, and sheep-raising, and other civilized pursuits. These figures make an aggregate of 161,000, which is considerably larger than the aggregate Indian population with which the War Department ever had directly to deal.

In the light of the figures above given, it will not do to say that the civil administration of Indian affairs has been a failure; nor will it do, in the light of history, to assert that military control is to be preferred to civil control. According to the census of 1890, the

TOTAL INDIAN POPULATION

of the United States is 844,704, which is made up as follows: On reservations or in schools under control of the Indian Office not taxed, 130,254; Indians incidentally under the Indian Office and self-supporting, are as follows: In Indian Territory, 25,357 are Cherokees, 3,464 Chickasaws, 9,998 Choctaws, 9,291 Creeks, and 2,539 Seminoles. There are also about 14,247 colored people (mixed Indian blood) living with and members of the above tribes. The total population of the five civilized tribes is therefore 84,671; Pueblos of New Mexico, 6,270; Six Nations and St. Regis of New York, 5,304; Eastern Cherokees of North Carolina, 2,885. Indians (98 per cent. of whom are not on reservations), taxed and self-sustaining citizens, counted in general in Montana, 35,287; Apaches at Mt. Vernon Barracks (prisoners), 37; Indians in State or Territorial prisons, 184; total, 53,373.

The census further shows: Total males taxed and untaxed, 80,715. Total males untaxed and on reservations, 63,780. Total females taxed and untaxed, 62,106. Total females untaxed and on reservations, 66,484. Ration Indians on reservations to whom rations are issued by the United States, 32,310.

SELF-SUPPORTING INDIANS

on reservations by farming, herding, root-digging, horse-raising, fishing, and hunting, 96,044. Total self-supporting Indians (33,567 taxed and not including the five civilized tribes), 128,611. The number of whites on the several reservations in the Indian Territory aggregates 107,987, as follows: In Cherokee Nation 27,176, in Chickasaw Nation 49,444, in Choctaw Nation 97,991, in Seminole Nation 96, in Creek Nation 3,280.

DOG DANCE OF THE SIOUX.

CHIPPEWA SCALP DANCE.

THE notes marked thus, ⌣ are performed with a tremulous voice, sounded: "High-yi-yi," &c.

CHAPTER XLI.

DOCUMENTS IN THE CASE.

GENERAL MILES' ADDRESS TO HIS SOLDIERS ON THE CLOSE OF THE WAR—
AN OFFICIAL OUTLINE OF THE CAMPAIGN—REGRET FOR FALLEN COM-
RADES—THANKS FOR EFFICIENT SERVICE—LETTERS FROM A MISSIONARY
AND FROM A BISHOP.

Soon after the return of the Indians to the Pine
Ridge Agency, General Miles issued an address to

ADDRESS TO THE TROOPS.

the troops, congratulating them on the close of the
war, as follows :

"Headquarters Division of the Missouri,
"In the field, Pine Ridge, S. D., Jan. 18, 1891,
"General Orders, No. 2.

"The Division Commander takes pleasure in announcing the satisfactory termination of hostilities
in this division. The disaffection among the Indians
was widespread, involving many different tribes.
The purpose of the conspiracy was to produce a
general uprising of all the Indians in the coming
Spring. The hostile element of the Sioux Nation
precipitated the movement by leaving their agencies,

546

defying the authorities of the Government, and destroying their property, that had been given them for the purpose of civilization. They assembled in large force in the almost impenetrable ground known as the Mauvais Terres of South Dakota, and from that rendezvous marauding parties robbed both white citizens and friendly Indians on their reservation and throughout the adjacent settlements.

CHECK THIS INSURRECTION.

To check this insurrection, orders were given for the arrest of the chief conspirator, Sitting Bull, who was on the eve of leaving his reservation to join those above mentioned. This was done on the 14th of December last. After peaceably submitting to arrest by the officials of the Government, he created a revolt which brought to his assistance large numbers of his followers, who assailed the Indian police. This resulted in his death, and final arrest of 300 of his people, and removed the principal part of the disaffected element from the Standing Rock reservation. The second arrest was that of Big Foot's party, December 21, 1890. This band was composed of outlaws from different tribes, who had defied the Government officials, and escaped during December 22, 1890.

"While these measures were being carried into execution, the troops were quickly moved between

PROTECTION TO LIFE AND PROPERTY.

the hostile element in the stronghold and the settlements, in such a way as to check their depredations and give protection to life and property of the citizens. Nearly the entire force of troops in the Department of Dakota, under General Ruger, were judiciously placed where they would give the most protection to the settlements and enable them to intercept hostiles, should they escape. Brief delays were necessary to put the troops in proper position, as well as to give time for the work of disaffection to be carried on in the hostile camp, and strengthen the loyal element. Gradually the troops were moved to such positions as to render resistance of the hostiles useless, and they were forced back to the agency. The escape of Big Foot made his recapture necessary. This was successfully done by a batallion of the 7th Calvary and Lieutenant Hawthorne's detachment of artillery under Major Whiteside, December 28, 1890, after which they were marched seven miles to Wounded Knee, and at 9 p. m. the command was joined by Colonel Forsyth, with the 2d Battallion of his regiment, with two Hotchkiss guns under Captain Capron, 1st Artillery, and Lieutenant Taylor's scouts. With this band of outlaws under control of the troops, the entire hostile camp moving in before them to surrender and within a short distance of the agency, it was hoped and expected that this serious Indian difficulty would be brought to a close without the loss of life of a single white man. While disarming Big Foot's band, on the morning of December 29th, after a portion of their arms had been surrendered, they were

incited to hostility by the harangues of one of their
false prophets, and in their attack and attempt to

INCITED TO HOSTILITY.

escape nearly all of the men were killed or wounded,
and the serious loss of life occurred to a large number of non-combatants. During the engagement,
some 150 of the young warriors that were moving
in to surrender, went to the assistance of Big Foot's
band and were engaged with the troops, and returning, made a vigorous attack upon the agency, drawing the fire of the Indian police and scouts. This
caused a general alarm, and upwards of 3000 Indians
fled from the agency to the canons and broken
ground adjacent to White Clay Creek, and assumed
a hostile attitude. The troops that were following,
however, checked their further movements. The
attempts of some of the warriors to burn buildings
near the agency the following day, resulted in a skirmish with the 7th Calvary, under Colonel Forsyth,
promptly supported by Major Henry, 9th Calvary.

"On January 1, 1891, a spirited engagement
occurred on White River between a body of warriors numbering upwards of 100 and Captain Kerr's
troops of the 6th Calvary, in which the Indians were
repulsed with loss. Major Tupper's battallion of
Colonel Carr's command of the 6th Cavalry moving
to his support. This was followed by several skirmishes between the Indians and the scouts under
Lieutenant Casey. While making a reconnoissance
the service sustained a serious loss in the death of

that gallant officer.   The troops under command of
Brigadier-General Brooke gradually closed their
lines of retreat and forced the hostiles by superior

UNDER THE GUNS OF THE COMMAND.

numbers back to the agency, where they are now
under the guns of the command and the control of
the military.

"While the service has sustained the loss of such
gallant officers and patriots as Captain Wallace,
Lieutenants Casey and Mann, and the brave non-
commissioned officers and soldiers who have given
their lives in the cause of good government, the

MOST GRATIFYING RESULTS.

most gratifying results have been obtained by the
endurance, patience and fortitude of both officers and
men.   The work of disarming the hostiles has in a
large measure been accomplished, but will be continued by a portion of the command now in the field,
and by the agency officials.   As soon as practicable
the troops will return to their stations, and will take
with them the assurance that their services have
been a great value to the country in suppressing
one of the most threatening Indian outbreaks, and
that they have been enabled to keep back the hostile Indians from the unprotected settlements to the
extent that not a citizen's life has been lost beyond
the boundries of the Indian reservations.   In announcing this fact, the Division Commander desires
to express his thanks and highest appreciation of
the royal and efficient service that has been render-

ed. The mention of individual names of either officers or soldiers for meritorious conduct will be deferred until sufficient time is given to ascertain each heroic act, in order that it may be properly recognized and duly rewarded.

"H. C. CORBIN, Assistant Adjutant-General.
"By command of Major-General Miles.
"(Official)."

The following letter, "unofficial," but not therefore less interesting, was written by Mrs. Charles

WIFE OF A SIOUX MINISTER.

S. Cook, wife of a Sioux minister, after the Wounded Knee battle, but before the final surrender:

"Pine Ridge Agency, S. D., Jan. 2, 1891.

" . . . You know, through the papers, of course, of the two battles fought ; how the first began while the Indians were being disarmed. Our soldiers, not expecting resistance, had not separated the men from their families, and as the troops were standing on three sides of a square, the firing caused a terrible slaughter of women and children, as well as men, and dreadful to say, the soldiers killed each other as well. This battle took place about eighteen miles from this agency, and the wounded were brought here, most of the Indians being placed in our church, where we have been caring for them ever since Monday night. It seems months, instead of days, since they were brought in !

"The second battle was fought only a few miles away, but was not disastrous to either side, though

the Indians had such advantage that but for the arrival of reinforcements, the Seventh Cavalry would
have been annihilated.

" The whole matter is heartrending to us who are
workers in the field. It is surely the result of a mis-

A MISTAKEN POLICY.

taken policy on the part of the Government; the
result of land-greediness, the result of unfulfilled
promises, the result of supposing the Indians to be
children, and treating them as such. The ghost-
dance mania is only a sort of final straw, as it was
really the thing that gave the Indians an outlet for
all the pent-up emotions of years, and how soon
they were in a state of wild frenzy, and kept themselves there by constant dancing and exhorting each
other to die, that they might meet their dead relations, and hasten the time when this country should
be their own again. All this is old to you now, for
it has been told and retold in the papers. When we
try to look forward to the end we are sick at heart,
for no one can tell what the end will be. We only

WHAT THE END WILL BE.

know that the Indians must yield in time, but before
that many men must die, and the Indians must begin
"civilization" all over again, if there are any left to
begin.

"So far the Christian Indians have remained
friendly, and are living in "tepees" around the
agency. They are more or less alarmed, naturally,
knowing the hostile Indians will be harder on them

than on the whites even ; for the hostiles are their fathers, brothers, sons and other relatives, and it is really wonderful that they stand as firm as they do. All our native helpers, Mr. Ross and the catechists, have been invaluable in caring for the wounded. We

CARING FOR THE WOUNDED.

have fifteen women and children in the church and fourteen in a tent near the soldiers' hospital tent. Miss Goodale, who most fortunately is with us, and two other ladies, are most indefatigable in their labors, cooking food and attending to the wounded. I never saw, and never dreamed of seeing, such an awful sight as these prisoners presented the night they were brought in. I know now what is meant by "gaping wounds" and "destitute condition." You know the number killed and wounded, I suppose— twenty-eight soldiers killed and thirty-eight wounded ; twenty-eight Indians killed and about 130 men wounded, and numbers of women and children. The wounded Indians were all women and children except four.

"Mr. Cook officiated at the burial of the soldiers

BURIAL OF THE SOLDIERS.

on Wednesday. They were placed in our cemetery temporarily. We expect Bishop Hare to-morrow for a few days' stay. We shall be glad to have his wise help and cheerful face. We do not think we are now in personal danger. Two nights, Monday and Tuesday, the troops were somewhat scattered and we slept in our clothes (the few hours that we slept at all), expecting an attack on the agency, which would have been a very serious thing, as the agency was not well protected, especially on Monday night. Now, new troops are here for the especial purpose of protecting the agency, leaving the other forces free to meet the Indians outside. Troops are surrounding the Indians and approaching them more closely all the time. We have had no winter yet, which is favorable to the Indians.

"Our Christmas Day services were attended by

OUR CHRISTMAS DAY SERVICES.

large congregations and the responses and singing were as inspiring as they always are. That evening and Friday and Saturday evenings, the Christmas tree was filled with gifts, and five congregations received their presents. We intended to give the first three evenings of this week to the remaining eight congregations, but, of course, all our plans had to be changed.

"We have been so thankful for the warm clothing, of which a great deal has been sent us, and which has been given to our own people and also to the wounded Indians, who had nothing. At present all is confusion. Our house is a centre for both white and red people, and we have no leisure moments except such as are stolen from duty or sleep. Remember me always in your prayers."

This letter from Bishop Hare, of Niobrara, is

LETTER FROM BISHOP HARE.

also of interest, as showing some effects of Church work among the redmen :

"Nine Sioux Indians, nobly working in the sacred ministry! About forty Sioux Indians helping them as licensed catechists! Forty branches of the Women's Auxiliary among the Sioux Indian women! Seventeen hundred Sioux Indian communicants! Sioux Indians contributing $3,000 annually for religious purposes! But what impression have all these solemn but cheering facts made upon the public mind, as compared with the wild antics of

WILD ANTICS OF THE HEATHEN.

the heathen Sioux Indians, which have excited the attention and stirred the feelings of the country, and daily occupied column after column of the newspapers for two weeks past? Alas! Alas! As we have written elsewhere, wickedness presents more vivid contrasts than virture does, its history is more picturesque, and has more of the element of the unexpected.

"The final outcome is yet to appear. But two or three possible issues ought to be guarded against.

"First. The ringleaders of this disturbance, which has alarmed the whole Northwest, covered the better Indians with shame, brought scorn upon their essays of civilization, robbed many of them of their hard-earned possessions and exposed them to personal peril, should not be left at liberty hereafter to repeat the baneful operation.

" Had several Indians whom we could name been consigned to Fort Marion or Fortress Monroe shortly after the Custer affair, we should not have the present complication to untangle.

"Not to speak of alarm and losses suffered by the whites, it is not satisfactory after years of patient labor to read, as is credibly reported from Pine Ridge Reserve: 'Much destruction of property and cattle has been going on for days. All the houses of the quiet Indians on the two branches of the Medicine Root, Porcupine Tail and Wounded Knee Creeks have been broken into, entered and robbed of all contents; the school-houses the same. Everything else which was of no use to the marauding Indians, was destroyed and scattered in every direction. The catechists' houses, those not standing near the chapels, have met with the same fate as the rest. Charley Turning-hawk, the catechist, had quite a store; a small bag of salt was all that was left. The catechists, Silas Opegila, Henry Red Shirt, Thomas Tyon, for certainty, are among the sufferers; they have nothing left.'

' Second. In dealing with these evil-doers, let

NO MERE REVENGE.

there be no mere revenge, much less indiscriminate revenge. This has not been indulged in in the past, and it will be noticed that Mr. Ashley, in his graphic narrative, reports that the friendly Indians have already fear of its repetition. He writes: 'They fear, however, that in the event of any trouble, their ponies will be taken from them, whether innocent or guilty, as was done once before, and they ought to be assured of protection.'

"Years ago indiscriminate punishment might be

apologized for, on the ground that the Indians were not individually well enough known to make discrimination possible, and • there was therefore no recourse in military operations but to make a general seizure of all Indian ponies and guns, and to otherwise treat the Indians, innocent or guilty, all alike. No such pretext can have place now. The names of all Indians are down on agency lists. Indians are known individually to teachers, missionaries and agents.

DISCRIMINATION.

"Discrimation is therefore quite practicable. It will be an event in Indian life of vast and far-reaching influence for good if, after this outbreak, the Indians discover that the power which bears the sword will do it ' for the punishment of evil-doers, and for the praise of them that do well.'

"Third. Let good sense and Christian charity arrest the tendency which this outbreak of wild passion will naturally have to dampen interest in Indian missionary and educational work, and to produce the feeling that such work has been in vain. It is surely a fact of vast import that, as is said elsewhere:

" ' Settlers have fled, not so much because of real dangers, as because of their fears, and while they have been fleeing, some white women in Indian camps have been pursuing their work without molestation and without alarm. I have visited several Indian agencies, and have late news from all the Sioux Indian country, but I have yet to learn of a single case of insult, much less of violence, offered to any teacher or missionary in any of the fifty odd stations scattered all over the disturbed districts in South Dakota.'

"And so far as we have information, the Indian clergy and helpers have stood the revival all about them of wild life without flinching, like an anvil when struck.

LIKE AN ANVIL WHEN STRUCK.

"Their terrible trials and faithfulness in them are surely a graphic argument that we should do more than ever to sustain them, and an assurance to us that, if we do our duty we can make others like them.

"The testimony which comes from the Pine Ridge Reserve shows that there is something in the work of the Church which the wild Indian, even when bent on plunder, respects, 'A curious and suggestive feature of this universal plundering and destruction,' writes the Rev. C. S. Cook, 'is the evident intentional sparing of the chapels and the adjacent mission houses: not one of them has been touched."

CHAPTER XLII.

VIEWS OF CAPTAIN R. H. PRATT OF THE CARLISLE INDIAN SCHOOL—YOUNG
INDIANS EDUCATED THERE DO NOT RETURN TO BARBARISM—VERY FEW
CASES WHERE TRAINING HAS NOT HAD PERMANENTLY GOOD RESULTS—
GROWTH OF CIVILIZATION AMONG THE INDIANS—URGENT NEED THAT THE
TRIBAL SYSTEM BE ABOLISHED.

Not many men in the United States have studied
the Indian question in all its phrases more carefully
or more practically, than Captain R. H. Pratt, the
head of the Indian school at Carlisle, Penn., and his
studies have been supplemented by a personal knowledge of Indians, that makes his opinion on all matters relating to the race, of great value. The Captain is not only a man of great executive ability, with
a clear idea of what should be done for the Indian,
but also courageous in expressing his views. He
has not always found himself able to agree with
others who have the interest of the Indian at heart;
but on all such occasions he has said so fairly and
squarely. But, whatever may be thought of some
of his views, there is no doubt that he has done a
noble work in the education of the Indian race, and

559

that he has earned the right to a respectful hearing when he has anything to say on the Indian question.

When the Indian troubles were at their height, in December, 1890, Captain Pratt talked at some length with a correspondent of *The New York Tribune*, about the war and the Messiah craze, and about Indian education. " First of all," he said, " I want to say a word about the often-made statement, that the Indian boys educated at this school, nearly all re-

RELAPSE INTO BARBARISM.

lapse into barbarism. This statement is almost entirely without truth. There are relapses, but the proportion is not great. During the last week, the Rev. Mr. Hubbard, a missionary among the Indians in the Indian Territory, for the last eighteen years, spent a day with me here. He stated that he knew upward of sixty of our returned students, and saw some of them every day, and that he knew of only one failure or relapse in the whole number. He is, however, a zealous friend of our cause, and probably would not see with as critical eyes as an enemy. We have scores of students throughout the reservations who are doing most excellent work in the face of the

DOING MORE EXCELLENT WORK.

greatest difficulty, teaching school, farming, working at their trades, and a large number form the best element in the force of scouts under the military and police forces for the agencies. They furnish most of the non-commissioned officers.

"This morning I am in receipt of an interesting

letter from Bird C. Seward, a full-blood Cheyenne, who was with us less than three years, and returned to his home on account of rheumatism. It is one of the letters I receive almost daily from returned students."

The Captain believes strongly in the policy of not sending the Indian boys back to their tribes, but of keeping them in the East. "Just read these letters, written by Richard Davis of West Grove, Penn.," he said, "and they will show you how much like our-

HOW MUCH LIKE OURSELVES.

selves the Indian is. He speaks of his work on the farm, his desire to put away a little money for a rainy day, tells whom he intended to vote for, and refers to his wife and children, just as any average white farmer would, only in better language, for he is well educated. Now, who is Richard Davis? Well he is a Cheyenne boy who belonged to the hostile Cheyennes whom we fought in 1874 and 1875, and who with his father and people, I, with others, under Generals Davidson and Mackenzie, chased and fought over the western part of the Indian Territory. After eight years with us, this young man married a Pawnee girl, and went into the employ of Mr. Harvey, of West Grove, Penn., and he has his little home, his wife and two children. He takes

HAS HIS LITTLE HOME.

care of Mr. Harvey's dairy, supplying Mr. Wana-maker's great store in Philadelphia with about eighty quarts of cream daily. As to his care of the stock and his performance of the duties intrusted to him, you can see in this letter what his employer says. I have plenty of like cases I could show you among our farmers, not only Cheyennes, but Sioux, Apaches, Navajos, Comanches, Pawnees, Kiowas, and others belonging to our most backward tribes.

"If you will examine carefully the results of educating Indian children at home, and compare them with the results in the oldest and best schools that have been established, you will greatly modify your views in regard to the possibilities of that sort of thing. To the casual observer it appears to be a good thing, but the results in no case that I know of have been at all commensurate with the outlay of time and labor. No spirit of American citizenship or

SPIRIT OF AMERICAN CITIZENSHIP.

individuality and independence has been generated. The results in every case have been simply to produce, as I said in my report, a so-called nation out of the tribe."

"Do you care, Captain," asked the correspondent, "to express any opinion as to the cause of the present dissatisfaction of the Indians?"

"Certainly," he promptly replied. "The Messiah craze is the natural result of the present reservation and tribal surroundings. From a life of activity in the chase, and almost unlimited freedom in roaming and war, the Indians have been crowded into a condition of enforced idleness on the reservations. Day after day around their camp-fires they talk of their past, simply because there is little or no future for them to talk about. The frequently

ENFORCED IDLENESS ON THE RESERVATIONS.

changed, almost infinitesimal and ignorant, inexperienced forces which the Government and the Church bring to bear upon them through agents and employes and missionaries, disturb little the onward flow of their superstition and savage rites. Civilization, like corn and other grains, is purely a crop raised by planting and cultivation, and the quality of the planting and the thoroughness of the cultivation, determine the crop. Any farmer planting only ten grains of corn or half a pint of wheat to the acre and demanding a yield of 100 bushels of the one and forty of the other per acre would be insane. By his scant planting, he invites weeds to grow and choke what he does plant. Are we any wiser in our scant planting of industry, education and civilization among the Indians? When I studied geography, all of Kansas and Nebraska was designated as the great American Desert. What a tremendous lie it was! From my experience, under proper influences, the alleged desert character of the Indian will as significantly fade away.

"The Messiah delusion flourishes only in the soil

THE MESSIAH DELUSION.

of superstition. The old, who have held on either openly or secretly to the past, and have longings for its return, are the principal ones affected by it. The crude notions they have received in regard to

Christianity have been utilized by their superstitious tendencies, and they hope for miracles. The disappointments they will suffer in not seeing the fulfilment of their desires and promises of their prophets will work the best cure. I have been inclined to think, and still think, that designing white men have inaugurated and have added much to the spread of the craze."

"Are you willing to say, Captain, in what respects, if any, you think the policy of the Government toward the Indians should be modified or changed?"

"I most emphatically think that the tribal relations should be broken up," replied Captain Pratt. "So do others who candidly study the Indian problem. But what is the use of talking about breaking up

BREAKING UP TRIBAL RELATIONS.

tribal relations of the Indians when we are continually bringing to bear old systems, or organizing new systems calculated to confirm and strengthen tribal relations? I look upon General Morgan's public school system for the tribes as being one of the most potent instruments ever used to accomplish the building up and strengthening of the tribal relations. I have no desire to antagonize the Commissioner. I say nothing to you here, nor have I said anything in my report, which I have not said to him in a much stronger way, personally, when we have met ; and if you read the proceedings of the Lake Mohonk Conference for 1889, you will find that when he presented his public school system there, which the conference adopted, I antagonized it just as I have in my report, and as I always have antagonized that idea. With the 775 children at Carlisle, I am strong, because they speak forty-seven differ-

FORTY-SEVEN DIFFERENT LANGUAGES.

ent languages, and there is little difficulty in getting them to unite on English. If they were all Sioux or Cheyenne, or Apaches, the progress would be far less, and the care very much greater. If half the students in this school were Anglo-Saxon and the other half Indian, the progress in the English language and Anglo-Saxon ideas for the Indian portion would be advanced 100 per cent. ; and placing one young Indian in a school with whites, if the school is of the same grade, forces him without his knowing it to make still greater progress than he could in a school where half were Indian and half whites."

A short time later, speaking on the same subject before the students of Mt. Holyoke College, Capt. Pratt said : "On New Year's Day I called to pay my respects to the Secretary of War and met the Inspector-General of the Army, who, in the Secretary's presence, spoke of Carlisle students being among the ghost-dancers ; that some of them at Pine Ridge were in a position to be shooting soldiers. I replied that across the Potomac, in sight of Washington, was Arlington, once the home of a celebrated and highly trusted servant of the Republic, whose ancestry was most distinguished and loyal in the darkest days of our history. He was educated at the public expense

and for many years served the country loyally.   In
his maturity, when his family and section declared
against the government, he was urged to remain
true, but he declined, and boldly went with his family
and led the forces of rebellion for four years, killing
our soldiers by the thousands.   Let us not find fault,
then, with a few young Indian children to whom we
give the merest smattering of an education, and send
back to their parents and reservation, if they go
with their families and parents into practices they
esteem right.   These young men are not savage
simply because they are born of savage parents.
Savagery and civilization are habits.   Formation

SAVAGERY AND CIVILIZATION ARE HABITS.

or change of habit is brought about by environment.
I urge that we environ the Indians with our civilization and they will become civilized.   Leave them in
the environment of the tribes and their savagery,
and they will remain tribal and savages.   We are
not born with language, or savagery, or civilization.
These come as a result of environment, not as a
result of birth.   They are not forced upon us, only
during the period of growth.   A person's habits
change after maturity.   If we continue to carefully
guard the Indians in their reservations and not allow
them the freedom of association and effort among us,
that other people have, we shall not lack material
for Wild West shows for centuries to come.

   " Over 5,000,000 immigrants came into the United
States between 1880 and 1890.   They and their

children are with us and part of us to-day, entering
the public school systems, scattering among our
people, coming into the environment of our institu-
tions. They abandoned their language and became
Americans. Two hundred and fifty thousand
already in America were Indians ten years ago, and
are still Indians because we will not allow them the

ARE STILL INDIANS.

environment of our American civilization that we
allow the others. Suppose these 5,000,000 foreign-
ers, instead of being scattered over the country, had
been sent to reservations, would they have made
any progress in becoming Americans? It is only
when we allow them to congregate in bodies that
they give us any trouble. Scattered and in contact
with our own people they become of us. The
policy of the churches to create Indian communities,
instead of inviting the Indian into our community, is
at the bottom of most of our difficulties. Massachusetts, in 1633, provided that Indians should own
lands in the communities of the Colony and share in
all social and political privileges. But the Church
people favored Indian communities and they do to-
day. What we must do is to broaden the policy of
inviting the Indians to come into our communities.
It has been a great success at Carlisle. The system
shows there is little more difficulty, in making
English-speaking, industrious, civilized men and
woman of Indians than there is in reaching the
same conditions with our foreign immigrants."

CHAPTER XLIII.

WHAT OF THE FUTURE.

THE CAUSES OF INDIAN DISCONTENT AND THE REMEDIES THAT SHOULD BE APPLIED—VIEWS OF THE INDIAN RIGHTS ASSOCIATION—AN OBJECT LESSON FROM THE SAN CARLOS RESERVATION—THE CHIRICAHUA TRIBES—SWINDLING THE INDIANS—CHARACTER OF THE FRONTIERSMAN—FAMILY AFFECTION AMONG THE INDIANS—LACK OF APPRECIATION OF THE POWER OF THE WHITES.

Every Indian war calls forth much philosophizing as to its causes and the blame therefor, and much prognosticating as to the future of the red race. The present time is no exception to the rule, but there seems to be rather more than ordinary agreement as to the wrongs suffered by the Indians, through either careless and ignorant or dishonest management.

The view of the Sioux taken by the Indian Rights Association, has been set forth officially in these terms:

"The Sioux Indians, among whom the disturbance exists, number approximately 28,000 souls. They subsist mainly on rations furnished by the Government, given them in payment for land ceded by them to the United States, although many of

568

them, under the guidance of agents and missionaries, have made laudable advances toward independance, and some of them are practically self-supporting.

"There are two well-defined parties among the Sioux (a fact pertinent to a consideration of the present trouble), a progressive party, almost wholly

A PROGRESSIVE PARTY.

Christian, which has been created and developed under the influence of missionaries, both white and native, of various religious bodies—Congregational, Presbyterian, Roman Catholic and Episcopalian— who for many years have labored devotedly among these Indians. This progressive party represents the 'new way,' new ideas and new hopes, the ideas of Christianity and of civilization. It is loyal to the Government, peacable and steadily increasing in influence, industry and vigor. A few of the native leaders of this party are educated and refined men, while its members as a whole lead exemplary moral lives.

Second, a heathen, non-progressive party looking backward to the days of the buffalo, predatory

LOOKING BACKWARD.

warfare, and unrestrained freedom, hostile to the advance of civilization, whether among the whites as a menacing force outside the reservation, or among the Indians themselves as a disintegrating force within. The occupation of the heathen party since reservation life began, has been the consumption of Government rations, dancing, wandering from place to place on visits to friends and relatives. This party has been represented by such men as Spotted Tail, Red Cloud, Sitting Bull, from whom nothing in the line of progress was hoped for or has been obtained· Such leaders were always openly or secretly at enmity with the Government and with the best interests of their people. They have discouraged

DISCOURAGED OR TERRORIZED.

or terrorized progressive Indians, have been a thorn in the side of good Indian agents, and the masters of poor ones. It is a fact that cannot be too strongly emphasized that no dangerous and powerful heathen party could have existed, had the Government fulfilled solemn promises and its manifest duty to provide for the education of these people."

The causes of the discontent which led to the war of 1890-1, were stated to be, in the belief of the Association, as follows:

"First. Ignorance, through the failure of the Government to supply education, and the sway of savage

SWAY OF SAVAGE IDEAS.

ideas in the minds of the non-progressive Sioux, which fostered latent hostility to the Government, which made them an easy prey to religious frenzy and suggested violence as a remedy for real or fancied wrongs.

"Second. Hunger and disease—the grippe among the adults, and measles among the children.

"Third. Distrust of the good faith of the Government, based on imperfect fulfilment of former promises and delay in the carrying out of the terms of the recent agreement.

"Fourth. The spoils system as applied to the management of Indian affairs, which has supplied feeble or unwise mangement at some of the agencies, has prevented continuity and harmony in the Government's work for the civilization of the Indians."

And this is the remedy proposed:

THE REMEDY PROPOSED.

"The first and most important requisite is a single, responsible, competent head for the management of Indian affairs, and charged with that duty only, who shall report directly to the President, and who shall be looked to by the country at large for a successful Indian management.

"An Indian service wholly free from the interference of partisan politics, which shall continue its

INTERFERENCE OF PARTISAN POLITICS.

policy and carry out its educational work undisturbed by changing Administrations.

"While we do not advocate the complete transfer of Indian management to the War Department, we believe that all the advantages which the advocates of that plan desire could be obtained by detailing many able and experienced army officers to serve as Indian agents, without the counterbalancing disad-vantages which we believe would result from so radical a change.

"This suggestion has especial force from the fact

that a few army officers have in the past served as Indian agents with excellent results.

"The appropriation of sufficient money by Congress to permit the education of all Indian youth and the maintenance of a thoroughly effective service. Manifestly, it is the part of wisdom to give enough money to do the work in hand if there be a thoroughly efficient executive officer to expend it."

A well informed writer in *The New York Times* has at considerable length urged the incompetence or dishonesty of agents as a prime cause of Indian

INCOMPETENCE OR DISHONESTY.

troubles. The agency at the San Carlos reservation, in Arizona, he says, is a fair sample of an agency of the first class, as they were rated a few years ago, according to the number of Indians fed. The San Carlos reserve is an almost rectangular area, cut out of the finest part of the centre of the Territory, running north and south about 130 miles and east and west about 40 miles. It is watered by the San Carlos and Gila Rivers and by many mountain streams flowing south into them, whose courses follow the richest grazing country of the world. The mountains of the region are covered with pine forests, succeeded at lower altitudes by the cottonwood and 'mesquite' of the lowlands. The soil is not rich, except where it is alluvial, but growing out of plateaus covered with volcanic rocks, one can travel for days through fields of wild barley growing waist high. It is not uncommon to find corn grow-

ing ten and fourteen feet high, nor to find farmers
who think it nothing unusual to gather three crops
of 'alfalfa' per year from the same ground.

This reservation is the home of the Apache

HOME OF THE APACHE.

nation proper. The name Apache is a corruption
of the Zuni and Moki terms 'Apachu,' which they
applied to the Navajos, and which means a large,
strong man. The Apaches are divided into tribes,
and named according to the locality of their homes.
The Tonto Apaches were probably the ones who
were most easily capabable of being made good
citizens, and inhabited the section known as Tonto
Basin, surrounded by the Sierra Ancha and the
Superstition Mountains. Until they leagued themselves with the hostile White Mountain Apaches
they had never given any trouble, but since 1880
they have been little better than any others. Their
nature is not so ferocious as that of the White Moun-

NOT SO FEROCIOUS.

tain Indians, and they are probably the most easily
led of the nation. The White Mountain tribe has
never been known to cultivate the land; their pas-
times are hunting in the Autumn, war and murder in
the Winter, and returning to the agency in the
Spring and Summer to draw their rations. The San
Carlos tribe are the politicians, and never make a
move without attaching themselves to the stronger
party. For many years they have been employed
as Government scouts, and no case of mutiny or

bad faith is known against them. Most of them live along the San Carlos River, close to the main agency buildings, and they were the main reliance of General Crook in his campign against the other tribes.

" The Chiricahua tribes, which dwelt in the mountains of the same name to the south, have always been the bane of the Territory. Back in the days before the war they overran the southern part of Arizona from the Pacific to the Rio Grande. Under Magnus Colorado, the father of Cochise, an Indian of shrewd sense and an able warrior, they probably committed more depredations than any other aborigi-

COMMITTED MORE DEPREDATIONS.

nal tribe. Magnus was finally captured by the California rangers under Colonel McClave in New Mexico and confined in an adobe hut, with two trusty sentinels to guard the windows. McClave understood his prisoner, and must have believed that he would make a better Indian under the sod than above it, for on one warm, sunny afternoon, when the chief was seated in his cell with his head bowed, probably concocting schemes of revenge, a soldier climbed upon the roof, and dropped an adobe brick down the chimney. It fell into the fireplace, close to the prisoner's feet and so startled him that he jumped to his feet and bounded to the window, when the sentinel on duty, thinking him about to make a break for liberty, shot him through the heart. None of his successors ever held the tribe so well

together, but many of them were most successful
raiders with smaller bands. His pupil in Indian

SHOT HIM THROUGH THE HEART.

warfare and protege, Victoria, kept many cavalry
and infantry companies on the jump for years, while
Geronimo's misdeeds are of too recent occurrence
to require mention.

"When General Crook went to Arizona, he found
all these Apache tribes banded together against
their enemy, the white man. This feeling and
Indian union were helped along by a succession of
dishonest agents, who openly said they had not gone
to Arizona for their health, and who generally left
with their pockets well lined. When the agency
was started, an Indian received about a pound of
beef a day, but as time went on the scales were

SCALES WERE TAMPERED WITH.

tampered with and the Indian stomachs went empty.
In an agency of 5,000 Indians an agent may misap-
propriate from $4,000 to $6,000 per month, on beef
alone, by allowing Indians to hunt on the reservation,
so that they may not be present at the weekly issue
of rations. By an easy system, these Indians are
carried on the rolls as fed, while in reality they get
nothing, and the difference, including coffee, sugar,
flour, salt, yeast powder, and beef, may be quietly
disposed of to the storekeepers of the adjacent
mining towns. The agent always puts his prices at a
little lower rate than the same articles could be
bought in San Francisco and shipped by rail, so the

tradesmen secure a larger profit, business booms, the agent is a popular man whom all stand by, and the Indian, exasperated by ill-treatment, goes on the war-path, killing everything white.

KILLING EVERYTHING WHITE.

By charging up on the rolls as issued that which has not been issued, there sometimes arises a great surplus of material which it may be difficult to dispose of. In 1879 there were in the Government buildings at San Carlos thirty-six Studebaker farm wagons which had been charged to the Indians as issued to them. At a low calculation these wagons could have been sold for $1,000 each, and would have realized a handsome steal for somebody. In addition to this, there was a heavy surplus of all other supplies, but the Indians broke out a few months too soon. The agent fled

THE AGENT FLED.

and was succeeded by the military, who had inventories made and the property taken up and properly credited to the Government.

It may safely be estimated that just about one-third of the supplies purchased for the Indians never reach them. A residence in the Indian country soon convinces one that there is in the East a great deal of maudlin sentimentality for the Indian, and on the other hand the honesty, thrift, noble character, and worth of the frontiersmen have been greatly overrated. This same frontiersman is the one who usually sells rifles and ammunition to the Indians. Why he should do so is very easily explained. Take, for example, the case of the teamster or driver of a

GREATLY OVERRATED.

"prairie schooner." He is always supplied with a rifle and cartridges. He makes his camps, when possible, in mining towns, and when his animals are unharnessed and fed for the night he goes out to "see the town." Everything is closed except the gambling saloons, and he is soon drawn in with the rest of the crowd to buck at "faro." It usually happens that he drives out of town without a cent. An endless road of the plains generally induces one to reflect and think. All he has is his rifle. It is worth in the towns about $20, but an Indian will give $60 for it, because selling arms to the Indians is illegal and the heavy penalty deters many from so doing. While eating his luncheon an Indian passes by and the trade is made. Our driver goes to the next town, purchases another rifle for $20, and has $40 more with which to buck the tiger again. One by one rifles are picked up in this manner by the Indians, until they are really better armed than

BETTER ARMED THAN OUR OWN SOLDIERS.

our own soldiers who still carry the old Springfield rifles, while many Indians have Winchesters and other styles of magazine guns.

In olden days, when any bad character disappered from the North and East with a Sheriff looking for him, it was generally said that he had "gone to Texas," and soon the initials "G. T. T." were as well understood as "F. F. V," are to-day. The cowboy of the northern plains is a much more respectable individual than those who have spread west from Texas across New Mexico and Arizona. Thus, "gone to Arizona" has become a common phrase. They practice every kind of villainy

EVERY KIND OF VILLAINY.

against the Indians, who reciprocate whenever a fair opportunity offers itself. Indian cattle are stolen, their brands obliterated, and run in with white cattle to be driven East. White cattle are always encroaching on Indian reservations, and schemes are always being formed to cut off so much of this or that Indian reserve. All this is resented and brooded over by the wise men of the tribes, and another Indian war is the result. Usually one finds a peculiar kind of freemasonry existing among bad characters of the same ilk, but in the case of the freebooting frontiersmen and the Indians there is no such sympathy.

About four years ago, some Apaches started a farm and cattle ranch near the headwaters of Coon Creek, Arizona, making every promise of good behavior, as earnestly as only Indians can promise. Many industrious white settlers of the better class had settled in the valley, but notwithstanding their objections the Indians were allowed to move in. It was not long before young colts began to disappear, and occasionally a young and tender lamb would be missing. Many complaints were made, but the agent, for reasons of his own, pigeonholed them. Finally the Indians were caught having a barbecue

HAVING A BARBECUE.

on stolen cattle, and the indignant citizens appealed to the courts and had the guilty bucks arrested. During their sojourn in jail an enterprising stock raiser living on Pinal Creek cast covetous eyes on the sleek, fat Indian cattle, which continued to grow fatter notwithstanding the fact of their master's absence, but there was one difficulty to be overcome. The Indians had long before recognized the uselessness of any ordinary hide brand, which could be blotted out with a red hot frying pan, and had marked their cattle by splitting the left ear lengthwise. Finally the Pinal Creek raiser decided to adopt a brand which was to cut off the left ear entirely. So, rounding up the Indian cattle he ob-

OBLITERATED THEIR BRAND.

literated their brand and initiated his own in one blow as it were, and incorporated them in his own herd. When the Indians were released they soon discovered the peculiar brand of their neighbor, and the troops were again called upon to settle the difficulty, and the Indian cattle were returned.

Another difficulty in the management of Indians is the constant friction existing between the War and Interior Departments. Any plan or suggestion offered by a military man is sure to be opposed by the civilian and vice versa. There is a little jealousy in this, but oftener it is a question of dollars and cents with the Indian agent, who can always make more when the army has no finger in the pie. One agent, rather more zealous, attempted to establish a rule that the troops could not pursue and arrest an Indian while on the reservation. Very soon the younger bucks practiced making small raids over the boundary of their haven of rest, only to return quickly with their booty and be exempt from punishment. Robberies, murders and cattle

ROBBERIES, MURDERS AND CATTLE THIEVING,

thieving became of such frequent occurrence that they brought down a storm of indignation on the agent's head, who reversed his decision.

The ill feeling between the subordinates of the two departments works to the great disadvantage of the army in some instances, as in the Chiricahua war of 1882, when the departure of 110 bucks from the reservation was not reported to army headquarters by the agent. As a consequence many innocent lives were sacrificed and the Valley of the Gila ruined. In raiding the valley this war party killed about fifty people, coming upon them unexpectedly through the agent's criminal and really

MALICIOUS NEGLIGENCE,

malicious negligence, when there were troops in readiness close by who could have prevented the massacres. Before the Western Union Company stretched its wires through the Territory, the Government had its own telegraph lines, and had placed them so well that almost any party of hostiles could be intercepted before it could escape over the frontier into Mexico. The Indians were bright, and it was not long before they conceived the plan of cutting the wires. Had they simply cut them, it would have availed them little, because linemen would easily have found the break; but they sometimes used to cut out sections of from 50 to 100 feet in length, and, substituting therefore a piece of dark, heavy cord so closely resembling the original wire, made discovery very difficult.

Among themselves—*i. e.*, between members of the same family—their practices are worthy of our

WORTHY OF OUR ADOPTION.

adoption. Parents are generally devoted to their children and wives to their husbands. To be sure, the noble red man expects his squaw or squaws to do all the work, while he rests and smokes, but in return he is their protector and will die for them.

In 1882 a party of Chiricahua Indians, after being badly whipped in Mexico by our troops, were being closely pursued. The wounded were being helped along, but many succumbed to their wounds and died on the trail. A small detachment of pursuers discovered and followed a newly-made path evidently leading to a small grove of "mesquite" trees, and, when arriving at that point, found four ponies tied around a newly-made grave. At one end of the freshly-turned earth was some food, neatly tied up in paper, for the use of the sleeping brave when he should awake in the happy hunting grounds. As some of the party were intimately acquainted with the hostiles, the grave was opened to see who the

HAPPY HUNTING GROUNDS.

occupant might be. Dressed in the clothes of a murdered white, and painted for war, there had been laid at rest the body of one of Victoria's most trusty and dangerous followers. The friendly scouts soon pulled the corpse out to search the clothes for any valuables. A small amount of money and a few trinkets were found; the ponies were driven along by the pursuing party and the dead brave left on the ground beside the open graves. In a few days the same detachment returned and, through curiosity, made a detour past the spot. To their astonishment they found that the body had been again interred, and the loose earth carefully smoothed over as before. His squaw, who had accompanied him in his flight, had probably remained weeping at his grave, unable to leave her

UNABLE TO LEAVE HER LOVER.

lover. At the approach of the detachment she had probably concealed herself, and imagine her wounded feelings as she saw him dragged from his resting place. As soon as the violators had gone she returned, and with loving care again put him at rest, and was doubtless near at hand to watch the second visit. There are many similar instances of devotion familiar to all who have lived among the Indians, and many equally ferocious and cruel acts of the same devoted squaws toward the helpless prisoners who fall into their murderous clutches.

It is very seldom that the Indians take prisoners, as most whites usually reserve one cartridge for themselves to use, if everything is lost and capture inevitable. It is not considered dignified for the Indian braves to torture prisoners, but they stand by to enjoy the scene while the squaws perpetrate

SQUAWS PERPETRATE EVERY DIABOLICAL OUTRAGE.

every diabolical outrage that their fiendish imagination suggests. Ears are cut off, then the nose, and sharp-pointed sticks are pressed into the eyes; where fire is used, the unhappy wretch is pinned to the ground, after which the fire is kindled on his stomach. Only a few years ago some American prospectors discovered a dead Mexican a few miles below the Arizona line. He had first been buried in the hot desert up to his neck; then his eyelids were cut off to make the exposure to the broiling sun more painful, while pieces of putrid meat were scattered on the ground around his head to attract swarms of "blowflies." The poor fellow's sufferings must have been intense, and he probably lived in that position for two whole days.

The Indian is a very queer mixture, and it re-

A VERY QUEER MIXTURE.

quires a long residence with him thoroughly to understand his character. Nearly all our agents in the West owe their appointments to political preferment alone, and fitness seems to be the last thing thought of, if considered at all. A professional "wire puller" from Ohio, after being defeated at the polls is usually appointed over the heads of competent citizens of the Indian country. Repairing the "fences" of his political superiors has not given him much insight into Indian management, but he cares little for that, because he regards his appointment as a reward for party services, and he resolves to make the most of it. He has no house rent, his food costs him nothing, and his clothes are purchased at an almost nominal price from Indian traders who expect return favors. The salary is very small and entirely out of proportion to the immense responsibilities of the post, and in that point Congress is culpable. What

CONGRESS IS CULPABLE.

man, capable of earning a decent living in a civilized section of the country, would dream of burying himself on an Indian reservation, surrounded by the refuse of the country's population, on a salary of $1,500 a year, were it not for the fact that he has hopes of making a large amount of money on the outside?

A few years ago it was a notorious fact that the San Carlos Agency was a grocery and feed store for the surrounding country—that is to say, any frontiersman could purchase his supplies there, have his animals shod there, and even purchase farming implements which had been sent for distribution among the Indians. During the administration of the Interior Department by Secretary Schurz the affairs of the agency were investigated and the agent indicted by the Territorial courts. An army officer was put in charge and kept there until the pressure

PRESSURE BROUGHT ON THE SECRETARY.

brought on the Secretary was so heavy that another civilian was sent out to relieve him. The military by careful work appeased all the disaffected Indians, and for the first time in many years San Carlos was quiet. The settlers in the Gila Valley felt secure, and did not dread finding themselves surrounded at daylight by a murderous band of Apaches. A reservation farm was started, waterways were built for irrigation, the ground was plowed, and everything seemed to be in a fair way to make the Indians an agricultural and self-supporting community, when the army officer was regretfully relieved by Mr. Schurz.

The new agent was not a dishonest man, but was lacking in almost every requirement for the successful management of Indians. The speculators, thieves, and general bad characters of the reserva-

BAD CHARACTERS OF THE RESERVATION.

tion who had been driven off during the military control now returned, and by ingenious arguments so prejudiced the new agent against anything military that he became a tool in their hands. The agent was a simple-minded individual, much more competent to manage a Sunday school class of a village parish than to deal with the shrewd scoundrels who surrounded him. He was warned and

advised to put the crowd off of the reservation ; but
the merchants of the surrounding towns, fearing a
diminution of profits, assured him that such action
would result in an Indian outbreak. Living at the
agency and among the Indians, the agent was unable to discover any signs of disaffection, until one
fine morning his chief of scouts was killed and the
agency buildings fired into. The outbreak would
never have occurred had not the Indians been deprived of more than half of their rations by the
greedy set of thieves who advised the agent. The
GREEDY SET OF THIEVES.
war caused by this agent's blunders lasted three
years, and was only quelled when General Crook
captured the marauding bands in Mexico and had
them transported to St. Augustine.

The Indian, as a rule, is deceitful and treacherous,
but his treatment has been such as to develop those
characteristics. Kindness is in a measure appreciated by them, but they are never so respectful as
when they understand that the power over them is
able and willing to punish them. They are singu-
larly ignorant of the preponderance of whites in
this country and of the immense resources of the
Government, and it is this ignorance which renders
their submission more difficult. The few Southwestern Indians who have been taken East to see
the sights have returned and related what they have
seen, but all to no use. Sneezer, a San Carlos
Apache of great influence with his tribe, was taken

to Washington, Philadelphia, Boston, and New York, with the hope that on his return he would be able to give the Indians such an account of the magnitude of our cities, the number of people, the extent of railways, and the power of the whites that they might be impressed, as it were, with some conception of the hopelessness of their struggle against

HOPELESSNESS OF THEIR STRUGGLE.

the advance of civilization. Sneezer went back and told his tribe of the wonders he had seen. Stone houses, ten stories high; street cars; railroads crossing States; the immense number of people; the grandeur of the cities; the immense steamers of New York Harbor, and the great lake along our coast, whose waters he said were salty. His former admirers and supporters listened, dumfounded and amazed. They wondered if their chief had become crazy. They questioned him again, and his answers only increased their astonishment, and with one accord they pronounced him bewitched and out of his mind. From a most powerful factor of the tribe he became a pitied lunatic, of less influence than a ten-year-old boy, and his tales of travel were repeated to children as we relate those of the Arabian Nights.

www.ingramcontent.com/pod-product-compliance
Lightning Source LLC
Chambersburg PA
CBHW020651270326
41928CB00005B/71